W9-AUB-398
3 1668 03294 3812

The American Family in the Colonial Period

The American Family in the Colonial Period

Arthur W. Calhoun

Dover Publications, Inc.
Mineola, New York

Bibliographical Note

This Dover edition, first published in 2004, is an unabridged republication of the work originally published in 1917 by the Arthur H. Clark Company, Cleveland (Ohio), under the title *A Social History of the American Family, Vol. I: Colonial Period.*

Library of Congress Cataloging-in-Publication Data

Calhoun, Arthur W. (Arthur Wallace), 1885–1979.
[Social history of the American family from colonial times to the present. 1, Colonial period]
The American family in the colonial period / Arthur W. Calhoun.
p. cm.
"An unabridged republication of the work originally published in 1917 by the Arthur H. Clark Company, Cleveland (Ohio), under the title A social history of the American family, vol. I: Colonial period"—Verso t.p.
Includes bibliographical references.
ISBN 0-486-43366-8 (pbk.)
1. Family—United States—History. 2. Women—United States—History. 3. United States—Social life and customs—17th century. 4. United States—Social life and customs—18th century. 5. United States—Social conditions—17th century. 6. United States—Social conditions—18th century. I. Title.

HQ535.C23 2004
306.85'0973—dc22

2004043838

Manufactured in the United States of America
Dover Publications, Inc., 31 East 2nd Street, Mineola, N.Y. 11501

To
MY MOTHER

CONTENTS

PREFACE

The three volumes* of which this is the first are an attempt to develop an understanding of the forces that have been operative in the evolution of family institutions in the United States. They set forth the nature of the influences that have shaped marriage, controlled fecundity, determined the respective status of father, mother, child, attached relative, and servant, influenced sexual morality, and governed the function of the family as an educational, economic, moral, and spiritual institution as also its relation to state, industry, and society in general in the matter of social control. The work is primarily a contribution to genetic sociology.

Not until such an investigation as lies back of these volumes has been undertaken is it possible to realize the absolute dearth of connected and systematic material on the general history of the American family as a social institution in relation to other social institutions and to "the social forces." In this as in so many other vital fields of human interest and action, everything has hitherto been taken for granted. In view, therefore, of the increasing attention given in recent years to the problems of the modern family, such as conditions of marriage, the birth-rate, the waning of home activities, the insurgency of the child, the economic independence of woman, sexual morality, divorce, and general family instability, it seems that the main lines of family evolution in the United States should be made accessible not merely to the professional student of sociology but also

*Only volume I of the three is available as a Dover reprint at the time of this printing.

to the thinking public. The present work is in answer to that realized need.

The first volume of the series covers the colonial period and sets forth the germination of the American family as a product of European folkways, of the economic transition to modern capitalism, and of the distinctive environment of a virgin continent. Usages imported from Europe are detailed and their gradual modification or overthrow under the influence of economic progress and the sway of the wilderness is exhibited. Variations between the geographical sections are traced to mesological and population differences but the general similarity of North and South is affirmed as a preliminary to the study of their divergence in the national period. In general, the colonial family is presented as a property institution dominated by middle class standards, and operating as an agency of social control in the midst of a social order governed by the interests of a forceful aristocracy which shaped religion, education, politics, and all else to its own profit. The characteristics of the family in the English colonies receive accentuation from a brief view of the French settlements by the Gulf.

In the second volume, the period from Independence through the Civil War is covered under five main heads: the influence of pioneering and the frontier, the rise of urban industrialism, the growth of luxury and extravagance, the culmination of the régime of slavery, and the consequences of the Civil War. Cleavages between East and West and between North and South are made manifest in this volume and the interaction of their several influences is noted. It is also made evident that all the alarming problems that to-day portend family disintegration or perversion were present in some degree in ante-bellum days and were even dwelt upon with alarm.

The third volume analyzes the factors that have consummated the revolution of the family during the past fifty years. Stress is laid on the advance of industrialism, urban concentration, the growth of the larger capitalism, the immigrant invasion, the passing of the frontier, the intensification of the struggle for the standard of living, the movements of rebellion and revolution represented by such manifestations as feminism and socialism, the development of volitional control of family evolution, and the outlook for a democratic future. At no previous point save in the last stages of chatteldom in the South does the economic factor extrude so overwhelmingly.

In common with the best recent historical works, due place has been given to "the Economic Interpretation," but with studied avoidance of fantastic exaggeration. The true claims of the dispassionate historical spirit have been held steadily in view. If it seem to the reader that undue attention has been given to pathological abnormalities, he should bear in mind that the American history with which most readers are familiar has been written by litterateurs or historians with little perspective save that which inheres in loyalty to the established order, in the attenuated atmosphere of the middle class, or in the desire to glorify the past, it may be of New England with its ancestral worthies, or of some other section in the romantic days. Those trained in the literature of such shallow schools naturally find it hard to put aside prepossessions and to refrain from confounding the disclosures of science with the product of the muck-raker.

Years of research, analysis, and rumination have gone

into the preparation of these volumes. Exhaustive investigation of source writings and secondary works together with painstaking reconstruction and interpretation of the course of events warrant the assurance that the present work is the most complete, fundamental, and authoritative treatment of the field that it covers. It is given to the public in the hope that it will call forth a vital interest in the further development of this aspect of our social history.

To William E. Zeuch, of Clark University, I am indebted for valued assistance. I also acknowledge special indebtedness to the libraries of the State Historical Society of Wisconsin, the University of Wisconsin, and the University of Tennessee for access to the principal sources of my material, and to my wife for assistance and inspiration in the progress of the manuscript. I shall also be under obligation to such critics of the work as shall point the way to intrinsic improvement in the presentation of so momentous a theme.

ARTHUR WALLACE CALHOUN.

Clark University, November, 1916

I. OLD WORLD ORIGINS–THE WIDER BACKGROUND[1]

American family institutions are a resultant of three main factors: the complex of medieval tradition evolved through the centuries on the basis of ancient civilization plus the usages of its barbarian successor; the economic transition from medieval landlordism to modern capitalism; and the influence of environment in an unfolding continent. It is necessary to begin this study with a survey of the European background.[2]

Medieval thought on the sex relation was inconsistent. Women were regarded, sometimes as perils, again as objects of worship. The extremes embodied themselves in celibacy and in the minne-cult. Which was the more pregnant of depravity it would be hard to say.[3]

Military mores are always, at bottom, disdainful of women. Chivalry with its sentimental immorality gave women hyperbolic praise in place of justice. Material advantage was the gist of medieval marriage. Women were an incident to their fiefs to be disposed of in loveless marriage. In the fifteenth century, cases of wives prostituted for gain to themselves and husbands were alleged in argument against matrimony. In the larger

[1] Compare Goodsell, *History of the Family*, chapters vii-viii. The appearance of this work warrants brevity in the introductory chapters of the present treatise.

[2] In introduction, see Bebel, *Woman and Socialism*, chapters i-iv; Cooke, *Woman in the Progress of Civilization*, chapters i-iii; Dealey, *The Family*, chapters i-iv; Goodsell, *History of the Family*, chapters i-ix.

[3] Compare Cornish, *Chivalry*, chapter xii.

medieval cities there were official brothels–municipal, state, or church perquisites. Strangers of note were supplied prostitutes at municipal expense. The woman who in despair killed her child was put to cruel death, while the seducer perhaps even sat among the judges. Adultery of wives met severe punishment.[4]

It may be that marriages turned out as well in the Middle Ages as now and that adultery was not more frequent. There was not wanting certain appreciation of woman as wife and mother. But over against modern divorce laxity may be set medieval ecclesiastical jugglery which sold divorces while pretending to prohibit them. In like manner ecclesiastical impediments to marriage could be removed for a fee.

It is impossible to harmonize medieval "love" with the strong emphasis laid by feudalism on female chastity. The desire for concentrated transmission of feudal estates to legitimate offspring tended to monogamy and wifely purity. Chastity became woman's main virtue. The wife's highest duty was to furnish a legitimate male heir to the family perquisites. Even the peasant sought marriage distinctly as a means of getting heirs. Chastity was not incumbent on men. A kind of restraint was, indeed, incumbent on the males of the nobility so far as women of their own class were concerned; for male relatives would visit swift punishment on the man that ruined a girl's prospects of becoming the broodmare to some noble house. But women of the working class were legitimate prey of the contemptuous bestiality of the nobles.[5]

The master-class encouraged and controlled marriage

[4] Bebel. *Woman and Socialism*, 73-75.

[5] On this paragraph, compare Meily, *Puritanism*, 33-35; Bebel, *Woman and Socialism*, 80.

among the menials as a means of propagating serfs and securing fees. The lord's power of intercourse with women of servile rank found expression in the *jus primæ noctis* which existed even into modern times.

It must be admitted that feudal days gave to women of the nobility a certain prestige and dignity. As chatelaines they even won military distinction in cases of siege. Prolonged separations emphasized the mutual needs of the two sexes. Life in the family remote from males of equal rank softened patriarchal asperities. The isolation of noble ladies exposing them somewhat to the lusts of base-born men required all knights to be their champions. Chivalry had, forsooth, its fairer side and performed a substantial service in grafting upon sex passion that romantic love which, distorted and perverted as it was by a sickly atmosphere in an age highly favorable to emotion rather than to reason, has become the basis of all that is fairest in sex relations to-day and holds the key to the future.

In the Middle Ages woman was in general an unrecorded cipher lost in obscure domestic toil and the bearing and rearing of numerous children. She generally welcomed a suitor at once for her one recourse was to lose her identity. Military slaughter tended to disturb the balance of the sexes and magnify the value of men. Perhaps the witch delusion which operated unbelievably to decimate the ranks of women was to their sex a blessing in disguise. But women in the Middle Ages probably enjoyed more equality with men than most of the time since.[6] Some held responsible positions and displayed executive ability. In Saxon England women could be present at the local moot and even at the na-

[6] Compare *Position of Women: Actual and Ideal*, 46-47; Abram, *English Life and Manners in the later Middle Ages*, 44.

tional Witanagemot. Norman rule reduced woman's rights, yet under feudalism women could hold high state office in default of male heirs.

In artisan circles, when the revival of commerce brought a wider market for the products of household industry, the patriarchal head of the family owned the product of all its toil. The standard of living in the home depended solely on his will. But gilds admitted women, and women often engaged in commercial pursuits along with their husbands or as their successors. In fourteenth century England, a married woman was permitted by law to act in business as if single in spite of her being under tutelage. In the craft gilds wife and daughters worked with husband and father at his craft. Journeymen could not marry but the master must have a wife of approved descent. The gild supervised the training of children; they were expected to follow their parents' craft. Some gilds forbade employment of wife and daughters and in the last days of the gilds this prohibition became a general rule. Girls were helped with money to marry or go into a religious house as they chose.[7]

Woman's subordinate position in marriage came down through old Teutonic usage. In the old days of ordeal she was incapable of appearing in the lists in her own defense and had to be represented by a protector who, in case of wives, was of course the husband. Even late in the Middle Ages "ein Weib zu kaufen" was the stock expression for getting married. The idea of sale was gone but its place had been taken by the notion of the transfer of authority. A woman was always under guardianship; the natural warden was the father; at

[7] On gild privileges for women, see Brentano, *History and Development of Gilds*, cxxxii; Lipson, *Introduction to the Economic History of England*, vol. i, 316-318.

marriage the wardship passed to the husband. The common law is voiced thus by a dramatic character: "I will be master of what is mine own. She is my goods, my chattels; she is my house, my household stuff, my field, my barn, my horse, my ox, my ass, my anything." The wife was merged in the husband; legally she did not exist.

Our traditional common law in cases of children and real estate left without a will gave a son, tho younger, inheritance before a daughter. In case of a daughter's seduction, her father's only recourse was on the ground that she was his servant and that the seducer had trespassed on his property and deprived him of the benefit of her labor. In nearly all the Teutonic codes the husband had the right to beat his wife. "Justice Brooke affirmeth plainly that if a man beat an outlaw, a traitor, a pagan, his villein, or his wife it is dispunishable, because by the Law Common, these persons can have no action."[8] "Wives in England," says an Antwerp merchant, 1599, "are entirely in the power of their husbands, their lives only excepted." Even in the eighteenth century, wife trading was an English custom.[9] Until the reign of George IV burning at the stake was the legal penalty for wives that murdered their husbands.[10]

Doubtless the reality of English life was less barbarous than the law; yet we are describing a man-made world in which economic dependence held woman in general to a servile level. Her training corresponded to her sphere. In medieval Europe peasant girls were taught to work in house and field, accept the conventional piety, barely to read and write, and then marry.

[8] Brace. *Gesta Christi*, 285-290.

[9] Earle. *Colonial Dames and Goodwives*, 26, 29.

[10] Yonge. *Site of Old "James Towne,"* 138.

All girls were taught the textile arts. Daughters of wealthy burghers had tutors and after the fourteenth century there were schools for them in most cities. Women in the castles had enjoyed the same education as men. The convents, also, had provided training for women. But the rise of the universities, boisterously masculine, detracted from the education of women and a studied contempt for women developed.

Many Renaissance writers gave woman a new recognition. At the Renaissance the position of women underwent a marked transformation. Some women became professors in Italian and Spanish universities.[11] Erasmus wrote of and for women, though not with entire approval of equal educational opportunities for them. He said the wise man is aware that nothing is of greater advantage to woman's morals than worthy knowledge. Toward the close of feudalism girls were sent from castles or wealthy burgher homes to the castles of high nobles to acquire polish. In the fifteenth century an increasing number of women – often of the prosperous middle class – found opportunities, though limited, for literary and classical education. Sir Thomas More believed that education may agree equally well with both sexes. Agrippa (in a work published in 1530) asserted woman's superiority over man and pointed to man's tyranny as the reason for woman's dearth of achievement.[12]

Like women, the younger children of the medieval dignitary were subordinate. Feudal lands were limited in area; hence title, property, rank, and power passed to one child – the oldest male. The family line was of huge social importance: status and worth depended on

[11] *Position of Woman: Actual and Ideal*, 53.

[12] Compare Cooke, *Woman in the Progress of Civilization*, chapter vi.

what one's forebears had done. Exaltation of the family in linear extension rather than expanse was vital to the prosperity of the landed class. In Germany, where the law of primogeniture was too lax, where all of a noble's children were noble and his estates free from entail, the continual multiplication of titles and subdivision of territories reduced most houses to relative poverty. The German noble might provide for younger sons by securing them appointment to some rich benefice but this practice augmented social unrest.

As chivalry sank in decadence the cities flourished and in them the busy, prosaic middle class whose rise burst forth in the Reformation. Bourgeois wives found complete satisfaction around the domestic hearth. In modest bourgeois circles small attention was given to the mental culture of children. Girls generally grew up under the sole supervision of their mothers, or at best enjoyed convent training directed to piety and domestic accomplishments, in which they became very proficient. Girls married even in their fourteenth year. Fathers attached no small importance to practical advantages in matrimony, and the longing of maidens for rich knights was widespread. It came to be no disgrace for a prince to marry a girl of the middle class, for such a match might serve as a means of reviving fading fortunes. Aeneas Sylvius (afterwards Pope Pius II) said of Germany about the middle of the fifteenth century: "Where is the woman (I do not speak of the nobility, but of the bourgeoisie) who does not glitter with gold? What profusion of gold and pearls, ornaments, reliquaries." By the sixteenth century, the castled knights saw the burghers living in houses that, to the dwellers in uncomfortable castles, seemed the height of luxury. The knights' ladies coveted the princely silks and velvets and jewels that decked the womenfolk of the bourgeoisie. Even when the medieval sumptuary laws forbidding the burghers to wear pearls and velvet were not disobeyed, the wives and daughters of the middle class could solace themselves with silks and diamonds. And to the noble lady, the exclusive privilege of wearing pearls and velvet was small comfort in default of the means of procuring them. The knights' attempts to rival the burghers brought on ruin. Switzerland saw a similar riot of conspicuous consumption.

Morals were lax. For the satisfaction of vanity and desire for enjoyment, the daughters of citizens often allowed themselves to be drawn aside from the path of womanly honor. In cases of seduction, where the suitor broke his word and tried to back out after betrothal, the practical father exacted rich compensation. The men were continually complaining against the women. In fifteenth century Germany children born out of wedlock were frequent, growing up in their father's house along with their half brothers and sisters; and for a long time no disgrace attached. Why should it in bourgeois circles, where there was no noble estate to be conserved?[13]

In the fifteenth century, with improved hygienic conditions and favorable material conditions, there were, not uncommonly, families of twelve, fifteen, or even more children. A chronicle gives the city of Erfurt an average of eight to ten children per family. Idealism was not wanting. Albrecht von Eyb, in his treatise *Whether a man ought to take a wife or not*, printed in 1472, seems to speak for the Germany of his day when he says:

Marriage is a useful wholesome thing: by it many a conflict and

[13] See Richard, *History of German Civilization*, 224; *Kulturgeschichte des Mittelalters*, 573-574.

> war is quieted, relationship and good friendship formed, and the whole human race perpetuated. Matrimony is also a merry, pleasurable, and sweet thing. What is merrier and sweeter than the names of father and mother and the children hanging on their parents' necks? If married people have the right love and the right will for one another, their joy and sorrow are common to them and they enjoy the good things the more merrily and bear the adverse things the more easily.

Yet the position of woman was not high: her sphere was the home, and she was seldom mentioned.

The Protestant Revolution changed markedly the old order of life. The movement that is known as the Reformation had a strong economic element.[14] It signified the rise to power of a new sovereign – the industrial, mercantile, commercial middle-class – which had long been falling heir to the power slipping from the hands of a decadent feudal aristocracy. Since the Reformation, the moneyed type has dominated the world.

Where this economic class was not strong enough, the Reformation proved abortive and spelled tragedy to the families that accepted it. Thus, in France, the Huguenots were forbidden to train their children in the faith. A royal decree in 1685 required that every child of five years and over be removed by the authorities from his Protestant parents. Protestant marriages were illegal and the offspring illegitimate. Girls were carried away to shame and parents had no power to interfere. Coligny was at first reluctant to publish his faith because of the suffering that would be entailed on his wife and household; but she preferred to be bold, so he avowed

[14] Adams. *Law of Civilization and Decay*, 187-208; Patten. *Development of English Thought*, 102-105, 117; Forrest. *Development of Western Civilization*, 291-298; Stillé. *Studies in Medieval History*, 443-445; Traill and Mann. *Social England*, vol. iii, 59; Pollard. *Factors in Modern History*, 46-50; Seignobos. *History of Medieval and Modern Civilization*, 283, 290-292.

his religion and held worship daily in his family. Not all families in the riven lands enjoyed such unison.

An understanding of the significance of this great social revolution is essential, both on account of its general influence on the European institutions from which our civilization is derived and from the fact that it was this revolutionary middle-class, stern, sober, prudential, industrial, driven into exile by temporary triumphs of reaction or coming freely in pursuit of opportunity and economic gain, that made America.

Feudal militancy had subordinated family life to the affairs of war. With the passing of the old chivalric notions a good deal of false sentiment died away and the attitude of men toward women was markedly altered. The Reformation developed a rather matter-of-fact view. The bourgeoisie may well claim the honor of being first to assert that romantic love is the ideal basis of marriage; but the constraints of private wealth have always operated to frustrate this ideal. Though suppression of convents curtailed woman's opportunity, the Reformation did remove the stain put on marriage and the family by the law of celibacy. Celibates began to marry. Luther, by word and example, glorified marriage and the family. He said: "O! what a great rich and magnificent blessing there is in the married state; what joy is shown to man in matrimony by his descendants!"[15] His recognition of the normal sex impulse to propagation appears in this utterance: "Unless specially endowed by a rare, divine grace, a woman can no more dispense with a man, than . . . with food, drink, sleep, and other natural needs. In the same way a man cannot do without a woman."[16]

---

[15] Richard. *History of German Civilization*, 253-255; Painter. *Luther on Education*, 113-116.

[16] Bebel. *Woman and Socialism*, 78.

Luther gave woman no chivalric admiration; yet, while emphasizing motherhood, he did not regard woman as a mere bearer of children. Marriage signified to him the moral restraint and religious sanctification of natural impulse. None should marry unless competent to instruct their children in the elements of religion. He emphasized the nurture of children, stressing honor to parents and reverence to God and making no distinction between boys and girls as to need of education nor between men and women as to right to teach. Home should be made a delight but firmness must not be sacrificed. According to him the wife's union to the husband is a fit symbol of the soul's union to Christ by faith. Whatever Christ possesses, the believing soul may claim as its own.[17]

It might be supposed that such liberal views, coming at a time when society thrilled with the longing to establish more firmly the individual personality by means of marriage and family life, would mean an era of emancipation for woman. But this did not immediately follow. The reformers did not recognize woman as in all points equal to man. "Let woman learn betimes to serve according to her lot" was their opinion. She was to be trained to faith and for the calling of housewife and mother. The home under the Reformation continued under the old laws. Woman was to be under obedience to the male head. She was to be constantly employed for his benefit. He chose her society, for he was responsible for her, and to him as a sort of Father Confessor she was accountable. Neither talent nor genius could emancipate her without his consent. At about the time of the Reformation it was said, "She that

[17] Compare Scherr, *Geschichte der deutschen Frauenwelt*, Band ii, 19-21; Vedder, *Reformation in Germany*, 124; Cooke, *Woman in the Progress of Civilization*, 358-359; Painter, *Luther on Education*, chapter vi.

knoweth how to compound a pudding is more desirable than she who skillfully compoundeth a poem." It was the maxim of Luther that "no gown or garment worse become a woman than that she will be wise." Abolition of convents brought a period of two or three centuries in northern lands during which the intellectual training of women largely ceased. Luther pictures the real German housewife–a pious, God-fearing woman, domestic toiler, comforter of man, a rare treasure–trustworthy, loving, industrious, beneficent, blessed. "When a woman walks in obedience toward God," says Luther, "holds her husband in love and esteem, and brings up her children well–in comparison with such ornament, pearls, velvet, and tinsel are like an old, torn, patched, beggar's cloak." It is evident that the faithful, unobtrusive, industrious German *Hausfrau* is the ideal woman of the Reformation.[18]

The reformers had large problems to solve. The Reformation spelled individualism and the decay of the modern family can be traced back to this source. The reformers were not fundamentally to blame. Marriage had been regarded in Germany as a civil contract, yet mystical elements were present such as the notion that marriage would purge away crime, in consequence of which view felons condemned to death would be released if some one would marry them.[19] At the time of the Reformation there was growing up a church theory which treated unblest marriages as concubinage.[20] Confusion arose from prevalent usage. It became customary in one town for betrothed to live together before

---

18 Compare Scherr, *Geschichte der deutschen Frauenwelt*, Band ii, 22-23; Otto, *Deutsches Frauenleben*, 94; Gage, *Woman, Church, and State*, 146-147; Cooke, *Woman in the Progress of Civilization*, chapter iv, 47.

19 Baring-Gould. *Germany, Present and Past*, vol. i, 159, 162, 163.

20 — *Idem.*

marriage. The consistory held such cohabitation to be true marriage. Luther wrote,

> It has often fallen out that a married pair came for me, and that one or both had already been secretly betrothed to another: then there was a case of distress and perplexity and we confessors and theologians were expected to give counsel to those tortured consciences. But how could we?[21]

Luther had slight thought of human interdependence. He looked at morals in a superficial way, as scarcely more than a department of politics belonging to the care of the state. Consequently he followed the secular theory of marriage. He said,

> Know that marriage is something extrinsic as any other worldly action. As I may eat, drink, sleep, walk, ride, and deal with any heathen, Jew, Turk, or heretic, so to one of these I may also become and remain married. Do not observe the laws of fools that forbid such marriages. In regard to matters of marriage and divorce . . . let them be subject to worldly rule since marriage is a worldly extrinsic thing.[22]

Of course Luther desired that the civil authority should be "pious." But not till the end of the seventeenth century was religious ceremony considered necessary to legal marriage among Protestants. Till then "conscience [common-law] marriage" sufficed.[23] Luther and other reformers also opposed restrictions to marriage.

For a time the new era threatened to return to pagan laxity and licentiousness. The reformers did not always avoid immorality in their loose handling of marriage. For instance, Luther says,

> If a healthy woman is joined in wedlock to an impotent man and could not, nor would for her honor's sake openly choose

[21] Baring-Gould. *Germany, Present and Past*, vol. i, 147, 154.
[22] Bebel. *Woman and Socialism*, 78-79.
[23] — *Idem*, 79.

> another, she should speak to her husband thus: "See, my dear husband, thou hast deceived me and my young body and endangered my honor and salvation; before God there is no honor between us. Suffer that I maintain secret marriage with thy brother or closest friend while thou remainest my husband in name. That thy property may not fall heir to strangers; willingly be deceived by me as you have unwillingly deceived me."

The husband should consent. If he refuses, she has a right to leave him, go elsewhere, and remarry. Similarly, if a woman will not perform her conjugal duty, the husband has the right to get another woman, after telling his wife his intention.[24]

Of course the author of such views was in favor of permitting divorcees to remarry. He even sanctioned bigamy. "I confess," he says, "for my part that if a man wishes to marry two or more wives, I cannot forbid him, nor is his conduct repugnant to the Holy Scriptures." Melanchthon advised Henry VIII. to commit bigamy rather than divorce Catherine. He and Luther, as a matter of shrewd politics, connived in the disgraceful bigamy of Philip of Hesse. Luther forgot all honesty in trying to cover the trail of this infamy, which he was unwilling for the "coarse peasants" to imitate. Catholics could well say, "Behold the fruits of the Reformation!" Kolde says, "It is highly probable that the beginning of the decline of Protestantism as a political power coincides with the marriage of the Prince of Hesse."[25]

Such laxity as the reformers exhibited correlates with the economic basis of the Protestant Revolution. Unlike feudal landed estates, bourgeois personalty was not especially appropriate to concentrated hereditary trans-

---

[24] On Luther's radicalism, see *idem*, 79-80.

[25] On Luther and bigamy, see Gage, *Woman, Church, and State*, 399; Vedder, *Reformation in Germany*, 350-355.

mission, as its items were transient and indefinitely increasable. Primogeniture, and even a closely restricted progeny, were no longer necessary to the perpetuation of class domination. The economic reason for the irrefragable feudal marriage was gone. Divorce found a lodgment in bourgeois theory and practice. As we have seen, a certain recognition began to be bestowed on illegitimates. As under Roman law, subsequent marriage of parents became a means of legitimizing them.[26]

It is not to be assumed that sex life in the Reformation period was purer than ordinary. The code of Charles V. was severe against sexual transgression and the sharp penalties denounced upon seduction, adultery, incest, unnatural lust, abortion, infanticide, etc. indicate the prevalence of these practices. Court records of the sixteenth century afford confirmatory evidence. The Protestant clergy declaimed zealously against sexual excess. Prostitutes were harassed and "fallen" women were relentlessly persecuted.

The Reformation was not in all particulars so radical as in its handling of the sex relation. For instance, Luther kept children within the pale of collective religion by accepting the view that faith of sponsors suffices for infants in baptism. It was left for more thorogoing sectaries to apply individualism to this rite also and abolish the baptism of infants.

In so short a space as can be given to this initial chapter it is impossible to harmonize all seeming contradictions in medieval and early modern sex and family life or to give an adequate perspective. It may suffice to remember that out of medieval confusion of thought and practice, out of a feudal society of class privilege

[26] Meily. *Puritanism*, 57-58.

and exploitation, arose by economic process a new social order which stressed the individual and his freedom and revolved around industry and commerce rather than around land ownership. This change of economic base demanded a revolution in thought and morals and new standards evolved to meet the emergency. A survey of England in this period of transition leads to the threshold of American colonization.

II. OLD WORLD ORIGINS-SPECIFIC SOURCES[27]

The *Paston Letters* introduce us to fifteenth century England. In them marriage seems to be in the main a matter of mercenary calculation and withal the chief business of family life. A girl informs her suitor how much her father will give her; if the amount is unsatisfactory he must cease his suit. When Margaret made a love match with a servant in the family her mother cut her off from inheritance tho she did leave twenty pounds to her grandson by this marriage. John Paston sometimes had two matrimonial projects on hand at once. After seeking his brother's advice in a number of cases he finally made a love match with an ardent young lady whose mother was favorable but whose father's economic sense made him hard to satisfy. One precocious youth begs his brother for help in wooing a young lady. "The age of her is by all likelihood eighteen or nineteen at the furthest. And as for the money and plate, it is ready whensoever she were wedded, and as for her beauty judge you that when you see her, and specially behold her hands."

Kindly feelings were not wanting. Marital relations seem to have been comfortable. There were close relations between brothers and when one Paston married, his mother wrote her husband to buy the new daughter a gown "goodly blue" or "bright sanguine." The rearing of children and their start in life were matters of grave concern. Judge Paston's marriageable daughter

[27] Compare Goodsell, *History of the Family*, chapter ix.

was generally beaten once or twice a week by her mother, sometimes twice in one day, and her head was broken in two or three places. When her brother aged sixteen was in school at London the mother sent instructions for the master as follows, "If he hath nought do well, nor wyll nought amend, pray hym that he wyll trewly belassch hym, tyll he wyll amend; and so did the last master, and the best that ever he had, at Cambridge." Such stringencies shadow the bright episodes of Paston affairs. The ill-treated daughter was anxious for a husband as refuge from maternal tyranny. Doubtless many an English maid felt like eagerness, for brutality seems to have been usual with British matrons in high life. Elizabeth Tanfield (1585-1639), Lady Falkland, while speaking to her mother always knelt before her.

The Tudor age found England busy with foreign enterprises, discovery of new worlds, commerce, trade – building up a solid basis of wealth and progress – absorption in economic and intellectual activities that left no time for "chivalry." The man ushered in by the revolution we have already traced was the modern approximation of the "economic man" – a type to whose senses women make a relatively mild appeal. The men of the sixteenth century were somewhat of modern men and regarded woman as a participant in the burdens and pleasures of life, not a being to be worshiped or shunned.

English women enjoyed rather more freedom than some of their continental sisters. A Dutchman of the sixteenth century writes to that effect concerning wives, noting also their fondness for dress and ease. He adds: "England is called the paradise of married women. The girls who are not yet married are kept much more rigorously and strictly than in the Low Countries." The Duke of Wirtemberg who was in England about 1592 remarked on the great liberty accorded women and recorded their fondness for finery; so "that, as I am informed, many a one does not hesitate to wear velvet in the street, which is common with them, whilst at home perhaps they have not a piece of dry bread." One observer says, "The females have great liberty and are almost like masters." [28]

Foreign observers tend to confine their attention to the middle and upper classes. The condition of the lower class, nevertheless, is of equal importance at least. Europe had been slipping toward the starvation point. Firewood was becoming a luxury in many parts of western Europe. Especially in England had the price of building materials risen to what seemed a very high point. Vagabondage was repeatedly the subject of cruel legislation. Any one might take the children of vagabonds and keep them as apprentices. In Henry VIII.'s day the culture of wool had desolated many homes. In order to extend pasturage greedy men resorted to force and fraud and ejected the husbandmen, occasioning thereby poverty, misery, and crime among those deprived of employment.

By the middle of the sixteenth century, castle architecture was being superseded. Even in the fourteenth and fifteenth centuries domestic arrangements had shown a tendency to improve. There was more desire for privacy. The sixteenth century revolutionized domestic architecture. Dissolution of the monasteries threw property into hands concerned more with pleasure than with defense.

---

[28] Traill and Mann. *Social England*, vol. iii, 785-786; Hill. *Women in English Life*, vol. i, 115-118.

In Elizabethan England peasant cottages usually had but two rooms, one for the servants, the other for the family. Substantial farmers had houses with several rooms. For some time housing had been a problem in London. The crowded condition of the city made it an unpleasant abode. Vacated palaces were transformed into tenements that would hold a score or more of families. Elizabeth issued an edict against the housing of different families in the same building but the proclamation was of course mainly futile. Even the people of the better class seem to have had no notion of privacy of daily home life. Rooms opened into one another. Often half a dozen rooms were so connected that some of them could be reached only by passing through several or all of the others. This was the case even with bedrooms. Frequently a large room was converted into several sleeping quarters by means of curtains.

The lure of the city was already felt. People flocked to London and wasted their substance in revels.

> When husband hath at play set up his rest,
> Then wife and babes at home a hungry goeth.
>
> The master may keep revel all the year,
> And leave the wife at home like silly fool.

It seems that country dames did not often share their husbands' trips to the capital. The wife of the city burgess also found ample employment in looking after the multitudinous duties of her household. Little attention was given to improving the education of women of the middle class. Sir Thomas Overbury's poem, "A Wife," expresses the sentiment of the age:

> Give me next good, an understanding wife,
> By nature wise, not learned much by art.

Some knowledge on her part will all my life
  More scope of conversation impart.

. . . . .

A passive understanding to conceive,
  And judgment to discern I wish to find.
Beyond that all as hazardous I leave;
  Learning and pregnant wit in woman-kind,
What it finds malleable maketh frail,
And doth not add more ballast but more sail.

Domestic charge doth best that sexe befit,
  Contiguous businesse so to fix the minde,
That leisure space for fancies not admit,
  Their leisure 'tis corrupteth womankinde.
Else, being placed from many vices free,
They had to heaven a shorter cut than we.

Books are a part of man's Prerogatives . . .

In the words of Gervase Markham [died 1637] also appears the ideal for the English housewife:

Next unto her sanctity and holiness of life, it is meet that our English housewife be a woman of great modesty and temperance, as well inwardly as outwardly; inwardly as in her behavior and carriage towards her husband, wherein she shall shun all violence of rage, passion, and humour, coveting less to direct than to be directed, appearing ever unto him pleasant, amiable and delightful; and, tho' occasions of mishaps, or the misgovernment of his will may induce her to contrary thoughts, yet virtuously to suppress them, and with a mild sufferance rather to call him home from his error, than with the strength of anger to abate the least spark of his evil, calling into her mind, that evil and uncomely language is deformed, tho uttered even to servants; but most monstrous and ugly when it appears before the presence of a husband; outwardly as in her apparel and diet, both of which she shall proportion according to the competency of her husband's estate and calling, making her circle rather straight than large.

She should avoid fantastic fashions and remember that

diet should be nutritive rather than epicurish. He says the housewife ought to understand medicine and nursing, cookery, gardening, care of poultry, making of butter and cheese, cutting up of meat, distilling, and the care of wool and flax. The average Elizabethan housewife was proficient in all these duties. Even if she did not have to perform them it was often necessary to train household servants. Their numerous retinue constituted a veritable *familia* – a burden of responsibility to mistress and master. For instance, John Harrington in 1566 drew up rules for his servants requiring them among other things to attend family prayers under penalty of two pence fine.

With the passing of convent life marriage was more essential to woman than ever. There were not husbands enough to go round. Girls that failed to find mates had a dark outlook – perhaps as drudges for their relatives. For an old maid the Elizabethans could think of no better employment than "to lead apes in hell;"[29] so a younger sister was rarely permitted to marry first. Girls married very young; unmarried daughters were undesirable members of the household. A poet makes a girl of fifteen lament that she has not found a husband; and he was probably not exaggerating. Fifteen or sixteen was a common age for marriage in Shakespeare's day. The maiden of twenty was regarded as a confirmed spinster. Sometimes girls were married so young that it was necessary to wait several years before they were old enough for actual wives. This may have been shrewd business but much immorality resulted from this child-marriage common in fashionable life.

[29] Compare Katherine in Shakespeare, "Taming of the Shrew," act ii, scene 1.

Courtship in the England of Elizabeth was bolder and ruder than to-day. It was, however, improper to propose to the girl before obtaining the parents' consent and as often as not it was they that conveyed the proposal to the girl. Old plays contain more references to the necessity of the lover's trying to win the mother's aid than the father's. A girl rarely dared, however, withstand the father's will for a marriage, and few lovers would risk the loss of a marriage portion through failure to obtain paternal assent to their suit. Lyly presents the situation vividly in these words:

> Parents in these days are grown peevish, they rock their children in their cradles till they sleep, and cross them about their bridals until their hearts ache. Marriage among them has become a market. What will you give with your daughter? What jointure will you make for your son? And many a match is broken off for a penny more or less, as tho they could not afford their children at such a price; when none should cheapen such ware but affection, and none buy it but love. . . Our parents . . . give us pap with a spoon before we can speak, and when we speak for that we love, pap with a hatchet.

He adds, "I shall measure my love by mine own judgment, not my father's purse or peevishness. Nature hath made me his child not his slave." The Elizabethan girl that opposed her father's choice was indeed treated like a slave. "Romeo and Juliet" and the "Two Gentlemen of Verona" reflect this fact and Ophelia's implicit acquiescence in her father's despotism shows what was expected of a well-bred English girl in Shakespeare's day.

Ceremonial betrothal often preceded marriage. It took place before a responsible witness, preferably a priest. After the ceremony the terms husband and wife could be applied and possibly the privilege of the marriage bed might be enjoyed. A like usage will be noted in the American colonies.

In a way children seem to have been esteemed in sixteenth century England. Bonfires were often built in celebration of a wife's pregnancy. Births were celebrated similarly and by other public rejoicing. But children among all classes were treated with severity. A Venetian noble who accompanied an ambassador from Venice to the English court in the sixteenth century wrote:

> The want of affection in the English is strongly manifested toward their children[,] for having kept them at home till they arrive at the age of seven or nine years, they put them out, both males and females to hard service in the homes of other people, binding them generally for another seven or nine years. And these are called apprentices, and during that time they perform all the most menial offices; and few are born who are exempted from this fate, for every one, however rich he may be, sends away his children into the homes of others; whilst he in return receives those of strangers into his own.

This sounds like a rigid system yet we find children described as "most ongracious grafftes, ripe and ready in all lewd libertie" through the fault of the parents and schoolmasters "which do nother teach their children good, nother yet chasten them when they do evill." Between the Reformation and the Civil War lay a century of peace. Men had time to know their children. Little ones figure prettily in memoirs, letters, and art. These children seem to have led happy lives for the most part.

In the seventeenth century, people looking back regretted the passing of the time when daughters were obsequious and serviceable, when

> There was no supposed humiliation in offices which are now accounted menial, but which the peer received as a matter of

course from the gentlemen of his household, and which were paid to the knights and gentlemen by domestics chosen in the families of their own most respectable tenants; whilst in the humbler ranks of middle life it was the uniform and recognized duty of the wife to wait on her husband, the child on his parents, the youngest of the family on his elder brothers and sisters.[30]

With the seventeenth century and the Puritan movement we come to the immediate sources of New England family institutions. It is particularly to the traditions and standards of the middle class, especially of the Puritan type, that we must look for the genesis of northern colonial life. Moreover in the southern colonies this class was stronger and the "cream of society" was weaker than southerners of aristocratic tastes like to admit. The New World environment, too, favored the standards of the middle class from which the immigrants came. This concurrence of geographic and social influences gives us our distinctive civilization. Our modern ideal of monogamy with equality and mutuality is not of aristocratic lineage. It comes up apparently from the "lower" classes where economic conditions forbade polygamic connections. Sumner says: "It is the system of the urban-middle-capitalist class. . . In the old countries the mores of the middle class have come into conflict with the mores of peasants and nobles. The former have steadily won."[31] Naturally so inasmuch as this bourgeoisie, drawing into itself the more enterprising sons of the peasantry and grasping the power that economic change wrested from the nobility, has dominated modern society.

Puritanism was an economic phenomenon.[32] The in-

[30] Hill. *Women in English Life*, vol. i, 125.

[31] Sumner. *Folkways*, 375-376.

[32] Compare Parce, *Economic Determinism*, 98, 102, 110; Patten, *Development of English Thought*, 81-98, 124-134; Meily, *Puritanism*, chapter iii.

fluence of the Renaissance had spread a belief in the pleasures of this world and a regard for the life of the flesh as good in itself. Such a view is the spiritual reflection of the increased comfort and plenty arising from even the limited economic progress of the middle ages. The inventions and changes of the fifteenth century made indoor life less barren and more agreeable and a new type of man was the result – a man that disliked the open country and became attached to home. Elizabeth introduced many new food plants from Italy. Domestic comfort began to enter the homes of the poor. They began to provide their cottages with chimneys. The use of window glass spread and pillows appeared on the beds of the common people. The new conditions made real family life possible. The home became the center of pleasurable activities. To have a wife a homemaker – one that could change into comforts the necessities that man produced – was so much the more desirable.

Under earlier conditions enjoyment had been sought in group festivities, which were likely to be unrestrained and licentious. The development of the modern home caused a divide in social life and gave those that were so disposed a more refined way of satisfying their desire for pleasure. Those in whom the bonds of morality and the ties of family life were strongest gradually withdrew from the coarser community revelry. The Protestant Reformers extolled family life and denounced communal pleasures, attributing their moral degeneration to the Catholic church. New economic conditions with their numerous luxuries offered a strong temptation to depart from ancestral simplicity and brought about a market for indulgences among those that desired to reconcile their moral feelings with conflicting economic tendencies. The bettering of economic conditions in the fifteenth century had, then, increased the evils of communal pleasures and also strengthened and intensified family life. Europe was at the parting of the ways. The "Puritan" was ready for a moral crusade against the growing dissipation and vice that threatened the family.

In the opening years of the seventeenth century refined English ladies preferred rural seclusion to the dissoluteness of the court of James I. Charles purified the court; yet the ladies stayed in the country.

It should be remembered that while Puritanism was of English growth the continent had a Puritanism of its own. The ordinary Dutchman of the seventeenth century stayed at home three hundred and sixty days in the year spending his time in the ancestral dwelling that his grandfather had built for him. In Germany, says Bebel,

> The merry, life-loving townsman of the middle ages became a bigoted, austere, sombre Philistine. . . The honorable citizen with his stiff cravat, his narrow intellectual horizon, his severe but hypocritical morality, became the prototype of society. Legitimate wives who had not favored the sensuality tolerated by the Catholicism of the middle ages, were generally better pleased by the Puritan spirit of Protestantism.

The Puritan emphasis on sexual restraint was of a piece with the general gospel of frugality so appropriate among a class of people trying to accumulate capital in an age of deficit. Urgent economic interests furthered the novel virtue of male chastity. The necessity of accumulation led the Puritan to reprobate all unprofitable forms of sin including markedly licentiousness, that prodigal waster. But male chastity, being less important than female in safeguarding legitimate inheritance, never has attained the sanctity enforced upon females.

The Puritan concept of home was negative. A home was made mainly by abstaining from other social relations. As we have seen, communal pleasures were morally dangerous or at least were so considered. Thus the Maypole had been associated with sex excitement and indulgence. Accordingly in 1644 the Puritan parliament forbade Maypoles. The Puritans also condemned music as one of Satan's snares and ruled it out of the family. They were too short-sighted to glimpse the remoter connections between rhythm and efficiency. The Puritan Englishman was unsociable, independent, full of biblical traditions which cultivated reverence for paternal authority and a desire for abundant paternity.

English families were among the largest in the world. The manor house, the parsonage, the doctor's and the lawyer's homes were swarming with children. The women married young and very frequently died in their youth from sheer exhaustion by child-bearing. Second marriages and double sets of children were found everywhere. Infant mortality was high.

The later Puritanism distorted childhood. Milton's father, tho a strict Puritan, was not harsh to his children, but the poet was the embodiment of unreasonableness and cruelty. The seventeenth century in Europe was an age of precocity. The Puritans, as we shall see in the colonies, were ready to promote this tendency. The fear of infant damnation made necessary the earliest possible conversion of the child. In seventeenth century England it was in Puritan households that the rod was most favored; for were not the little ones until conversion children of wrath requiring to have the devil well whipped out of them? Calvinism retarded, thus, what had been a promising movement away from the rod. If the Puritan wife "obeyed her husband, calling him Lord" she required at the same time strict obedience and honor at the hands of her children.

Nevertheless in some homes of much religious strictness the children were most tenderly dealt with. The fact that so many mothers died young may have been a factor in causing women to train their infants prematurely.

A man's family included his entire household from chaplain to kitchen boy, and for their welfare – soul and body – the master considered himself accountable. He ruled at least the lower of them with the rod.

Girls of the seventeenth century, like their predecessors, married early. While daughters were yet at school or even in the nursery, careful parents were already pondering the selection of husbands. Children were often married at thirteen. Daughters were usually allowed at least the right of refusal but they do not seem to have been prone to make objection. Both Puritans and cavaliers were ready to advise their children, "Let not your fancy overrule your necessity," "Where passion and affection sway, that man is deprived of sense and understanding." Mercenary marriages were in keeping with the nature of the hard-headed middle-class that took to Puritanism. It is surprising that the majority of the seventeenth century marriages of which we hear seem to have turned out so well.

Under the early Stuarts the education of women continued to be seriously regarded but it is doubtful whether the high standards of the Tudor ladies were preserved save in select circles. A volume published in London in 1632 declares that "the reason why women have no control in Parliament, why they make no laws, consent to none, abrogate none, is their original sin." The Cromwellian period brought no improvement in the condition of woman. Ministers still preached her responsibility for the fall, and warnings were thundered against her extreme sinfulness. Milton's views were derogatory of woman. He says: "Either . . . polygamy is a true marriage, or all children born in that state are spurious, which would include the whole race of Jacob, the twelve tribes chosen by God. . . Not a trace appears of the interdiction of polygamy throughout the whole law, not even in any of the prophets." *Paradise Lost* inculcated many views inimical to woman. Milton was a tyrant over his own house, unloved by any of his series of wives or by his daughters. He did much to strengthen the idea of woman's subordination to man: "He for God; she for God in him;" or as Eve puts it–"God thy law, thou mine."

The idea that learning was a waste of time for a woman was beginning to assert itself but did not meet with universal acceptance. The education of women was generally neglected: some women of high rank could not write. The mother was generally found at home superintending the education of her daughters. As housewife she was supposed to order thoroly her household.

We must not suppose that the Puritan husband was always a despot. There were many happy marriages.[33] Cromwell's wife wrote to him: "My life is but half a life in your absence, did not the Lord make it up in Himself." He wrote to her: "Thou art dearer to me than any creature, let that suffice." Colonel Hutchin-

[33] Traill and Mann. *Social England*, vol. iv, 220; Byington. *The Puritan in England and New England*, 222-231; Coxe. *Claims of the Country on American Females*, vol. ii, 15; Young. *Chronicles of the First Planters of the Colony of Massachusetts Bay, from 1623 to 1636*, 432.

son, one of the Ironsides, was a model husband, full of tenderness and devotion. The age shows many illustrations of beautiful family relations. John Winthrop writes to his wife thus: "My only beloved spouse, my most sweet friend, and faithful companion of my pilgrimage, the happye and hopeful supplye (next Christ Jesus) of my greatest losses." He addresses her at various times as – "My truly beloved and deare wife. . . My sweet wife. . . My most deare and sweete spouse. . . My deare wife, my chief love in this world." Mrs. Winthrop declared that her husband loved her; and "she delighted to steal time from household duties to talk with her absent lord." John Cotton addresses his wife as "Dear wife and comfortable yoke-fellow . . . sweetheart."

The seventeenth-century lady who, owing to her shortage of money or to other disability, had failed of marriage enjoyed none of the present recourses. She could not properly set up bachelor quarters. It was customary for the mistress of a house to have a gentlewoman as assistant and such a position afforded a natural occupation for an unmarried relative or friend tho the "position was often not much better than that of a superior lady's maid." "Even before their marriage, if they had no homes, and in the hard and troublous times of the Civil War, girls not infrequently accepted an offer of this description."[34]

While the spirit of Puritanism drew sharp lines around the family and strengthened its stakes, there were Reformation influences, as we have seen, that tended to unsettle the family (along with other social institutions). The Renaissance and the Reformation

[34] Bradley. *The English Housewife in the Seventeenth and Eighteenth Centuries*, 24.

worked out in the elevation of the individual and tended to cause the decline of the family as a social unit. Every man was to stand on his own feet. Laxity of opinion and teaching on the sacredness of the marriage bond and in regard to divorce goes back to continental Protestants of the sixteenth century. It was reflected in the laws of Protestant states in Europe and in the codes of New England. The Reformation was not immediately a great ethical force. The effect of Protestant liberty was at first bad because it set men free to violate social standards. Rights were magnified; duties approached zero. Reformers' later writings lament horrible moral deterioration of the people.

Strange sects arose. In 1532 John Becold of Leyden arrived at Münster with a great number of believers. He pretended to receive revelations, one of which was that God willed that a man should have as many wives as he pleased. John had fifteen and encouraged polygamy among his followers. It was counted praiseworthy to have many wives and all the good-looking women in Münster were besieged with solicitations. (It is noteworthy that there was a surplus of woman in Münster at the time. Such a situation favors polygamy.) A later leader, Jan Wilhelms, had twenty-one wives.

Save at Münster polygamy was never even proposed by Anabaptists. Nevertheless dangerous influences were spreading. It was at Norwich among an offshoot of Anabaptists that Brown (Separatist) established his first congregation. In the eyes of the Brownists marriage was only an ordinary contract requiring neither minister nor magistrate. Francis Johnson, third chief of the Brownists, justified bundling with other men's wives. The Pilgrims were Brownists. Robertson attributes the Plymouth communism to Brownist influence. It may be that some of the sexual looseness and trouble with people marrying themselves (in New England) was a reflection of the extravagances of the European sectaries.

To some the doctrines and practices of the Friends seemed dangerously loose. This sect believed marriage to be an ordinance of God, not requiring the intervention of a clergyman. The bride and the groom took each other in presence of the meeting and signed a certificate which was then signed by the audience. For a time such marriages were illegal but in 1661 a decision was rendered in their favor. This was an important victory as enemies were raising questions as to legitimacy and property under such marriages. Fox claimed scripture in support of the Friends' practice. "Where do you read," he says, "from *Genesis* to *Revelation* that ever any priest did marry any?"

But the Friends found it necessary to censor marriage. Fox says, "Many had gone together in marriage contrary to their relations minds; and some young, raw people, that came among us had mixt with the world. Widows had married without making provision for their children by their former husbands," etc. So it was ordered that all bring their marriages before the meetings. Fox opposed marriage of too near kindred, hasty remarriages, and child marriages. He advocated a register of marriages. None were to marry without parents' or relatives' certificate. The Quakers in England were demanding (1655) equal rights for women, abolition of lewd sports, and establishment of civil marriage. The Quakers were a species of Super-Puritans.

Had the unsettling, secularizing, individualistic tendencies of the Protestant movement gone altogether without counteraction the family would doubtless have approached a stage of disintegration comparable to that of to-day. Milton's liberal divorce ideas are notorious. Puritan advocacy of divorce was stimulated by the trading-class opposition to feudalism.[35] Indissoluble marriage, vital to feudalism, was a convenient point of attack. (Present outcry against "the divorce evil" comes chiefly from the ritualistic churches, themselves survivals of feudalism.) But the original ground of monogamy – the necessity of restricted and ascertained progeny as heirs – remained and monogamy was consequently retained with divorce as a loophole. An additional support of monogamy continued in the fact that the order of exploitation established by the bourgeoisie like its feudal predecessor kept most men too poor to afford a plurality of wives.

There was sufficient canniness in the Calvinist to prevent excess of riot. The Puritans were men of business and where the financial pawn is at stake marriage is likely to be relatively stable. The significance of Calvin's position (for the purpose of this study) will be very evident if we remember the make-up of the colonial population. Through all the colonies ran the creed of Calvin whose doctrines lived in the Puritan, the Dutch Reformed, the Huguenot, the Scotch-Irish. It may be well therefore to cite the position of this man whose teachings influenced so deeply the foundations of America.

From our point of view at least, Calvin's doctrine of marriage lacks consistency and, judged by present notions, his conception of the marriage relation is by no means a high one. True, he does liken the conjugal

[35] Meily. *Puritanism*, 58.

relation to that existing between Christ and the believer and insists that it must be supported by mutual fidelity but when all is said marriage is, according to his teaching, simply a vent to passion, a last resort when self-control fails. (The Westminster larger catechism enumerates among "the duties required in the seventh commandment . . . marriage by those that have not the gift of continency.") Woman, wife, thus became a channel for lust, tho even in matrimony due restraint and moderation were to be observed.

Children were to be kept in strict subjection. "Those who violate the parental authority by contempt or rebellion, are not men but monsters. Therefore the Lord commands all those who are disobedient to their parents to be put to death."[36]

Obviously this stern doctrine of the family was calculated to develop an institution under paternal supremacy with the wife a mere adjunct to her lord's desires and the children minor slaves of his will. Such results are easier to secure than the masculine fidelity with which Calvin idealized his teachings. It will be found that, in broad outline, the colonial family reflected the type approved by Calvin, tho not without mollifications induced by fatherly love or by the limits of wifely and filial patience, or imposed by the sense of the community.

Inasmuch as the first English colony of the North was formed by sojourners from Holland it is well before proceeding to the study of colonial life to examine the influences to which the Pilgrims were subject during their stay in the low countries.

In Leyden the (Dutch) people generally were betrothed or married very young. Sometimes the be-

[36] On Calvin, see his *Institutes*, vol. i, 344-345, 360, 364-367.

trothal was of considerable duration and the betrothed pair enjoyed great liberty. At the end of the sixteenth century marriage was solemnized in church, tho somewhat privately, but inside of ten years it became almost entirely a civil ceremony, celebrated in presence of the magistrate. Pastor Robinson agreed "that the ceremonies of marriage and burial, being common to all men, whether Christian or heathen, were no part of the services of the church, and should be performed . . . by a civil magistrate."

Some other features of Dutch life seem to have influenced American life through the Pilgrims. One was the high position of women. The women of Netherlands in the sixteenth century were distinguished by beauty of form and vigor of constitution. Unconfined, travelling alone and unafraid, they had acquired manners more frank and independent than women in other lands, while their morals were pure and their decorum undoubted. The women of the Dutch Netherlands in the sixteenth and seventeenth centuries were more highly educated, better protected by the laws, and more prominent in station than any of their contemporaries.[37] On the wife's judgment, prudence, foresight, everything hinged. In business, women's opinions were sought and valued. They often engaged unquestioned in business independent of their men-folk. Holland was the only country where boys and girls were educated alike in the same schools. In most cities husband and wife were responsible for each others' debts. According to Moryson the husbands were veritable slaves and he tells of one wife who said that her husband "had newly asked

[37] Compare Van Rensselaer, *The Goede Vrouw of Mana-ha-ta, 1609-1760*, 10-13; Motley, *Rise of the Dutch Republic*, vol. i, 98; Cockshott, *The Pilgrim Fathers*, 116, 117.

her leave to goe abroade." "I may boldly say," he remarks, "that the women of those parts, are above all others truly taxed with this unnatural domineering over their husbands." The high position of woman was not approved by English writers. Guicciardini, also, writes: "The Women governe all, both within doors and without, and make all bargains, which joyned with the natural desire that Women have to bear rule, maketh them too imperious and troublesome."

The rights of wife and children were very carefully secured. A wife could bequeath her dowry as she pleased and, if childless, could will to her kin, after her husband's death, half of what he had acquired after marriage. Should husbands "either break in life-time, or be found banckerouts at death the wives are preferred to all debtors in the recovery of their dowry." The influence of this usage on Plymouth law will be suggested in the study of that colony, as also the influence of the Dutch law of inheritance which provided for far greater equality among members of the family than prevailed in England.

In Holland estates were usually left to be divided equally among all the children. Thus few received enough for maintenance and it was necessary to learn self-support. A son could not be disinherited save for certain causes approved by law and a father must leave at least one-third his estate for his children. Moreover, upon the death of their mother the children could require their father to divide his goods with them "lest he should waste all."

Dutch influence had something to do with the broad liberal policy of the first generation of Pilgrims. Moreover, the Pilgrims had during their twelve years in Holland an excellent experience in family training. The schools were Dutch and home training was necessary.

Conditions in Holland were not sufficiently favorable to invite permanent residence.

> For [says Bradford] many of their children, that were of best dispositions and gracious inclinations, having learned to bear the yoke in their youth, and willing to bear part of their parents burdens, were oftentimes so oppressed with their heavy labors, tho their minds were free and willing, yet their bodies bowed under the weight of the same and they became decrepit in their early youth. . . Many of their children . . . were drawn away by evil examples into extravagant and dangerous courses, getting the reins off their necks, and departing from their parents.

This was one of the considerations that led to migration to America.

III. COURTSHIP AND MARRIAGE IN COLONIAL NEW ENGLAND

In essentials the marriage usages of the United States run back to the period before the Revolution. The American colonist of English stock was a home-builder from the beginning. It was because the hazards of life at home made it impossible to gather a competence for their children that the religious enthusiasts sought a settled habitation over seas.[38] These sturdy Englishmen came, not as individual adventurers, but as families. If men came alone it was to prepare the way for wife and children or sweetheart by the next ship and they came to stay. The success of English colonization as contrasted with the more brilliant but less substantial French and Spanish occupation of the new world is due to its family nature.

The white colonial population of New England was pure English save for some Scotch-Irish in New Hampshire and Huguenots in Massachusetts and Rhode Island. This homogeneity of the North Atlantic colonies makes it possible to study them as a group and simplifies the understanding of their cultural lineage.

Marriages began at an early date in the new world. Love-making must have been a welcome pastime on the interminable voyages of those days and chaperonage seems to have been unknown in colonial life. Men took long rides with the damsel on the pillion behind them. Certainly the Puritans, sharply struggling, fru-

[38] Smythe. *Conquest of Arid America*, 12, 14.

gal, and homekeeping, did not multiply social functions as means for intercourse of youths and maidens. Till the singing-school came to save the day, regular opportunities for young New Englanders to become acquainted with prospective mates were apparently few. But even in New England, maidens enjoyed large liberty, for the neighborhoods were at first composed of approved families and in any case it was impossible in the wild, rough, new land, where every hand was needed for urgent labor, to think of secluding girls. To such influences we may trace the liberty of the modern American girl. Untoward results sometimes ensued, even in supposedly staid colonial days, before the primitive simplicity was adequately safeguarded.

Love and marriage at first sight brought romantic interest to the wilderness life where existence without home connections offered no attraction to serious men. In more than one instance a lonely Puritan came to the door of a maiden he had never seen, presented credentials, told his need of a housekeeper, proposed marriage, obtained hasty consent, and notified the town clerk, all in one day. On one occasion a bold fellow removed a rival's name from the posted marriage notice, inserted his own, and carried off the bride. After his death she married the first lover. Another Lochinvar kidnapped a bride-to-be on the eve of marriage.

In some parts of Connecticut courtship was carried on in the living-room in the presence of the family. Sara Knight, who journeyed from Boston to New York and back in 1704, notes the Puritanism of people along the way who would not allow harmless kissing among the young people. An earlier English traveller gives a cheering glimpse of Boston: "On the South there is a small but pleasant common, where the gallants, a little before sunset, walk with their Marmalet-Madams till the nine o'clock bell rings them home to their respective habitations."

In at least one noteworthy case the maiden did the courting. Cotton Mather writes:

> There is a young gentlewoman of incomparable accomplishments. No gentlewoman in the English Americas has had a more polite education. She is one of rare witt and sense; and of a comely aspect; and . . . she has a mother of an extraordinary character for her piety. This young gentlewoman first addresses me with diverse letters, and then makes me a visit at my house; wherein she gives me to understand, that she has long had more than an ordinary value for my ministry; and that since my present condition has given her more of liberty to think of me, she must confess herself charmed with my person, to such a degree, that she could not but break in upon me, with her most importunate requests, that I should make her mine, and that the highest consideration she had in it was her eternal salvation, for if she were mine, she could not but hope the effect of it would be that she should also be Christ's. I endeavored faithfully to set before her all the discouraging circumstances attending me, that I could think of. She told me that she had weighed all those discouragements but was fortified and resolved with a strong faith in the mighty God for to encounter them all. . . I was in a great strait how to treat so polite a gentlewoman. . . I plainly told her that I feared, whether her proposal would not meet with unsurmountable opposition, from those who had a great interest in disposing of me. However I desired that there might be time taken. . . In the meantime, if I could not make her my own, I should be glad of being any way instrumental, to make her the Lord's. . . She is not much more than twenty years old. I know she has been a very aiery person. Her reputation has been under some disadvantage. What snares may be laying for me I know not. [The gossip that arose about this case became such a nuisance that] all the friends I have . . . persuade me, that I shall have no way to get from under these confusions but by proceeding unto another marriage. Lord help me, what shall I do? [39]

[39] Mather's *Diary* (Massachusetts Historical Society *Collections*, seventh ser., vol. vii), part i, 457-458, 477.

The fathers seem to have relied much on the Lord in their courtship. On the occasion of his widowhood Mather wrote: "I have committed unto my Lord Jesus Christ the care of providing an agreeable consort for me, if my support in the service of his church . . . render it necessary or convenient." Later he thinks that the Lord is arranging things tho the people are worrying him about matches. It would be hard for them to tell, one might suppose, how much had been done by divine agency, inasmuch as match-makers were common. Thus Sewall writes of his second wife: ". . . My loving wife, who was the promoter of the match [of daughter Judith] and an industrious contriver of my daughter's comfortable settlement" has died. "I need your prayers that God . . . would yet again provide such a good wife for me, that I may be able to say I have obtained favor of the Lord; or else to make it best for me to spend the remnant of my life in a widowed condition."

Parents had, of course, a profound interest in their children's matrimonial outlook. We find Judge Sewall craftily and slyly endeavoring to ascertain whether his daughter Mary's prospective suitor had previously courted another girl. Later we read: "In the evening Sam Gerrish came not; we expected him; Mary dress'd herself; it was a painfull disgracefull disapointment." A month later the delinquent lover returned and finally married Mary, who died shortly and thus opened the way for a speedy remarriage to his first love.

Zeal for parental authority shows itself in legal attempts to restrain eager suitors from their unauthorized courting of "men's daughters and maids under guardians . . . and of mayde servants." As late as 1756, Connecticut recognized the right of parents to dispose of children in marriage. In New Haven, 1660, Jacob Minline went into the room where Sarah Tuttle was, seized her gloves, and then kissed her. "They sat down together; his arm being about her; and her arm upon his shoulder or about his neck; and hee kissed her, and shee kissed him, or they kissed one another, continuing in this posture about half an hour." Father Tuttle sued Jacob for inveigling his daughter's affections. When asked in court whether Jacob inveigled her affections she answered "No;" so the court fined Sarah rather than Jacob, calling her a "bould virgin." She answered "she hoped God would help her to carry it better for time to come." At the end of two years her fine was still unpaid and half of it was remitted.

In spite of all the seeming parental tyranny that prevailed in colonial days young women seem to have exercised considerable independence in love affairs. Betty Sewall, to her father's dismay, refused several suitors. Once he writes urging her to think well before she dismisses a certain suitor but telling her, nevertheless, that if she can not love, honor, and obey the man, her father will say no more.

Parents were not, indeed, legally supreme over their children's espousal. The general authority pursued its own ends and might work against the parental authority as well as with it. In a new country, needing population, it was natural that pious authorities should frown upon any discouragement of legitimate increase. The interests of the community took precedence over the private interests of parents, guardians, and masters. Marriage was normally undelayed. Appeal to a magistrate was in order in case of unreasonable opposition by those in charge of the young people. Thus unruly parents could be brought to terms.

Parents could be held to account for evil results of unreasonable opposition. In 1679 a couple being convicted of fornication before marriage, the case was held over and parents summoned to show why they denied the young couple marriage so long "after they were in order thereto." Such a decision would be distasteful to those that regarded as a divine gift the parental power to dispose of a child in marriage. We can imagine how it would impress the colonial gentleman who once expressed the opinion that "virgin modesty . . . should make marriage an act rather of obedience than choice . . . and they that think their friends too slow-paced in the matter give certain proof that lust is the sole motive."

Breach of promise sometimes occurred. Suits seem to have been rare; but cases were sometimes brought against both men and women and there are instances of damages assessed in behalf of men as well as for women. Such episodes suggest the economic element in marriage.

The European tendency to mercenary marriage carried over to the new world. Capital was naturally in urgent demand. Marriage was accorded matter-of-fact treatment. No sentiment was presupposed and it was easy for marriage to degenerate into a mere bargain. Emanuel Downing, one of the ablest Puritans, writes in 1640 of his matrimonial projects for children and niece, for which maiden he had secured a "varie good match," a member of the church with an estate of four hundred or five hundreds pounds. Governor Winthrop was Mrs. Downing's brother and guardian to the little orphan girl, Rebecca Cooper, "a verie good match," an "inheritance" on whom Downing and his wife had pitched as a fit wife for their son. Without speaking to the girl they wrote to the governor. He refused

> For the present, for these grounds. First: The girle desires not to mary as yet. Secondlie: Shee confesseth (which is the truth) hereself to be altogether yett unfitt for such a condition, shee being a verie girl and but fifteen yeares of age. Thirdlie: When the man was moved to her shee said shee could not like him. Fourthlie: You know it would be of ill reporte that a girl because she hath some estate should bee disposed of soe young, espetialie not having any parents to choose for her. . . If this will not satisfy some, let the court take her from mee and place with any other to dispose of her. I shall be content. Which I heare was plotted to accomplish this end.

There was doubtless point to the Massachusetts law of 1646 that no female orphan during her minority should be given in marriage except with the approbation of the majority of the selectmen of her town.

Luce Downing was persuaded by her mercenary parents' statement of pecuniary benefits to wed Mr. Norton to her father's delight, who wrote: "Shee may stay long ere she meet with a better unless I had more monie for her than I now can spare." But the girl's affections were vacillating; she seemed to be proposing to jilt Norton. His brother wrote a pointed letter to the governor about her vagaries. More liberal settlements were made; so she married Norton. The crassly monetary philanderings of Sewall[40] illustrate splendidly the mercenary spirit pervading the match-making of the New Englanders.

The useful function of widows in colonial economics appears in the frank words of one worthy who says,

> Our uncle is not at present able to pay you or any other he owes money to. If he was able to pay he would; they must have patience till God enable him. As his wife died in mercy near

[40] Summarized in Goodsell, *History of the Family*, 360-363; Earle, *Customs and Fashions in Old New England*, 43-56.

twelve months since, it may be he may light of some rich widow that may make him capable to pay; except God in this way raise him he cannot pay you or any one else.

Benjamin Franklin, in the New England *Courant* of December 11, 1721, lampoons economic marriage thus:

ON SYLVIA THE FAIR – A JINGLE

A Swarm of Sparks, young, gay, and bold,
Lov'd Sylvia long, but she was cold;
Int'rest and pride the nymph control'd,
So they in vain their passion told.
At last came Dulman, he was old,
Nay, he was ugly, but had gold,
He came, and saw, and took the hold,
While t'other beaux their loss consol'd.
Some say, she 's wed; I say she 's sold.

Speculating fops are hit in the *Courant* of January 29, 1722:

Adv. Several journeymen gentlemen (some foreigners and others of our own growth), never sully'd with business, and fit for town or country diversion, are willing to dispose of themselves in marriage, as follows, viz: Some to old virgins, who, by long industry have laid up £500, or proved themselves capable of maintaining a husband in a genteel and commendable idleness. Some to old or young widows, who have estates of their first husband's getting, to dispose of at their second husband's pleasure. And some to young ladies, under age, who have their fortunes in their own hands, and are willing to maintain a pretty, genteel man, rather than be without him.

N.B. The above gentlemen may be spoke with almost any hour in the day at the Tick-Tavern in Prodigal Square, and will proceed to courtship as soon as their mistresses shall pay their tavern score.

The genuine matrimonial advertisement put in its appearance in 1759. In the Boston *Evening Post*, Feb. 23, 1759, appeared:

To the ladies. Any young lady between the age of 18 and 23 of a midling stature; brown hair, regular features and a lively brisk eye: of good morals and not tinctured with anything that may sully so distinguishable a form possessed of £300 or 400 entirely her own disposal and where there will be no necessity of going through the tiresome talk of addressing parents or guardians for their consent: such a one by leaving a line directed for A.W. at the British Coffee House in King Street appointing where an interview may be had will meet with a person who flatters himself he shall not be thought disagreeable by any lady answering the above description. N.B. Profound secrecy will be observ'd. No trifling answers will be regarded.

We have ample evidence that fashionable courtship was permeated by a constantly economic spirit. Happy husbands were ready to sue their fathers-in-law if they proved too tardy or remiss in the matter of the bridal portion.[41] For years Edward Palmer worried the Winthrops about their sister's (his first wife's) dowry, long after he had taken a second wife. In 1679 James Willet, who had married Lieutenant Peter Hunt's daughter Elizabeth, claimed that the father had promised one hundred pounds as inducement. He sued for payment but lost and had to pay costs. Still the marriage seems to have been honorable and happy. Judge Sewall after his daughter's death higgled with her father-in-law over her dowry and grief did not dull his shrewdness.

As has already been suggested, the entrance to matrimony was well guarded in colonial New England. The law required previous publication, parental consent, and registration. Throughout New England except in New Hampshire the law enforced for nearly two centuries the publication of the banns three times preliminary to marriage. Sometimes consent of parents was included in the notice of banns. New Hampshire law, breezy

[41] Earle. *Customs and Fashions in Old New England*, 62.

foreshadowing of western recklessness, made possible "unpublished" marriage for such as would pay two guineas for a license. Considerations of revenue were the spring of this radicalism. Sometimes parsons kept a stock of these licenses on hand for issue to eloping couples at a profit.[42] Runaway marriages without publication were not considered very respectable; strictness in regard to marriage was as much in the interest of the state as for the satisfaction of parents.

New England called a halt to the growing tendency to make marriage an ecclesiastical function. Marriage was declared to be a civil contract, not a sacrament, and to require no priestly intervention. In the early period the Puritans were ordinarily more careful than Calvin who called the conjugal relation "sacred." They were satisfied with calling it "honorable." The publication of banns was ordinarily set for a public lecture or training day rather than on the Sabbath. The administration of the marriage law was a local function, performed by town officers. The Pilgrims had adopted the views of the Dutch Calvinists as to marriage; they held that neither Scripture nor the primitive Christians had ever authorized clergymen to perform marriage services, but that marriage with its civil obligations and connection with property rights as well as its importance in a business way to the state should be a strictly civil contract to be entered into before a magistrate. Thus William Bradford writes:

> May 12 was the first marriage in this place; which according to the laudable custom of the low-cuntries, in which they had lived, was thought most requisite to be performed by the magistrate, as being a civill thing upon which many questions about inheritances doe depende with other things most proper to their cognizance, and most consonante to the Scriptures.

---

[42] Earle. *Customs and Fashions in Old New England*, 76.

Civil marriage was not only the custom; it was the only legal form. Winthrop reports an interesting case.

> There was a great marriage to be solemnized at Boston. The bridegroom being of Hingham Mr. Hubbard's church, he was procured to preach and came to Boston to that end. But the magistrates . . . sent to him to forbear. The reasons: . . . For that his spirit had been discovered to be averse to our ecclesiastical and civil government; and he was a bold man and would speak his mind. 2. We were not willing to bring in the English custom of ministers performing the solemnities of marriage, which sermons at such times might induce; but if any ministers were present, and would bestow a word of exhortation, etc., it was permitted.

Opposition to a religious ceremony existed at a late date. A Huguenot clergyman was haled to court in 1685 for solemnizing marriages in Boston. He agreed to desist but presently forgot his promise. For some reason he saw fit to depart the same week for New York.

In the early years of the colonies the English usage of ceremonial betrothal persisted. In Plymouth this observance was known as pre-contract. Cotton Mather says: "There was maintained a solemnity called a contraction a little before the consummation of a marriage was allowed of. A pastor was usually employed and a sermon also preached on this occasion." One minister preached from *Ephesians*, vi, 10, 11, in order "to teach that marriage is a state of warfaring condition." The moral tendency of this half-way marriage must have been bad.

In many towns disorderly marriages – many of them, doubtless, between Quakers – were punished. Cases of self-betrothal seem to have been frequent and an observer writes that "there are those who practice no formality of marriage except joining hands and so live."

The possible connection of such laxity with Brownism has already been suggested. Clandestine marriages were frequent enough to be troublesome. The second generation at Plymouth developed radicalism. One fancy was the performance of marriage by unauthorized persons. Some couples dispensed with celebrant altogether. Men were fined for disorderly marriage. In Boston in 1641, Governor Bellingham gave scandal by suddenly marrying a woman who was about forming a contract with another. The banns had not been legally published and he married himself. He was prosecuted but refused to leave the bench of the court. Amid excitement the case was postponed and it was not again called up. Some couples were fined every month till they were properly married.

A Rhode Island act of 1647 outlaws the simple marriage by agreement. The Rhode Island colony records contain the case of a couple who had married themselves before witnesses. The woman had been legally separated from her husband, who got away with most of her estate. So she took up with George Gardener for her maintenance but was oppressed in spirit because she judged him not to be lawfully her husband. She petitioned to have her property and live apart. The assembly stigmatizes her as an abominable fornicator. The pair had owned each other as man and wife for eighteen or twenty years. Each was fined twenty pounds and ordered "not to lead soe scandalose life." Thereafter such marriages were to be proceeded against as for fornication. Due rules for marriage should be observed. Exception was made in favor of those then irregularly living as man and wife. They must live together.

A New London scapegrace insisted on taking up

with a woman and making her his wife without ceremony. The affair was a scandal to the community. A magistrate, meeting the couple on the street, accosted them thus: "John Rogers, do you persist in calling this woman, a servant, so much younger than yourself, your wife?" "Yes, I do," retorted John. "And do you, Mary, wish such an old man as this to be your husband?" "Indeed I do," she said. "Then, by the laws of God and this commonwealth," was the disconcerting reply, "I, as a magistrate, pronounce you man and wife."

Such were the difficulties that beset the fathers in their attempt to steer a safe middle course between ceremonial and common law marriage.

During the "tyranny" following 1686 the laws requiring marriage by civil magistrate were abrogated. Referring to Charlestown, Mr. Edes writes that the Reverend Charles Morton "was the first clergyman in this place to solemnize marriages, which previously to 1686 were performed only by civil magistrates."

As it became apparent that the Reformation church was a safe constituent of the new economic order, distrust of ecclesiastical functionings faded. In 1692 (the year Plymouth was merged in Massachusetts) the clergy were first authorized by the new province to perform marriages. The following is found for Connecticut in 1694:

> This court for the satisfaction of such as are conscientiously desireous to be marryed by the minister of their plantations do grant the ordayned ministers of the severall plantations . . . liberty to joyne in marriage such persons as are qualified for the same according to law.

Opposition to religious ceremonial abated and presently ministers of all denominations were allowed to perform the ceremony. Neal in his *History of New England* wrote:

> All marriages in New England were formerly performed by the civil magistrate, but of late they are more frequently solemnized by the clergy, who imitate the method prescribed by the church of England except in their collects, and the ceremony of the ring.

Nevertheless the Puritan contention has prevailed. Marriage was secularized and brought under control of the civil law and to-day when a minister performs the ceremony it is as an agent of the state that he acts.

The settlers in the New World gradually introduced more ceremony and gayety into their weddings. Asceticism could not outlive the age of deficit. In wealthy families a handsome outfit was usually provided for the adornment of the bride. Rude merriment attended New England weddings. There was sometimes a scramble for the bride's garter. The winner was supposed to gain luck and speedy marriage. In Marblehead the bridesmaids and groomsmen put the newly married pair to bed. It is said also that the bridal chamber was the scene of healths drunk and prayers offered. Judge Sewall was slighted on one occasion. He says that "none came to us" (after he and his elderly bride had retired). This usage of visiting the bridal chamber was doubtless a reminiscence of the day when every marriage was a tribal concern whose issue was vital to group life.

It was customary to allow the bride to choose the text of the sermon on the Sabbath when she appeared as bride. Brides were sometimes commendably clever in this matter. Thus Asa Somebody and his bride were edified by a discourse on the words: "And Asa did that which was good and right in the eyes of the Lord his God." Another favorite was: "Two are better than one; because they have a good reward for their labor. For if they fall the one will lift up his fellow; but woe to him that is alone when he falleth; for he hath not another to help him up." In some places the bride and groom seated themselves prominently in the gallery and in the midst of the service rose and rotated slowly several times for the edification of the congregation.

Even the small number of negroes in New England was a problem. In 1705 in Massachusetts we find that intermarriage between a white person and a negro or mulatto was forbidden by statute and a fine of fifty pounds fixed upon any person officiating at such marriage. It was also ordered that "no master shall unreasonably deny marriage to his negro with one of the same nation." Masters were responsible for the fines incurred by their slaves for sex offences; hence it might be less trouble to allow regular wedlock. Common-law marriage seems to have been valid but there were public legal marriages among Massachusetts slaves. Their banns were published in regular form.

The dependence of negro marriage on the master's good will is illustrated by a bill of sale of a negress in Boston in 1724 which recites that "Whereas Scipio, of Boston . . . free negro . . . purposes marriage to Margaret, . . . servant of . . . Dorcas Marshall: now to the intent that the said intended marriage may take effect, and that the said Scipio may enjoy the said Margaret without any interruption," etc. she is duly sold with her apparel for fifty pounds.

The later Massachusetts act (1786) prohibiting the marriage of whites to Indians, negroes, or mulattoes and declaring such marriages void was not repealed till 1843.

There were throughout New England regular marriages of white men with Indian women. In slavery days in Massachusetts it was to the advantage of negroes to take Indian wives, for the children of such unions would be free.

That economic interest was stronger than moral sense in the hearts of the fathers is shown in a formula for slave marriage[43] prepared and used by Reverend Samuel Phillips of Andover (1710-1771):

> You S. do now in the presence of God, and these witnesses, take R. to be your wife; promising that so far as shall be consistent with the relation which you now sustain, as a servant, you will perform the part of a husband towards her; and in particular you promise that you will love her; and that, as you shall have the opportunity and ability you will take a proper care of her in sickness and health, in prosperity and adversity; and that you will be true and faithful to her, and will cleave to her only, so long as God in his Providence, shall continue your and her abode in such place (or places) as that you can conveniently come together.

Similar words were repeated to the woman.

[43] Howard. *History of Matrimonial Institutions*, vol. ii, 225-226.

IV. THE NEW ENGLAND FAMILY—PRESTIGE AND FUNCTIONS

To the Pilgrim and the Puritan the home and the church were preëminent treasures. Yet it is hard to say whether family or property constituted the Puritans' chief treasure. The two interests interacted.

The early Puritans married young. Madam Knight wrote (1704) of Connecticut youth: "They generally marry very young, the males oftener as I am told under twenty years than above." Girls often married at sixteen or under. Old maids were ridiculed or even despised. A woman became an "antient maid" at twenty-five. But there is no evidence that child marriages, so common in England at the time, were ever permitted in America.

A man or woman, however, without family ties was almost unthinkable. Such an anomaly could not be tolerated. Even apart from the weight of this sentiment, it is easy to see that marriage would be almost the only honorable refuge for a woman. But New England family policy pressed as heavily upon the unattached man as on the isolated woman. Bachelors were rare and were viewed with disapproval. They were almost in the class of suspected criminals. They were rarely allowed to live by themselves or even to choose their places of abode but had to live wherever the court put them. A Massachusetts act of 1631 forbade hiring any person for less than a year unless he were a "settled housekeeper." In Hartford solitary men were taxed twenty shillings a week. A New Haven law runs thus: in order to

> Suppress inconvenience, and disorders inconsistent with the mind of God in the fifth commandment, single persons, not in service or dwelling with their relatives are forbidden to diet or lodge alone; but they are required to live in "licensed" families; and the governors of such families are ordered to "observe the course, carriage, and behavior of every such single person, whether he or she walk diligently in a constant lawful employment, attending both family duties and the public worship of God, and keeping good order day and night or otherwise.

Similar measures are found in the other colonies. Bachelors were under the special espionage of the constable, the watchman, and the tithing-man. There was, moreover, a positive premium on marriage in addition to the freedom gained. Many towns assigned building lots to bachelors upon marriage. It is not strange that bachelors were scarce.

Old maids, too, were rare and hard-off. The question of the "aimless and homeless" condition of single women troubled the selectmen. Grants seem to have been made of "maid's lots" but the policy was questioned. In 1636 we find this entry: "Deborah Holmes refused land, being a maid (but hath four bu. of corn granted her. . .) and would be a bad precedent to keep house alone." Later we find the Bay Colony allowing single women to follow approved callings. But marriage was, normally, prompt. A man writing from the Piscataqua colony says, "A good husband, with his wife to attend the cattle and make butter and cheese will be profitable, for maids they are soone gonne in this countrie."

There were, however, a few notable spinsters. The Plymouth church record of March 19, 1667, notes the death of "Mary Carpenter sister of Mrs. Alice Bradford, wife of Governor Bradford, being newly entered into the ninety-first year of her age. She was a godly old maid never married."

John Dunton wrote in glowing terms of one ideal "virgin."

> It is true an *old* (or superannuated) maid in Boston is thought such a curse, as nothing can exceed it (and looked on as a *dismal* spectacle) yet she by her good nature, gravity, and strict virtue convinces all (so much as the fleering Beaus) that it is not her necessity but her choice that keeps her a virgin. She is now about thirty years (the age which they call a thornback) yet she never disguises herself, and talks as little as she thinks of love.

This maid must have been very singular to deserve as much space as she received. The eulogist dilates at length on her modesty and propriety. "She would neither anticipate nor contradict the will of her parents" and "is against forcing her own, by marrying where she can not love; and that is the reason she is still a virgin."

Taunton, Massachusetts, was founded by an "ancient maid" of forty-eight. Winthrop's *Journal* for 1637 contains this item: "This year a plantation begun at Tichcutt by . . . an ancient maid, one Mrs. Poole. She went late thither and endured much hardship and lost much cattle."

In case of the decease of husband or wife remarriage was prompt. The first marriage in Plymouth colony was that of Edward Winslow, who had been a widower only seven weeks, to Susanna White who had been a widow not twelve weeks. The case was exceptional but in the new land there was no place for ceremonial mourning in such a case. It was fitting that Winslow should be at the head of a household and the White children needed a father especially as their mother was taken up with the care of an infant. Later the governor of New Hampshire married a lady whose husband was but ten days dead. Such frequent and hasty espousals were not altogether due to the impossible condition of a man or woman without a partner in the midst of a wilderness with all the families fully occupied in caring for their own. They were common in England.

A few concrete cases of colonial remarriage will make the usage vivid. Peter Sargent, a rich Boston merchant, had three wives. His second had had two previous husbands. His third wife had lost one husband, and she survived Peter, and also her third husband, who had three wives. His father had four, the last three of whom were widows. One reverend gentleman, facing death, confidently told his wife that she would soon be well provided for. "She was very shortly after very honorably and comfortably married unto a gentleman of good estate" and lived with him nearly two score years.

"Mistress" was attached to the names even of young girls. This usage makes it hard sometimes to ascertain whether a bride was a widow. But it is certain that widows were at a premium in colonial days. Perhaps the principal reason for this fact was the one indicated in the previous chapter in the discussion of economic marriage. It is hard to explain otherwise why men passed by the maidens and took the widows. And among these there was room to choose, for the number of colonial widows was huge. In 1698 it was said that Boston was full of widows and orphans, many of them very helpless. It is safe to say that the helpless ones went longest desolate. Their miserable condition emphasized again the importance of normal family connections. So we need not be surprised to find a choice widow whose love for her departed husband was reputed to be "strong as death" speedily marrying again.

So important was proper family relation that persons living apart from their spouses were sometimes ordered to get their partners or clear out. The well-being of the community was conceived to depend on rigid family discipline and if a man had no family he must find one. Thus New England law provided that "married persons must live together, unless the court of assistants approve of the cause to the contrary." In Rhode Island in 1655 we find it "ordered that Thomas Gennings shall go and demand his wife to live with him, but in case she refuse, he shall make his addresse to the Generall Court of Commissioners for redresse in the case." In 1660 the Connecticut court ordered

> That noe man or woman, within this colony who hath a wife or husband in forraigne parts, shall live here above two years, upon penalty of 40s. per month upon every such offender and any that have been above three years already, not to remaine within this colony above one yeare longer upon the same penalty, except they have liberty from the General Court.

It was not uncommon for immigrants to leave their spouses in Europe. Sometimes, as we shall see later, this was simple desertion, but by no means always. Thus a letter from England to Mr. Gibb in Piscataquay reads:

> I hope by this both your wives are with you according to your desire. I wish all your wives were with you, and that so many of you as desire wives had such as they desire. Your wife, Roger Knight's wife, and one wife more we have already sent you and more you shall have as you have wish for them.

Occasionally a wife was disinclined to come to America. Governor Winthrop wrote to England in 1632:

> I have much difficultye to keepe John Galope heere by reason his wife will not come. I marvayle at her womans weaknesse, that she will live myserably with her children there when she might live comfortably with her husband here. I pray perswade and further her coming by all means. If she will come

> let her have the remainder of his wages, if not let it be bestowed to bring over his children for soe he desires.

Reverend Mr. Wilson had a hard time persuading his wife to cross. Even a cleverly interpreted dream did not avail. He sent back comfortable reports, and finally recrossed the ocean after her. Then, after much fasting and prayer, she finally agreed to "accompany him over an ocean to a wilderness." These cases were not typical. Wives were ordinarily willing to try the new world.

It is evident that the family was regarded as an instrument to be used deliberately by the community for social welfare.

In the colonial records of Connecticut (1643), it is declared that

> The prsprity and well being of Comon weles doth much depend vvpon the well gouerment and ordering of prticuler Familyes, wch in an ordinary way cannot be expected when the rules of God are neglected in laying the foundation of a family state.

In Massachusetts during the period between 1660 and 1672, it was ordered that

> [The] selectmen of every town, in the several precincts and quarters wher they dwell, shall have a vigilant eye over their brethren and neighbors to see, first that none of them shall suffer so much barbarism in any of their families, as not to endeavor to teach . . . their children and apprentices so much learning as may enable them perfectly to read the English tongue and knowledge of the capital laws.

Once a week children and apprentices are to be catechized "in the grounds and principles of religion" and they are to be bred and brought up in some honest lawful calling "profitable for themselves and the commonwealth," if their parents "will not or can not train them up in learning to fit them for higher employments." Neglect of parental duty "whereby children and servants become rude, stubborn and unruly" is penalized by the removal of the children into better hands until they come of age. It seems that the law was for a time unenforced, "sin and prophaness" increased "and the ensnaring of many children and servants by the dissolute lives and practices of such as do live from under family government." The laws were ordered enforced and a list to be made of young persons living "from under family government, viz., do not serve their parents or masters as children, apprentices, hired servants, or journeymen ought to do, and usually did in our native country, being subject to their commands and discipline." Masters and heads of families were to take effectual care that their children and servants did not violate the Sabbath laws. Selectmen were to see to it that parents educated their children, for "many parents and masters are too indulgent and negligent of their duty."

Plymouth also took action: "Forasmuch as the good education of children and youth is of singular benefit and use to any commonwealth; and whereas many parents and masters either through an over respect to their own occasions and business or not duly considering the good of their children and servants, have too much neglected their duty in their education," parents are to be watched so that they properly teach their children. If after admonition and repeated fine negligent parents did not improve, the children were to be taken away and placed with masters where they would receive training and government. It should be remembered in this connection that the Plymouth people for a long period were in bondage to the capitalists that financed the original expedition, and consequently had to absorb all their energies in a sordid struggle for material interests. But pioneer life puts a damper on culture.

In the records of Connecticut (1665-1677) we find the following:

> Whereas reading the Scripture, cattechizing of children and dayly prayer with giueing of thanks is part of God's worship and the homage due to him, to be atended conscientiously by euery Christian family to distinguish them from the heathen whoe call not upon God, and the neglect of it a great sin . . . this court do solemnly recommend it to the ministry in all places, to look into the state of such famalyes, convince them of and instruct them in their duty [etc. Townsmen were to assist ministers] but if any heads or gouernors of such famalys shall be obstinate and refractorie and will not be reformed, that the grand jury present such person to the county court to be fined or punished or bownd to good behavior, according to the demeritts of the case.

The tithing-man was the censor of New England family life. His power entered every home. He looked after family morals and saw to the maintenance of family government, that all single persons were attached to some family, that children and servants were properly taught and trained at home and kept from disorderly and rude practices abroad. By a town order of Dorchester in 1678 it was required "that the tithing men in their severall precincts should inspect all inmates that do come into each of their precincts either single persons or families, and to give spedy information thereof unto the selectmen from time to time or to some of them that order may be taken about them."

Under such supervision it was a risky thing to have visitors. The harboring of strangers, even relatives from other places, often brought difficulty between citizens and magistrates and frequently caused arbitration between towns. Thus, in Connecticut, "Goodman Hunt and his wife, for keeping the counsels of the said William Harding, baking him a pasty and plum cakes, and keeping company with him on the Lord's day, and she suffering Harding to kiss her," were ordered to be sent out of town "within one month after the date hereof, yea, in a shorter time if any miscarriage be found in them." A Dorchester widow was not allowed to entertain a visiting son-in-law. Another woman was fined in 1671 "under distress" for housing her own daughter tho the latter (a married woman) said the bad weather kept her from home.

This prying authority would have been resented by as keen a people as the New Englanders had it been imposed by external authority. In later days they quickly remembered the English maxim, "every man's house his castle." James Otis in his speech on writs of assistance said, "One of the most essential branches of English liberty is the freedom of one's house. A man's house is his castle; and whilst he is quiet is as well guarded as a prince in his castle. This writ would totally annihilate this privilege." One can imagine the indignation when an officer whom Justice Walley had summoned for breach of the Sabbath used his power to search that dignitary's house from cellar to attic. Probably even the building laws imposed by the local authorities for fire-protection would have been looked at askance if they had been imposed by an alien power.

The reader has, of course, noted the religious cast of the family function. The fathers adopted the maxim that "families are the nurseries of the church and the commonwealth; ruin families and you ruin all." The maintenance of family religion was universally recognized in early New England as a duty and was seriously attended to in most families. Daily the scriptures were read and worship was offered to God. Fathers sought for their children, as for themselves, "first the kingdom of God and His righteousness" (which, somehow, unfortunately for morality, seemed to sanction forms of sin that filled the pocketbook). The religious influence pervaded family, school, society. Yet as early as 1679 a "Reforming Synod" at Boston said, "Family Worship is much neglected" and by 1691 a lament arose over the decay of piety and family religion. This was just one year after the appearance of the *New England Primer* which was certainly calculated to stem such a tide of evil. Catechism learning was enforced by law. But even in 1716 Mather thought it necessary, in the assembly of ministers, to "propose a motion . . . that no family in the country be without a *Bible* and a catechism; and that all children of a fitt age, be found able to read."

Theophilus Eaton, first governor of New Haven, was a shining example of the true patriarch.

> As in his government of the commonwealth, so in the government of his family, he was prudent, serious, happy to a wonder; and altho he sometimes had a large family, consisting of no less than thirty persons, yet he managed them with such an even temper, that observers have affirmed that they never saw a house ordered with more wisdom. He kept an honorable and hospitable table; but one thing that made the entertainment thereof the better, was the continual presence of his aged mother, by feeding of whom with an exemplary piety till she died, he insured his own prosperity as long as he lived. His children and servants he mightily encouraged in the study of the scriptures, and countenanced their addresses to himself with any of their inquiries; but when he saw any of them sinfully negligent about the concerns either of their general or particular callings, he would admonish them with such a penetrating efficacy, that they could scarce forbear falling down at his feet with tears. A word from him was enough to steer them.

Special laws for the further safeguarding of the family may be mentioned. For years the general court of Massachusetts acted as guardian of widows and orphans. The Body of Liberties decreed that "no man shall be deprived of his wife or children . . . unless by virtue of some express law of the country established by the General Court and sufficiently published."

But the laws were not solely in the interest of the individuals affected. The Plymouth colony ordered that "no one be allowed to be housekeepers . . . till such time as they be allowed and approved by the governor and councill;" also "no servant coming out of his time or other single person [is] suffered to keep house or be for him or themselves till . . . competently provided of arms and ammunition according to the orders of the colony." In case of certain youthful offenders Massachusetts ordered (1645) that "their parents or masters shall give them due correction and that in the presence of some officer if any magistrat shall so appoint." Again, 1668,

> This court taking notice, upon good information and sad complaints, that there are some persons in this jurisdiction, that have families to provide for, who greatly neglect their callings, or misspend what they earn, whereby their families are in much want, and are thereby exposed to suffer, and to need relief from others, This court for remedy of these great and unsufferable evils, do declare that . . . such neglectors of families are comprehended among [such idle persons as are subject to the house of correction].

Such legislation is an interesting rival of maximum wage laws as is also the provision of 1703-1704 that children of parents unable to maintain them are to be bound out.

In spite of legal subordination and occasional actual sacrifice to the public interest the New England family was not without individuality. One of the causes of the failure of the early communism lies right here.

> The yong-men that were most able and fitte for labor and service did repine that they should spend their time and strength to work for other men's wives and children without any recompense. . . And for men's wives to be commanded to do service for other men, as dressing their meate, washing their cloathes, etc., they deemed it a kind of slaverie; neither could many husbands well brooke it.

After assignments of land were made to each household "Women and children helped plant the family lots, altho they would have considered it a great hardship to work in the common field."

The Puritan censorship of family life was enforced by the arm of the law. But the Quakers, who could not control the civil power, maintained ecclesiastical oversight in behalf of moral training, sectarian solidarity and exclusiveness, parental control over courtship, and general propriety as in the following query: "Do no widows admit proposals of marage too early after the death of their former husbands, or from widowers sooner after the death of a former wife than is consistent with decency?"

The New England aristocracy possessed marked pride of family. Sumptuary laws were designed to maintain the distinction between rich and poor. One law provided that the wearing of gold or silver ornaments, silk ribbons, etc. should cause assessment at one hundred fifty pounds. The law exempted families of magistrates or "such whose quality and estate have been above the ordinary degree tho now decayed."

Ministers' families almost constituted a nobility. John Adams, who was only the son of a small, middle-class farmer, met with opposition from members of the flock of the minister whose daughter he was courting.

The Adams family was thought scarcely fit to match with the minister's daughter, the descendant of so many worthies. It so happened that her father was well disposed to the young man and after the ceremony had occurred saw fit to deliver an "Apology" from the text, "John came neither eating bread nor drinking wine, and ye say: 'He hath a devil.'"

True to their noble rank the reverend families tended to marry into each other. For a century and a half such marriages were very numerous. It seemed to be according to social propriety for ministers' sons to marry ministers' daughters. Pastors often married into the family of their predecessors–often the daughter, sometimes the widow. Many families may be cited as exhibits of interrelationship among ministers. The "Mather Dynasty" is a conspicuous case in point. Richard Mather's second wife was the widow of John Cotton. Their children, Increase Mather and Mary Cotton, were as brother and sister but were married and became the parents of Cotton Mather. The sons, grandsons, and great-grandsons of Richard Mather entered the ministry. The girls in the same generations married ministers. Thus the Mather blood fertilized the remote quarters of New England.

Family integrity reached beyond death. Much solicitude was felt by the New England people for the salvation of kindred. In many communities each family had a burying-place on the home-farm. Thus the dust of the dead consecrated the family devotion and the ancestral home of the living. Sewall considered a visit to the family tomb and the sight of the coffins in it an "awful yet pleasing treat" and Joseph Eliot said "that the two days wherein he buried his wife and son were the best he ever had in the world."

In the rapid expansion of New England families there developed a tendency to the formation of patriarchal clans. Aubury noted the great number of half-finished houses. A man would build and occupy half of the structure; when his son married, the new couple finished and moved into the other half. The families were thus separate, yet united by the common sheltering roof. Often, too, as already suggested, the family circle was expanded into a real "familia." In the household of the prosperous Massachusetts merchant were indentured servants, male and female, generally young, working out their time. Wage employees, even those used in his business, commonly ate at his family table, and lived under his roof. All such were, of course, under the paternal care of the house-father. Besides these, were unattached female relatives, who often lived with their kindred.

Careful as the new Americans were of their own families, and censorious as the aristocracy was of the families of the hard-pressed plebeians, they found themselves unable (or unwilling) to safe-guard the family relations of their slaves. Slavery can scarcely respect the family integrity of the servile class. Aside from the lust of males of the master race, is the economic motive that severs families for business reasons. Sewall, who was sufficiently cool-blooded in his own matrimonial ventures, was distressed at the thought of "how in taking negroes out of Africa and selling of them here, that which God has joined together men do boldly rend asunder; men from their country, husbands from their wives, parents from their children." Nor did the process end with the voyage from Africa. There was really no protection of marriage or sanction of marital or parental rights and duties. Who could be depended on to vindicate the slave if the whim of a master "unreasonably" denied marriage? The owner of a valuable female slave had to consider the risks of motherhood as compared with the accession of a slave child which would be little worth. And as for males Sewall refers to the well-known temptation masters have to connive at their fornication lest they should have to find wives for them or pay their fines. And it is certain that, in spite of Puritan regard for parenthood and the care of children, they separated mothers from their offspring.

One Massachusetts town hands down in tradition the memory of "raising slaves for market."[44] But the breeding of slaves was not, in general, regarded favorably in that colony. It seems to have been unprofitable. Negro children were, indeed, sold by the pound but the market was sadly sluggish, for negro babies were advertised in Boston to be given away like puppies and sometimes money was offered to any one that would take them.[45] Thus economic interest hoodwinked the Calvinist conscience as it always hoodwinks or swamps the conscience of the master class in matters of class dominance.

Some show must, of course, be made of approximating the relations of the disinherited to those of the privileged class. Thus in 1745 a negro slave obtained a divorce for his wife's adultery (with a white man) and in 1758 the Superior Court decided that a child of a female slave "never married according to any of the forms prescribed by the laws of the land" by another slave who "had kept her company with her master's

---

[44] Moore. *Notes on the History of Slavery in Massachusetts*, 69.

[45] Earle. *Customs and Fashions in Old New England*, 89; Moore, *op. cit.*, 57.

consent" was *not a bastard.* The reader will recall the mockery of slave marriage previously mentioned.

Slavery never took deep root in New England. The climate was against it. The fewness of the negroes tended to make race questions less urgent than in the South. Some of the farmers ate with their slaves. Madam Knight complained that in Connecticut slaves were allowed to sit and eat with the masters. "Into the dish goes the black hoof as freely as the white hand." Hawthorne says concerning the slaves of New England:

> They were not excluded from the domestic affections; in families of middling rank, they had their places at the board; and when the circle closed around the evening hearth its blaze glowed on their dark shining faces, intermixed familiarly with their master's children.

But the system was evil at best, and did violence to the fundamentals of morality. There might be cause to wonder that the subordinating of the marital interests and family ties of the servile class to monetary considerations did not demoralize the family institutions of the masters, were it not that bourgeois marriage is itself an economic institution subordinating love to money, and further that in a society marked by class cleavage each social level preserves its own ethic, more or less distinct and insulated from that of the other classes. And we need only note the present-day phenomenon of "the divided conscience" in order to appreciate the incongruities that economic interest can perpetrate. The colonial conscience was able to witness even the shocking system of white servitude with its ruinous effects. Massachusetts tried to sell children of Quakers to Barbadoes but could find no shipmaster base enough to take them.[46]

[46] Moore, *op. cit.*, 33.

V. THE POSITION OF WOMEN IN THE NEW ENGLAND COLONIAL FAMILY

The rigors and dangers of pioneer life constituted colonial New England a man's world. Life conditions allowed a type of patriarchism that found affinity in the Old Testament regime. Views as to proper relations between husband and wife, parent and child, or between man and maid before marriage, came directly from the scriptures, as for example Calvin's views quoted in an introductory chapter. Byington thinks that "The Courtship of Miles Standish" gives us a very correct picture of the social and family life of the Pilgrims. The proxy wooing suggests the patriarchal story of Isaac.

Inasmuch as the husband was the patriarch, woman found in matrimony but limited freedom. Sewall reports a wedding address by Mr. Noyes in which he said that: "Love was the sugar to sweeten every condition in the married relation." It is to be feared that there was no superabundance of sugar in the Puritan domestic economy. An excess of male despotism is more probable. One man that abused his wife asserted in good ancestral phrase that she was his servant and slave.

Woman was indeed "a sweet sex" but her sphere was narrow. Altho it was a woman that gave the first plot of ground for a free school in Massachusetts, education even in common schools was withheld from girls until it was found necessary to allow them to attend during the summer (while the boys were busy fishing) in order to hold school moneys.[47] One Connecticut town voted not to "waste" any of its money in educating girls.[48] One small maiden sat for hours daily on the schoolhouse steps in order to catch as much as possible of the lessons going on inside. By the middle of the eighteenth century girls were sometimes sent to the city to finishing school. In 1788 Northampton voted not to spend any money on the education of girls. It was well into the nineteenth century before the New Englanders thought education for girls desirable. Mrs. John Adams said: "It was fashionable to ridicule female learning. . . Female education in the best families went no further than writing and arithmetic; in some few and rare instances, music and dancing." Woman's only chance for much intellectual improvement was to be found in occasional contact with the learned, and in the families of the educated class. The only useful instruction in practical affairs was received from the mother. When Governor Winthrop's wife lost her mind her Puritan women friends attributed the calamity to her desertion of her domestic duties and meddling in man's sphere. Governor Winthrop believed that the young wife of the governor of Connecticut had gone insane "by occasion of giving herself wholly to reading and writing." Had she "not gone out of her way and calling to meddle in such things as are proper for men, whose minds are stronger, etc., she had kept her wits, and might have improved them usefully and honorably in the place God had set her."

There were, indeed, during the colonial period some women conspicuous for their brilliancy and mental attainments; but their field was cramped. The principal

[47] Gage. *Woman, Church, and State,* 407.

[48] *Scribner's Magazine,* vol. I, 762.

charge against Mrs. Hutchinson was that she had, contrary to Paul, presumed to instruct men. Anne Bradstreet, daughter of Governor Dudley and wife of a governor, the mother of eight children, and a faithful performer of household and social duties, felt the pressure when she essayed to write poetry. She says:

> I am obnoxious to each carping tongue
> Who says my hand a needle better fits,
> A poets pen all scorn I should thus wrong,
> For such despite they cast on female wits:
> If what I do prove well, it won't advance,
> They'l say it 's stoln, or else it was by chance.
>
> . . . .
>
> Let Greeks be Greeks, and women what they are
> Men have precedency and still excell,
> It is but vain unjustly to wage warre:
> Men can do best, and women know it well
> Preheminence in all and each is yours;
> Yet grant some small acknowledgement of ours.

In such an atmosphere it is not strange if, as Fisher says of the colonies in general, "Married women usually became prudes and retired from all amusements and pleasures."

Mrs. Adams writing in 1778 says: "I regret the trifling, narrow, contracted education of the females of my own country." She quotes some writer thus:

> If women are to be esteemed our enemies, methinks it is an ignoble cowardice, thus to disarm them, and not allow them the same weapons we use ourselves; but if they deserve the titles of our friends, 'tis an inhuman tyranny to debar them of the privileges of ingenuous education, which would also render their friendship so much the more delightful to themselves and us. . . Their senses are generally as quick as ours; their reason as nervous, their judgment as mature and solid. . . Nor need we fear to lose our empire over them by thus improving their native abilities; since, where there is most learning,

> sense, and knowledge, there is always observed to be the most modesty and rectitude of manners.

John Adams expressed his belief in the education of women. He said that great characters usually have some woman about them and that much of their larger success and the greatness of their lives is due to her influence. But in his opinion *femmes savantes* are contemptible. Mrs. Adams thought however that "if we mean to have heroes, statesmen, and philosophers, we should have learned women."

One writer waxes poetic in his portrayal of the ideal woman. "Mrs. R—— had a round and pretty face, with gentle manners; kept her house well, her only pride to be neat and orderly. . . . The hyacinth follows not the sun more willingly than she her husband's pleasure." Dunton remarks, in like vein, of Mrs. Stewart of Boston: "Her pride was to be neat and cleanly, and her thrift not to be prodigal, which made her seldom a non-resident of her household." It was a hard life – full of drudgery and of daily monotony. In old letters we find great rejoicing over small luxuries or labor-saving contrivances that found their way to the busy housekeeper.

Among the Puritans no spirit of chivalry prevailed. The Massachusetts colony had a law that women suspected of witchcraft be stripped and their bodies scrutinized by a male "witch-pricker" to see if there was not the devil's mark upon them. When in 1656 two Quaker women came to Boston from Barbadoes the deputy-governor apprehended and jailed them. They were in prison five weeks – till a ship was ready to deport them. Endicott would have had them flogged. At Hartford, 1645, a man was fined "for bequething his wyfe." A Boston paper of 1736 contains the following:

> The beginning of last week a pretty odd and uncommon adventure happened in this town, between two men about a certain woman, each one claiming her as his wife, but so it was, that one of them had actually disposed of his right in her to the other for fifteen shillings this currency, who had only paid ten of it in part, and refus'd to pay the other five, inclining rather to quit the woman and lose his earnest; but two gentlemen happening to be present, who were friends to peace, charitably gave him half a crown apiece to enable him to fulfil his agreement, which the creditor readily took, and gave the woman a modest salute, wishing her well and his Brother Stirling much joy of his bargain.

The reader will recall what was said in a previous chapter about the usage of wife-sale in England.

On woman rested the burden of interminable childbearing. Large families were the rule. Families of ten and twelve children were very common. Families of from twenty to twenty-five children were not rare enough to call forth expression of wonder. Josselyn (1673) remarks: "They have store of children."

"Steeped in the Old Testament" where they read, "Lo, children are an heritage of the Lord: and the fruit of the womb is his reward. As arrows are in the hand of a mighty man; so are children of the youth. Happy is the man that hath his quiver full of them," and living in an empty land, the springs of fecundity were strong. Large families were eagerly welcomed. Boston had as little land to spare as any New England town but in the allotments women and children received a full share. In Brookline the early allotments were in proportion to the size of the family. As bait for immigrants, Gabriel Thomas wrote of the new world:

> The Christian children born here are generally well-favored and beautiful. . . I never knew any to come into the world

> with the least blemish . . . being in the general . . . better-natured, milder, and more tender-hearted than those born in England.

Equal praise was given to the children of Virginia. It was also asserted that the average family was larger in America. The question of pioneer fecundity receives larger attention in the next volume but it is cited here in order to emphasize the burden laid upon woman by primitive standards.

Some specific illustrations may be of service. Speaking of a worthy, Mather said:

> He was twice married. By his first wife, the vertuous daughter of parents therein resembled by her, he had six children. But his next wife was a young gentlewoman whom he chose from under the guardianship and with the countenance of Edward Hopkins Esq., the excellent governor of Connecticut. . . By the daughter of that Mr. Launce, who is yet living among us, Mr. Sherman had no less than twenty children added unto the number of six which he had before. . . One woman [in New England] has had not less than twenty-two children: whereof she buried fourteen sons and six daughters. Another woman has had no less than twenty-three children by one husband; whereof nineteen lived unto men's and women's estate. A third was mother to seven-and-twenty children: and she that was mother to Sir William Phips, the late governor of New England, had no less than twenty-five children besides him; she had one and twenty sons and five daughters. Now unto the catalog of such "fruitful vines by the sides of the house" is this gentlewoman Mrs. Sherman to be enumerated. Behold thus was our Sherman, that eminent fearer of the Lord, blessed of Him.

Green, the Boston printer, had thirty children. William Rawson had twenty by one wife. The reverend S. Willard, first minister of Groton, was one of seventeen children and himself had twenty. The reverend Abijah Weld of Attleboro, Massachusetts, had fifteen children.

The reverend Moses Fisher had sixteen. Of Mrs. Sara Thayer, who died in 1751, a local poet wrote:

Also she was a fruitful vine,
The truth I may relate, –
Fourteen was of her body born
And lived to mans estate.

From these did spring a numerous race,
One hundred thirty-two;
Sixty and six each sex alike,
As I declare to you.

And one thing more remarkable,
Which I shall here record:
She'd fourteen children with her
At the table of our Lord.

One worthy colonist died in 1771 leaving a progeny of one hundred eight children, grandchildren, and great-grandchildren. Another Massachusetts man died about the same time, leaving one hundred fifty-seven issue alive, including five great-grandchildren.

In the seventeenth century, in spite of early marriage and very high birth-rate, increase was offset by frightful mortality of children; so that the slaughter of womanhood in incessant child-bearing was relatively vain. Significant is the inscription on a Plymouth grave-stone: "Here lies —— —— with twenty small children.

Perhaps there is danger of overdrawing the harsh lines in colonial family life. There was real affection in many cases between Puritan husbands and wives. A few love letters offer proof. And the New Englanders wrote many eulogies of their wives. Ministers sounded in tedious sermons the piety of colonial women and poets sang their charms. A colonial writer (supposedly President Clap of Yale, 1740-1766) pays this tribute to his wife:

> [The Lord had apparently supplied his want of a woman of serene temper, and piety.] And if it happened at any time that we seemed not altogether to agree in our opinion or inclination about any lesser matter we used to discourse upon it, with a perfect calmness and pleasancy; but she did not choose to debate long upon any such thing but was always free and ready enough to acquiesce in the opinion or inclination of her husband. And such was her kind and obliging carriage to me, that I took great pleasure in pleasing her in everything that I could. . . And if at any time she had any just and necessary occasion to correct her children or servants she would do it with a proper and moderate smartness so as effectually to answer yet without the least passion or ruffle of mind. . . [If her husband was remiss in anything, she gently intimated it to him, and (he says) she was usually right.] She always went through the difficulties of childbearing with a remarkable steadfastness, faith, patience, and decency. . . Indeed she would sometimes say to me that bearing, tending and burying children was hard work, and that she had done a great deal of it for one of her age, (she had six children, whereof she buried four, and died in the 24 year of her age.) yet would say it was the work she was made for, and what God in his providence had called her to, and she could freely do it all for Him.

Minister Clap in his diary speaks thus of his wife:

> She exceeded all persons that ever I saw, in a most serene, pleasant, and excellent temper and disposition, which rendered her very agreeable and lovely to me, and all that were acquainted with her. I lived with her in the house near eleven years, and she was my wife for almost nine, and I never saw her in any unpleasant temper. Indeed I took great pleasure in pleasing her in everything which I thought I conveniently could; and if she erred in anything of that nature, it was sometimes in not insisting upon her own inclination so much as a wife may modestly do. [When he concluded to marry again he prayed:] If it be thy holy will and pleasure, I entreat thou wouldst bestow upon me one who is of a healthy constitution, chaste, diligent,

prudent, grave and cheerful – one who is descended from credible parents, who has been well educated in the principles of religion, virtue, industry, and decent behavior. And may be the desire of mine eye, as well as the delight of my heart.

Back in the seventeenth century, the century of Puritanism, Anne Bradstreet wrote

To my Dear and Loving Husband

If ever two were one, then surely we.
If ever man were loved by wife, then thee;
If ever wife was happy in a man,
Compare with me ye women if you can.

I prize thy love more than whole Mines of gold,
Or all the riches that the East doth hold.
My love is such that Rivers cannot quench,
Nor ought but love from thee, give recompence.

Thy love is such I can no way repay,
The heavens reward thee manifold I pray.
Then while we live, in love lets so persever,
That when we live no more, we may live ever.

Thomas Shepherd, pastor at Cambridge from 1636 to 1649, wrote on the death of his second wife that the Lord mixes mercy and affliction.

My dear, precious, meek, and loving wife [has died in childbirth leaving two dear children. The Lord threatened to proceed in rooting out my family like Eli's.] I saw that if I had profited by my former afflictions of this nature, I should not have had this scourge. . . This loss was very great. She was a woman of incomparable meekness of spirit, toward myself especially, and very loving; of great prudence to take care for and order my family affairs, being neither too lavish nor sordid in anything, so that I knew not what was under her hands. . . The death of her first-born . . . was a great affliction to her. . . She . . . was the comfort of my life to me. . . When her fever began . . . she told me . . . we should love exceedingly together because

> we should not live long together. . . Thus God hath much scourged me for my sins, and sought to wean me from this world.

It was not prudent for the Puritan husband to be publicly demonstrative. Captain Kemble of Boston sat two hours in the public stocks (1656) for his "lewd and unseemly behavior" in kissing his wife "publicquely" on the Sabbath upon his doorstep when he had just returned from a voyage of three years.[49]

Even such a scandalous wight as Captain Underhill had some regard for wifely wisdom. Against his will he had been prevailed upon by his wife to wear his helmet to battle against the Indians and it had saved his life. So he writes:

> Let no man despise advice and counsel of his wife, tho she be a woman. It were strange to nature to think a man should be bound to fulfil the humor of a woman what arms he should carry; but you see God will have it so that a woman should overcome a man. What with Delilah's flattery and with her mournful tears, they must and will have their desire, when the hand of God goes along in the matter. . . Therefore let the clamor be quenched I daily hear in my ears, that New England men usurp over their wives, and keep them in servile subjection. The country is wronged in this matter as in many things else. Let this precedent satisfy the doubtful for that comes from the example of a rude soldier. If they be so courteous to their wives, as to take their advice in warlike matters, how much more kind is the tender affectionate husband to honor his wife as the weaker vessel? Yet mistake not. I say not that they are bound to call their wives in council, tho they are bound to take their private advice (so far as they see it make for their advantage and their good).

On his trips with circuit court John Adams used to keep his wife regularly informed of his experiences. She does not appear to have often replied to these letters. To do so would have been difficult, in that day of

[49] Earle. *Colonial Dames and Goodwives*, 136.

slow post, with him on the move. She was in closest sympathy with the development of his mind toward the Revolution. She bids adieu to domestic felicity, perhaps until they shall meet in another world. By her prudence during her husband's period of preoccupation in public affairs, she saved him the embarrassment of poverty in later years. She was a moderating influence upon his fieriness.

It is evident that practice in the best families in respect to woman's place outstript legal theory as implied in such a law as that of Massachusetts to the effect that "any conveyance or alienation of land or other estate whatsoever, made by any woman that is married, any child under age, ideott or distracted person, shall be good if it be passed and ratified by the consent of a generall court." The pater familias was not absolute in his authority, even in the eyes of the law. Massachusetts provided that "no man shall strike his wife, nor any woman her husband, on penalty of such fine, not exceeding £10 for one offence, or such corporall punishment as the county court shall determine." The Plymouth law was the same. The Body of Liberties (1641) ordained that "everie marryed woeman shall be free from bodily correction or stripes by her husband, unless it be in his own defence upon her assault. If there be any just cause of correction complaint shall be made to authoritie assembled in some court, from which only she shall receive it."

Wives enjoyed large protection from early laws. A man was not permitted to keep his wife on remote and dangerous plantations but must "bring her in, else the town will pull his house down." A man might not leave his wife for any length of time nor "marrie too wifes which were both alive for anything that can appear otherwise at one time." Nor must he even use "hard words" to her.[50]

The question of wifely subjection was not in all cases a simple one. In Rhode Island Mr. Verin's wife used to go out the back way to the adjoining house of Roger Williams to listen to his religious talks. Verin forbade her and the matter came up to the council. It was objected that a motion to censure Verin would mean that "men's wives and children and servants could claim liberty to go to all religious meetings, tho never so often." One Arnold asserted that "when he consented to that order" for religious liberty, "he never intended it should extend to the breach of any ordinance of God, such as the subjection of wives to their husbands," etc. One Green replied "that if they should restrain their wives etc, all the women of the country would cry out of them, etc." Arnold alleged that the desire to be gadding about was not prompted altogether by woman's conscience. Governor Winthrop notes that some members of the church at Providence suggested that if Goodman Verin would not allow his wife entire liberty to attend meeting on Sunday and weekly lectures as often as she desired "the church would dispose her to some other man who would use her better." The final action condemned Verin (1638). "It was agreed that Joshua Verin, upon the breach of a covenant for restraining of the libertie of conscience, shall be withheld from the libertie of voting till he shall declare the contrarie." He soon left Providence. Williams wrote of Verin:

> He hath refused to hear the word with us (which we molested him, not for this 12month) so because he could not draw his wife, a gracious modest woman, to the same ungodliness with

[50] Earle. *Customs and Fashions in Old New England*, 68.

him, he hath trodden her underfoot tyrannically and brutishly; which she and we long bearing, tho with his furious blows she went in danger of her life, at the last the major vote of us discard him from our civil freedom, or disfranchise.

Women's property interests received a measure of legal protection. It was enacted in Plymouth in 1636 (perhaps under the influence of Dutch law) that when lands were seized to satisfy the creditors of a deceased man the part reserved for the support of wife and children could not be touched. In 1646 the consent of the wife was made necessary to the sale of houses or lands. This measure was reënacted in 1658. Massachusetts (1647) allowed the widow one-third of her husband's estate as dowry. Previously the Body of Liberties had provided that "if any man at his death shall not leave his wife a competent portion of his estate, upon just complaint made to the general court she shall be relieved."

In Connecticut "when any man dieth intestate leaving an estate his widdow" shall have besides the third part of his real estate during her life "a part also of his personall estate equall to his eldest child, provided it exceed not a third part of the sd personall estate, which said part of her husband's personall estate shall be her own forever" (1696). The records of Connecticut show that "in the first settlement of the colony land was of little value in comparison with what it now [1723] is, by which means it became a general custom, that the real estate of any person" descending to his daughters "became . . . the proper and sole estate of their husbands, and might be by him alienated or disposed of without the knowledge or consent of such wives; and a great number of estates having been thus settled and so remain at this day. . ." Hereafter such real estate is not to be alienable without the wife's consent. In Rhode Island the dower right was used as a check on wives. It was ordained that a married woman "that elopeth with her adventurer" should lose her dower of lands.

The reasonableness of provision for the widow is expressed in the case of a woman of Plymouth colony thus: "Joane Tilson her husband dying without will, and forasmuch as she hath bine a true laborer with him . . . that shee shall have £30 sterling out of the said estate."

In Rhode Island, 1671, Mr. R. Waterman died intestate. The town council allotted the widow the enjoyment of house and lot, other lands and meadows, with the cattle, for her "maintenance and the bringing up of the orphans five small children." In December, 1699, a curious agreement was made between George Potter and Rachel, his wife. She had with his

> Consent and in hope of more peaceable liveing, withdrawn herself and removed to Boston for some time: and now finding it uncomfortable so to live and I being desirous to come together againe, doe here for her further incouragement and to prevent after strifes and alienations propose these Artikles. 1. She has given some things to her children. I shall never abraid her nor seek a return to them. 2ly. Our house and land, if I dye before my wife, she shall have it during her widowhood and bearing my name. In case of marriage she shall enjoy 1/3, other 2/3 to my nearest relations – at her decease her 1/3 to return. 3ly. I will not sell or mortgage any house or lands. 4ly. I promise to dwell in all loving and quiet behavior. All moveables she shall possess at my desease. 5ly. I Rachel Potter if it appear I have desposed of more than one bed since our departure, said bed shall be returned.

Such an agreement suggests an approach to equality, freedom, and mutuality between husband and wife.

A few instances of bequests to wives may reflect in a

measure the regard of husband for wife. Thomas Man gives his wife the use of all the household goods so long as she remains a widow. If she remarried, three-fourths of the goods should go to the daughters, one-fourth to the mother. In 1787 John Potter made considerate provision for his wife. A good riding beast, saddle and bridle with one good cow was to go to either son with whom she might choose to live. Firewood was to be brought to her room and she was to have everything to make her happy. If she should marry, these bequests were to go to the daughters. This conditioning of bequests on abstinence from remarriage illustrates the concept of the wife as an annex to the husband rather than as an individual personality.

Intestate settlements are an index of public opinion. This fact makes significant such a case as that when William Turpin died intestate in 1711, leaving a widow and three children. The son William agrees with his "mother-in-law" [step-mother?] to allow her the room now occupied by her in his father's house for life with benefit of fire, etc. If she needed a physician the expense was to be borne out of her own estate.

Tho the home was not sacred from the invasion of the state in case of parental unfitness, nevertheless, in the normal home domestic ties were manifold and strong in these simple days before economic evolution had banished or even considerably weakened home industries. The normal home was an almost self-sufficient unit. The wife attended to all manner of household manufactures after the fashion set by the virtuous woman in the last chapter of *Proverbs*.

But the impression that the colonial dame performed Herculean labors is a myth. These *tours de force* were rarely performed by a one-woman household. The wife bore and reared children and superintended the house; but she did not do the heavy work if there was need of her services in other lines. Some families had numerous trained and capable servants. In the country daughters not needed at home worked in neighbors' households until married. Many families in town and country took bound children to raise for the returns from their labor. They were generally children of neighbors or friends. They were not always well treated. The commonest helpers were the unmarried sisters of husband or wife. Moreover, most of the large families of earlier times were the offspring of at least two mothers,[51] and the later wives had fewer children. The first wife would get quickly six or seven children and die exhausted by maternity and labor. The next wife, young and sturdy, would take hold and bring up the family, some of whom were likely old enough to be of help. She would have three or four children, perhaps at longer intervals. If a third wife supervened she had a strong corps of assistants. The number of women that actually performed unaided the fabled tasks while bearing and rearing many children was probably not much greater than now. Many children died before their rearing was much of a tax. The typical family included several adult unmarried women, unpaid servants of their kindred. Often they filled a place of honor and esteem but in many cases they labored bitterly in dishonor – "old maids" in the sense that made the term one of intense reproach. These toiling spinsters are forgotten and their toils have been put down to the account of their married sisters. The existence of such a supply of high-class cheap labor de-

[51] Compare Hall and Smith, *Marriage and Fecundity of Colonial Men and Women*, in *Pedagogical Seminary*, vol. x, 275-314.

pressed the wages of domestic servants, and formed a tradition that has remained unto this day as a weight upon household service.[52]

The presence of a number of unmarried females in the household gave grounds for the enforcement of the Mosaic prohibition of marriage within forbidden degrees. We can imagine that the home would not have been very harmonious if the wife had felt that her sisters living in the same house were potential rivals and successors. In colonial days the family connections were closer than now and it was not unreasonable that persons related even by marriage should have been prohibited from marrying each other. Such restrictions would make less constrained and precarious the intercourse of large groups of kinsfolk. Whether or not the colonists were conscious of this reason for the "forbidden degrees" it is tolerably sure that these restrictions would not have lingered had they been altogether anachronistic.

In fact the barriers could scarcely be maintained. In 1691 Hannah Owen and Josiah Owen were adjudged to be "within the line of kindred or affinity forbidden" and ordered to cohabit no more. Hannah "owned that she was said Josiah's own brother's relict." To Josiah, who had brought about the marriage, nothing was done. The woman was ordered to "make a public acknowledgement of her sin and evil before the congregation at Braintree on their Lecture Day, or on the Lord's Day." Samuel Newton of Marlborough married his uncle's widow and had two children by her. The marriage was declared void "by the word of God as also by the law of England;" and they were forbidden to continue

[52] MacGill. "Myth of the Colonial Housewife," in the *Independent*, vol. lxix, 1318-1322.

in their "incest." In Massachusetts, 1695, a bill against incest was passed by the slight margin of twenty-seven to twenty-four.

> The ministers gave in their arguments yesterday in writing; else it had hardly gone, because several have married their wives' sisters, and the deputies thought it hard to part them. 'Twas concluded on the other hand that not to part them were to make the law abortive, by begetting in people a conceipt that such marriages were not against the law of God.

This law forbade marriage with wife's sister or niece. A few years later Samuel Sewall wrote to his cousin who had asked advice about a proposed marriage to the widow of his cousin-german. Samuel advised against the marriage on the ground of doubtful degrees and cited the Assembly's annotations on *Leviticus*, xviii. The gist of this is that as far as the ties of kindred love reach, so far the prohibition of marriage extends. Marriage should be with more remote persons "that so charity might be more diffusive; and not so contracted to one's kindred as it was among the Jews." Sewall says the Indians seldom marry so near as cousins-german and surely we ought not to have to go to school to them. Besides the saints disapprove. How much the Connecticut saints disapproved of what they considered incest is apparent from the law that he who married a sister-in-law was punished (and the wife too) with forty lashes on the bare back and forced to wear a letter "I" sewed on the outside of arm or on the back.

But not all women were content to constitute domestic problems. The spirit of self-reliance was, in case of necessity, as quick and steady in women of at least the later colonial period as now. But even in the early days, as suggested in our reference to the exploits of "ancient maids," women could do things. Governor

John Winthrop Junior's affairs in New Haven seem to have been placed in the care of Mrs. Davenport, wife of the Reverend John. There even were women voters in the New England colonies.[53] Advertisements from 1720 to 1800 show that women were teachers, embroiderers, jelly-makers, cooks, wax-workers, japanners, mantua makers, dealers in crockery, musical instruments, hardware, farm products, groceries, drugs, wines and spirits; and Hawthorne noted one colonial woman that ran a blacksmith shop. Peter Faneuil's account-books show dealings with many Boston tradeswomen, some of whom bought thousands of pounds' worth of imported goods in a year. On the list of Salem conspirators against taxation may be found the names of five women merchants. Women also published newspapers.[54] Most of these took charge on the death of a husband, brother, or son who had been editor. Sometimes they substituted for their male relatives in case of sickness or press of affairs. Women in New England coast towns were urged to participate actively in foreign commerce by sending a "venture" when a vessel departed with a cargo. Mrs. Grant, a business woman of Newport, who assumed charge of the business on her husband's death, found out that her lawyer was a rascal; so she rushed into court, pleaded a case for herself, and won the verdict. For nearly a century and a half after the landing of the Pilgrims there were practically no women wage-earners, however, outside of domestic service.

Colonial women were not altogether out of the "great world," the world of fashion. There were no fashion papers in the old days, but dolls dressed in the latest

[53] Björkman and Porritt. *Woman Suffrage—History, Arguments, Results*, 5; Stanton, et al. *History of Woman Suffrage*, vol. i, *footnote* 208.

[54] For details see Stanton et al., *History of Woman Suffrage*, vol. i, 43-44.

styles were exhibited. The following is a New England advertisement of the eighteenth century:

> To be seen at Mrs. Hannah Teats', a baby drest after the newest fashions. . . Lately arrived from London. Any ladies that desire to see it may either come or send. . . If they come . . . two shillings, and if she waits on 'em it is seven shillings.

Back in the early days Nathaniel Ward, minister at Ipswich (1634-1636), expressed disgust with extravagant fashions.

Writers tell us in glowing terms of woman's high position in colonial New England. Elliot says in *The New England History*: "In New England, women were never made the slaves, or inferiors of men; they were co-equal in social life, and held a position superior to that held by them in England." Dexter tells us that

> The Plymouth colony was the first in this country if not in the whole world, to recognize and honor woman. From the very outset, she had her rightful place at her husband's side as her children's head. And the Plymouth wives and mothers . . . were worthy of the men by whose side they stood. They represented in character and experience the best type of womanhood of that age. The same thing was true of the colony of Massachusetts Bay.

Warfield writes:

> There was material for Hawthorne's masterpiece even in Massachusetts Bay . . . but the current ran deep and strong through simple lives, finding their inspiration and happiness in the family, its home life, its bonds of affection, its widening circuit as younger generations cut their way westward through the forest. The familiar picture of the Puritan father [which Warfield seems to think overdrawn] is that of a man burdened with the responsibilities of life for himself and for his children. The companion piece is a mother who is a shield and a comforter, sharing the faith of her husband but manifesting its gentler aspects; not less anxious for the moral conduct of her

> offspring, but more confident of the value of a ministry of love. . . Throughout the colonies for the greater part of their history, the wife and mother dominated the home, ruling it with a light hand and a loving sway. The home life was very simple. The home training was reduced to a narrow field of purpose. The boys were to be fitted to go forth and earn a living, setting up homes for themselves as soon as possible. The girls were trained to become housewives.

Of course such generalizations partake of idealization. These pictures of the matriarchate of love are too idyllic. Warfield's generalization would be rather poetic even for our day.

VI. THE STATUS OF CHILDREN IN THE NEW ENGLAND COLONIAL FAMILY

If one were to infer the colonial attitude toward children from the prevalent fecundity he might guess that children were held in great esteem. The inference would be only partly correct. Dependent on men for the opportunity to live, women were the instruments of male gratification and did not realize their degradation. They were the vicarious sacrifice to the peopling of a continent. The children were providential accidents, prized, indeed, in a rather instinctive fashion by a people soaked in Hebraism, and living close to the line of annihilation, or, if more prosperous, requiring heirs that their hoard of goods might pass on with distinction and men to occupy the continent against all comers.

Colonial childhood is largely hidden in obscurity. Letters and diaries contain little mention of the children save the record of births and deaths and maladies and the like. Children were "to be seen not heard," and not seen too much either. There was no purpose to make the child appear valuable or noteworthy to himself or others. Scientific child study was a thing of the future.

Yet the family of moderate means was in many ways better off in America than in England and children profited by the improvement. It was difficult at first to rear children in the new country. In the bareness and cold of Massachusetts, mortality of infants was frightful. One man had sixteen children. The first was only a year and a half old when the second was born. When the baby was four days old the older child died. This calamity was five times repeated. Married nine years the mother had one child living and five dead. With freezing homes, bad diet, and Spartan treatment it does not seem strange that a large proportion of seventeenth century children died in infancy. This was the case even in the most favored families; thus of Cotton Mather's fifteen children only two survived him and of Judge Sewall's fourteen only three outlived their father.

This curtailment in face of the vacancy of a limitless continent enhanced the value of children. This increased esteem is obvious in colonial laws and children began to acquire that growing sense of their own importance that has at length illumined "the century of the child."

The colonists still believed in astrology; hence the very minute of the child's birth was recorded. Parents searched for names of deep import, and this with a view to their influence on the child's life. Quack medicines and vile doses were in evidence even tho it seems that Locke's *Thoughts on Education* published in England in 1690 was popular in the new world. It occurs on many old library lists in New England and among the few volumes on the single book shelf. His precepts were diffused on the pages of almanacs, the "best sellers" (save the *Bible*) of all eighteenth century books. From him came such practical suggestions as "always wetting children's feet in cold water to toughen them; and also have children wear thin-soled shoes that the wet may come freely in." It was urged that boys should go hatless and nightcapless as soon as they had hair. Josiah Quincy at three years was taken from his warm bed, winter and summer, carried to the cellar kitchen, and dipped three times in water just from the pump. He said that in his boyhood he sat more than half the time with wet feet without ill effects. Many Revolutionary heroes grew up under Locke's strenuous rules of dietary and sleeping. If his embargo on "physic" was too little followed, it was a cause for regret. But less beer was consumed in America than in the Old World, and more milk – a change beneficial to colonial children.

Nothing was allowed to interfere with due observance of religious form. The infant must be taken to the fireless church for baptism on the first Sabbath after birth no matter if ice had to be broken in the font. He went in the arms of the midwife – a great colonial dignitary. One parson practiced immersion till his own children nearly succumbed under the ordeal. It is said that the meeting-house contained sometimes a little wooden cage or frame to hold babies too young or feeble or sleepy to sit up. One would suppose that the interminable sermons in icy churches must have been responsible for many deaths.

The century of colony-planting, the seventeenth, was, in Europe, an age of precocity. The same atavism characterized the American colonies. A stern theology contributed to this distortion of childhood. Michael Wigglesworth, "the most popular versifier of early New England Puritanism," in his *Day of Doom*, which countless children had to learn, represents children deceased in infancy as pleading with the judge that if Adam, the author of original sin, is saved, they should also be. Christ tells them that if Adam had stood true they would have been glad to enjoy the reward; so they ought to be satisfied to take the penalty. Edwards, in a sermon, describes parents in heaven "with holy joy upon their countenances" at the torment of their little ones. This view of the depravity of child nature made it necessary to seek infantile conversion. Children from their earliest years were confronted with the terrors of hell from which they could escape only by following what they were taught and abstaining from everything they would naturally want to do. Cotton Mather writes:

> I took my little daughter Katy [aged four] into my study and there told my child that I am to dy shortly and she must, when I am dead, remember everything I now said unto her. I sett before her the sinfull condition of her nature and charged her to pray in secret places every day. That God for the sake of Jesus Christ would give her a new heart. . . I gave her to understand that when I am taken from her she must look to meet with more humbling afflictions than she does now she has a tender father to provide for her.

This was thirty years before he died.

Judge Sewall records the distress of his daughter Betty who burst out in a sudden cry, fearing she would go to hell.

> She was first wounded by my reading a sermon of Mr. Norton's; text "Ye shall seek me and shall not find me." And those words in the sermon "Ye shall seek me and die in your sins" ran in her mind and terrified her greatly. And staying at home she read out of Mr. Cotton Mather, "Why had Satan filled thy heart," which increased her fear. Her mother asked her whether she prayed. She answered "yes" but feared her prayers were not heard because her sins were not pardoned. . . [Two weeks later he writes:] Betty comes in as soon as I was up and tells me the disquiet she had when wak'd. Told me she was afraid she should go to hell; was like Spira not elected. Ask'd her what I should pray for, she said that God would pardon her sin and give her a new heart. I answered her fears

as well as I could, and prayed with many fears on either part. Hope God heard us.

Jonathan Edwards tells of Phebe Bartlet who at four was greatly affected by the talk of her brother converted a little before at about eleven. Her parents were not used to directing their serious counsels to their children, especially not to her as they thought her too young. But they watched her after her brother's talk listen earnestly to the advice they gave to the other children. She retired to pray several times daily. She one day told her mother her fear she should go to hell. Her mother quieted her, told her she must be a good girl and pray every day and that she hoped God would give her salvation. Later the child experienced salvation. When questioned she said she loved God better than father or mother or sister or anything. Then she cried for fear her sister would go to hell. At church she did not spend her time in child fashion. She went once with bigger children to a neighbor's lot to get plums. Her mother reproved her gently for taking them without leave. She had not known it was wrong. Distressed over her sin she retained her aversion to the fruit for a considerable time tho the other children were not much affected.

Anne Dudley at six or seven tells her grief at her "neglect of Private Duteys" in which she is too often lax. At sixteen recognizing herself as "carnall and sitting loose from God" she accepts the smallpox as a "proper rebuke to her pride and vanity." Nathaniel Mather tells us in his diary:

> When very young I went astray from God and my mind was altogether taken with vanities and follies, such as the remembrance of them doth greatly abase my soul within me. Of the manifold sins which then I was guilty of, none so sticks upon

> me, as that, being very young, I was whittling on the Sabbath Day, and for fear of being seen I did it behind the door. A great reproach of God! a specimen of that Atheism I brought into the world with me.

Children on the streets mouthed the current phrases and during the Hutchinson trial jeered at one another as believers in the "Covenant of Works" or in the "Covenant of Grace."

In many cases parental zeal for education overstimulated and forced baby minds. One of the most precocious was a girl born in Boston in 1708. In her second year she knew her letters and "could relate many stories out of the Scriptures to the satisfaction and pleasure of the most judicious." At three she knew most of the catechism, many psalms, many lines of poetry, and read distinctly; at four she asked many astonishing questions about theology. (Her father was president of Harvard.) A letter of Jonathan Edwards written at twelve sounds like the work of a grown man. Boys entered Boston Latin School as young as six and a half. They often began Latin much younger. Infants of three were sometimes taught to read Latin words as soon as English. One minister used to throw the book at a child of five for his slowness in learning Latin. Timothy Dwight is said to have committed the alphabet in a single lesson and could read the Bible before four and taught it to his comrades. At six he wanted to study Latin. Being denied he went at it alone and studied through the Latin grammar twice. He would have been ready for college at eight if the grammar school had not closed. In 1799 a boy of fourteen was graduated at Rhode Island College.

In other respects than education and religion precocity was taken for granted. Until the Revolution boys became men at sixteen, paid taxes, and served in the militia. Girl orphans were permitted at fourteen to choose their own guardians. When Governor Winthrop's son John was only fourteen, the governor made the boy executor of his will. He evidently considered a boy of fourteen or fifteen mature.[55] Such curtailment of infancy as colonial precocity exhibits evidences the simplicity of colonial civilization. It was a crime against childhood. Children of to-day would be nervous invalids if they were driven by uncanny fear to morbid introspection such as afflicted the young Puritans.

Those that survived infancy, tho probably as dearly loved as are children to-day, were denied all the normal sources of joy and happiness. Childish manners were formal and meek. Parents were addressed as "esteemed parent" or "honored sir and madam." A pert child was generally thought to be delirious or bewitched. One son of a stern Puritan said that "he never ventured to make a boy's simple request of his father, to offer so much as a petition for a knife or a ball without putting it into writing in due form." Children were now and then favored with a visit to some sainted person who would bless them or warn them to flee from the wrath to come. Everybody went to funerals. There was a dire scarcity of anything worthy to be called children's literature. The children of to-day would hardly be attracted by such advertisements as these: "Small book in easey verse Very Suitable for Children, entitled the Prodigal Daughter or the Disobedient Lady Reclaimed: adorned with curious cuts, Price 6d." "A Token for Children. Being the exact account of the Conversation and Holy and Exemplary Lives of several

[55] Compare Earle, *Child Life in Colonial Days*, chapter ix, "Childish Precocity."

Young Children." Or Mather's work, "Some Examples of Children in whom the Fear of God was remarkably Budding before they died; in several Parts of New England." How glad the children, after the first quarter of the eighteenth century, must have been to get *Mother Goose*! Of course to the stern Puritan, inexorably utilitarian, what afforded amusement seemed sinful. Child nature being depraved and wicked must be dampered. Play instincts were inexcusable.

The sense of parental responsibility was strong. When Cotton Mather's child fell into the fire the father wrote: "Alas for my sin, the just God throws my child into the fire!" A similar disaster led him to preach on "What use ought parents to make of disasters befalling their children?" Again he was led to preach on "What parents are to do for the salvation of their children."

Home discipline was relentless. Stern and arbitrary command compelled obedience, submissive and generally complete. Reverence and respect for older persons were seldom withheld. Adults believed in the rod as an instrument of subjugation. John Robinson, the Pilgrim preacher, said,

> Surely there is in all children (tho not alike) a stubbernes and stoutnes of minde arising from naturall pride which must in the first place be broken and beaten down that so the foundation of their education being layd in humilitie and tractableness other virtues may in their time be built thereon. It is commendable in a horse that he be stout and stomackfull being never left to his own government, but always to have his rider on his back and his bit in his mouth, but who would have his child like his horse in his brutishnes?

A little book of etiquette apparently widely circulated in colonial days contains directions for the table behavior of children:

> Never sit down at the table till asked, and after the blessing.

> Ask for nothing; tarry till it be offered thee. Speak not. Bite not thy bread but break it. Take salt only with a clean knife. Dip not the meat in the same. Hold not thy knife upright but sloping, and lay it down at right hand of plate with blade on plate. Look not earnestly at any other that is eating. When moderately satisfied leave the table. Sing not, hum not, wriggle not. Spit nowhere in the room but in the corner. . . When any speak to thee, stand up. Say not I have heard it before. Never endeavor to help him out if he tell it not right. Snigger not; never question the truth of it.

Some children were indulged and parents did the best they could for them and grieved at their death. Touchingly significant is the brief note left by one: "Fifty years ago today died my little John, Alas!" Giles Corry refused to plead on the charge of witchcraft because he had been informed that if convicted of felony the inheritance of his children would be forfeit to the crown. Even the discipline of eminent Puritans reveals kindliness of spirit. Cotton Mather writes: "My children are with me. I have now three of them (and my wife's kinswoman) at my table. . . I will have my table talk facetious as well as instructive, and use much freedom of conversation in it. . . I will sett before them some sentences of the Bible." He published a booklet (which was "much desired") on *A family Well-ordered; or an Essay to Render Parents and Children Happy in one another.* He tries to train his children in goodness and piety.

> I first beget in them a high opinion of their father's love to them, and of his being best able to judge, what shall be good for them. Then I make them sensible, tis a folly for them to pretend unto any witt and will of their own . . . my word must be their law. . . I would never come to give a child a blow; except in case of obstinacy or some gross enormity. To be chased for a while out of my presence I would make to be looked upon, as the sorest punishment in the family. . . The

stanch way of Education, carried on with raving and kicking and scourging (in schools as well as families) tis abominable; and a dreadful judgment of God upon the world. . . [He prays with his children; sets before them heaven and hell, etc. He would use their games to make them think of piety and goodness.] I would put my children upon chusing their several ways of usefulness, and enkindle in them as far as I can, a mighty desire of being useful in the world, and assist them unto the uttermost."

It was a child of this man that, dying at two years and seven months, "made a most edifying end in prayer and praise."

The reverend Jonathan Edwards of Northhampton was careful and thoro in his paternal discipline but his children reverenced, esteemed, and loved him.

He took the utmost care to begin his government of them when they were very young. When they first discovered any degree of self-will and stubbornness, he would attend to them until he had thoroly subdued them, and brought them to submit. Such prudent discipline, exercised with the greatest calmness, being repeated once or twice, was generally sufficient for that child, and effectually established his parental authority, and produced a cheerful obedience ever after. [He conversed with his children] singly and closely about the concerns of their souls. . . In the evening after tea, he customarily sat in the parlor with his family, for an hour, unbending from the severity of study, entering freely into the feelings and concerns of his children, and relaxing into cheerful and animated conversation, accompanied frequently with sprightly remarks, sallies of wit and humor. But before retiring to his study, he usually gave the conversation by degrees a more serious turn, addressing his children with great tenderness and earnestness on the subject of their salvation. . . He was utterly opposed to everything like unreasonable hours on the part of young people, in their visiting and amusements, which he regarded as a dangerous step toward corrupting them and bringing them to ruin. And he thought the excuse offered by many parents for tolerating this practise in their children – that it is the custom, and that the children of other people are allowed thus to practise, and therefore it is difficult and even impossible to restrain them – was insufficient and frivolous, and manifested a great degree of stupidity. . . He allowed none of his children to be absent from home after nine o'clock at night, when they went abroad to see their friends and companions; neither were they allowed to sit up much after that time, in his own house, when any of their friends came to visit them. If any gentleman desired to address either of his daughters, after the requisite introduction and preliminaries, he was allowed all proper opportunities of becoming thoroly acquainted with the manners and disposition of the young lady, but must not intrude on the customary hours of rest and sleep, nor on the religion and order of the family.

We are expected to believe that the Edwards young people went betimes cheerfully to bed. Incidentally the passage throws significant side-light on the relaxing of the hold of Puritanism. Many a stern Puritan family in America succumbed to the easier ways of the Church of England.

The letters of John Adams are full of interest from the standpoint of family training at the end of the colonial period. Thus in 1774, he writes to his wife:

Let us . . . my dear partner, from that affection which we feel for our lovely babes, apply ourselves, by every way we can, to the cultivation of our farm. . . Above all cares of this life, let our ardent anxiety be to mould the minds and manners of our children. [Again]: Pray remember me to my dear little babes, whom I long to see running to meet me and climb up upon me under the smiles of their mother. . . For God's sake make your children *hardy, active*, and *industrious*; for strength, activity, and industry will be their only resource and dependence. [Once more]: Remember my tender love to little Abby; tell her she must write me a letter. . . I am charmed with your amusement with our little Johnny. Tell him I am glad to hear he is so good a boy as to read to his mamma for her entertainment, and to keep himself out of the company of rude children. Tell him I hope to hear a good account of his accidence and nomenclature when I return. . . The education of our children is never out of my mind. Train them to virtue. Habituate them to industry, activity, and spirit.

Later he is distressed at illness of the family, and laments the death of his mother-in-law. He says the children were better for her influence. John Quincy, aged seven, writes a bright little letter to his father telling of his lessons and reading and hope to see his father. When the boy is ten, the father writes to him recommending certain formidable historical reading. His letters to his wife refer repeatedly to the need of training the children in good habits. She says on one occasion:

I often point them to their sire–
engaged in a corrupted state,
wrestling with vice and faction.

These letters disclose a human interest and spirit in family life, which, while not lax, is remote from fanaticism.

In addition to home training the New Englanders provided schools. Each town had a school. By 1649 some degree of education was compulsory in every New England colony except Rhode Island. School in New England ran seven or eight hours a day. Children took a live interest if we may judge by a juvenile couplet–

New teachers, new laws,
New devils, sharp claws.

Pioneering caused school interest to wane. In consequence of the loss of six hundred men in King Philip's War, schools were abandoned.

From Judge Sewall and Jonathan Edwards comes the impression that Puritan children were priggish, morbid, and doleful. Thanks to these worthy men the odd little creatures whose pictures have descended to us figure in our fancy as intolerable theologs. But the evidence is ample that the children of the Puritans no more relished the weary sermons beyond their depths, with their lurid threats of hell, than children of to-day relish the imprisonment of the rigid schoolroom or the tedium of Sunday clothes. Boys and even girls at church were a pest to the parson and had to be put under town surveillance. Laws passed at the close of King Philip's War confessed that the war was a judgment on the colony for the "disorder and rudeness of youth in many congregations in time of the worship of God, whereby sin and profaneness is greatly increased." John Pike of Dedham received sixteen shillings in 1723 for "keeping the boys in subjection six months." When rehired he exacted twice as much. Similar episodes took place everywhere. In Harwich, it was voted "that the same course be pursued with the girls" as with the boys, and at Farmington in 1772:

> Whereas indecencies are practised by the young people in time of Publick Worship by frequently passing and repassing by one another in the galleries; intermingling sexes to the great disturbance of many serious and well minded people – Resolved that each of us that are heads of families will use our utmost endeavor to suppress the evils.

One might suppose that the corralling of the boys on the back benches at church promoted the "Rude and Idel Behavior" which a Connecticut justice entered in his note-book thus:

> Smiling and larfing and intiseing others to the same evil. . . Pulling the hair of his nayber Veroni Simkins in the time of public worship. . . Throwing Sister Penticost Perkins on the ice on the Sabath day between the meeting hows and his place of abode.

But in spite of strict family discipline human nature in the colonies was much like human nature elsewhere. The amusements of the young were sometimes scandalous. There are numerous accounts of "mixt dancings, unlawful gamings, extravagance in dress, light behavior" and such-like offences. As early as 1657, Boston deemed it wise to pass a law as follows:

> Forasmuch as sundry complaints are made that several persons have received hurt by boys and young men playing at football in the streets, these therefore are to enjoin that none be found at that game in any of the streets, lanes or enclosures of this town under the penalty of 20s. for every such offence.

Sewall writes on one occasion:

> Joseph threw a knop of brass, and hit his sister Betty on the forehead so as to make it bleed and swell; upon which and for his playing at prayer time, and eating when return thanks, I whipped him pretty smartly.

But tho the judge could manage his own children his graceless grandchildren were a sore trial. Sam Hirst, the son of timid Betty, lived with his grandfather for a while. On April 1, 1719, the Judge wrote:

> In the morning I dehorted Sam Hirst and Grendall Rawson from playing idle tricks because 'twas first of April: They were the greatest fools that did so. [March 15, 1725]: Sam Hirst got up betime in the morning, and took Ben Swett with him and went into the Comon to play Wicket. Went before anybody was up, left the door open: Sam came not to prayer at which I was much displeased. [Two days later]: Did the like again, but took not Ben with him. I told him he could not lodge here practicing thus, So he log'd elsewher.

"What little hope of a happy generation after us," runs a seventeenth century plaint, "when many among us scarcely know how to teach their children manners!" Extreme Puritanism, indeed, did not last long in full strength. The reverend Ezekiel Rogers, a Puritan preacher who lived at the time when extreme Puritanism was waning, wrote in 1657:

> Do your children and family grow more godly? I find greatest trouble and grief about the rising generation. Young people

are little stirred here; but they strengthen one another in evil by example and by counsel. Much ado have I with my own family.

Just before the Revolution a little girl of eight came from the Barbadoes to her grandmother in Boston to attend school. The young lady left her grandmother's roof in great indignation because she was not allowed wine at all her meals. Her parents took her part saying that she had been reared as a lady and must have wine when she wished it. Thus imported looseness, together with the economic advance that relegated asceticism to the rear, contributed in the later days to the decline of Puritan rigor.

Colonial law upheld, of course, paternal authority. A Massachusetts law reads thus: "Forasmuch as it appeareth by too much experience, that divers children and servants do behave themselves disobediently and disorderly, towards their parents, masters, and governors [and this not many years after the founding of Massachusetts!] to the disturbance of families, and discouragement of such parents and governors," authority is given to magistrates to summon offenders and have them punished by whipping or otherwise. Furthermore, "upon information of diverse loose, vaine, and corrupt persons . . . which insinuate themselves into the fellowship of the young people . . . drawing them both by night and by day from their callings, studyes, and honest occupations and lodging places to the dishonor of God and grief of their parents, masters, teachers," therefore "persons under government not to be entertained in common houses." New Haven made persons trading with or abetting minors, etc., liable to punishment. Massachusetts in 1694-1695 made a further law: "Whereas complaint has been made by sundry inhabitants of this province that have sustained great damage by their sons and servants deserting their service without consent of their parents or masters," being encouraged aboard ships, a penalty is imposed on shipmasters for entertaining sons or servants without leave. Massachusetts had a law against excess of apparel on children and servants. "Also if any taylor shall make or fashion any garment for such children and servants . . . contrary to the mind and order of their parents and governors; every such taylor shall for the first offence be admonished; and for the second . . . forfeit double the value of such apparel or garment."

The law had to take cognizance of the fact that America was a sort of reformatory for parents in the old country to use. As early as 1647 a law was passed as follows: "Whereas sundry gentlemen of quality and others, ofttimes send over their children unto this country, to some friends here, hoping (at least) thereby to prevent their extravagant and notoris courses," but they manage to get credit and go on in extravagance to the grief of friends, therefore merchants giving credit without authority shall lose the debt.

For incorrigible disobedience to parents the colonists, in accordance with Moses and Calvin, prescribed the death penalty. The Connecticut statute reads:

> Forasmuch as incorrigibleness is also adjudged to be a sin of death, but noe law yet amongst us established for the execution thereof . . . it is ordered, that whatsoever child or servant . . . shall be convicted of any stubborn or rebellious caridge against their parents or gouernors, wch is a forerunner of the forementioned evell, the gouernor or any two magistrats haue liberty and power fro this court to commit such prson or prsons to the house of correction, and there to remayne under hard labor and severe punishment, so long as the court or the major part of the magistrats shall judge meet.

The Piscataqua colony had the following law:

> If any child or children above 16 yrs. old of competent understanding, shall curse or smite their natural father or mother, he or they shall be put to death unless it can be sufficiently testified that the parents have been very unchristianly negligent of the education of such children. . . If any man have a rebellious or stubborne son of sufficient years and understanding, viz. 16 years of age or upwards, wch shall not obey the voice of his father or the voice of his mother, yt when they have chastened him will not hearken unto them . . . such son shall be put to death, or otherwise severely punished.

The Bay Colony statute was to the same effect. The capital laws of Connecticut recognize an additional mitigating circumstance in case of the smiting, etc., of parents: "unless . . . the parents . . . so provoke them by extreme and cruell correction that they have been forced thereunto to preserve themselves from death, maiming." This law is buttressed with proof texts. There is no record of the actual infliction of the death penalty in Massachusetts and probably none elsewhere.

Regarding the distribution of property among children we find that the Puritan colonists legally repudiated the feudal principle of male preference and primogeniture, tho granting a double portion to the eldest son (in some colonies). In 1627 De Rasures, a visitor to Plymouth, found that "In the inheritance they place all the children in one degree, only the eldest son has an acknowledgement for his seniority of birth." The Massachusetts law of 1641 provides that

> When parents die intestate, the elder sonne shall have a double portion of his whole estate reall and personall, unless the general court upon just cause alleged shall judge otherwise. When parents die intestate having noe heirs male of their bodies their daughters shall inherit as copartners, unless the general court upon just reason shall judge otherwise.

Connecticut law of 1699 directs that children shall share equally in the estate of intestates. An example of the principle of equality is found in the Plymouth records. The court ordered in the case of a man dying without will that after the wife's share was deducted "the younger children bee made equal to the elder in what they have had, and for the remainder, after that is done, that it bee equally devided amongst all the children in equall proportions." The special privilege of the eldest son did not last long.

The usage of equal distribution may be derived from "the custom of Gavelkind in Kent" from which region many of the first colonists of New England, especially Connecticut, came. Campbell, however, traces back to Dutch law our principle of equal division of land among the children of an intestate.[56] His interpretation, tho suggestive, is too superficial. The decline of male primogeniture is essentially a phenomenon of the passing of feudalism – a system of society based on the ownership of land, limited in quantity and demanding military service of the holders. As soon as society ceased to center in military land-holding, the foundation of male primogeniture crumbled. In America land was too abundant to become an insignium of nobility. In the North the aristocracy was based on the ownership of increasable commodities and commerce rather than of land; society was only incidentally and temporarily military; so there was no need of limiting inheritance to the first-born male. Campbell's account of Dutch usage itself hints at the connection of primogeniture with feudal institutions. Our interpretation gets to the bottom of that association.

---

[56] Campbell. *The Puritan in Holland, England, and America*, vol. ii, 452-453.

In so far as the old aristocracy lingered English traditions as to primogeniture retained their hold inasmuch as parents could use their discretion if they made a will. Not always were estates divided evenly in New England. Usually the sons were set above the daughters. The larger the estate the greater was likely to be the discrimination. The father of Sir William Pepperell left his daughters five hundred pounds each in addition to previous advances. Then, after a few bequests, the whole large estate went to the future baronet, whereat the daughters and sons-in-law were greatly disappointed. It was the theory in Rhode Island that the father should provide for his sons and thus for other men's daughters.

Disinheritance was sometimes used as a means of discipline. The marriage of a daughter with an unwelcome swain was often prohibited by will: "not to suffer her to be circumvented and cast away upon a swaggering gentleman."

One might wonder how parents could provide for twelve, eighteen, or twenty-four children let alone have anything to leave them. But children of that period were soon able to contribute to the family store. When a host of the children were boys it was doubtless a relief to the weary mother when a lot of them went to sea, as in an eighteenth century news item from Portsmouth, New Hampshire:

> There are now living in this town, a lady and gentleman who have not been married more than twenty years, and yet have eighteen sons; ten of whom are at sea, and eight at home with their parents.

But it must have been a problem for the reverend Abijah Weld to rear his fifteen children on his salary of about two hundred and twenty dollars, tho he had a small farm. Moreover he entertained freely and gave to the poor. Reverend Moses Fisher with his sixteen children and a salary never over ninety pounds, usually only sixty pounds paid mainly in corn and wood, managed to send three sons to college and he married off all his daughters.

But high fecundity and child labor are consorts. The colonial home was a little world within whose bounds woman found her life, under whose roof the children could, if need were, learn all that was necessary for their future careers. The Puritans, as has been seen, were strong for the training of children for their duties here and beyond. Higgeson in *New England's Plantation* (1629) tells that "Little children here by setting of corne may earne much more than their own maintenance." Less than a decade after Higgeson's rejoicing at the possibilities of child labor in agriculture, Johnson was praising the people of Rowley who "built a fulling mill and caused their little ones to be very diligent in spinning cotton wool." The ruling element was not disposed to allow idleness among the poor. In Plymouth in 1641 it was ordered "that those that have relief from the townes and have children and doe not ymploy them that then it shal be lawful for the Towneship to take order that those children shal be put to worke in fitting ymployment according to their strength and abilities or placed out by the Townes." In Massachusetts, 1641, "it is desired and expected that all masters of families should see that their children and servants should be industriously implied so as that mornings and evenings and other seasons may not bee lost as formerly they have bene." In 1642 the orders were more definite. To keep cattle, alone, was not to be industrious in the Puritan sense of the word, and such children are also to "bee set to some other impliment withall as spinning upon the rock, knitting, weveing tape, etc." The same year it was decreed that all unruly poor children were to be bound out for service. A law of the general court of 1643 authorizes constables to whip runaway bound boys. *New England's First Fruits* (1642) appeals to Englishmen to stir up "some well-minded to cloath and transport over poore children, boyes and girles, which may be a great mercy to their bodies and soules."

In 1656 Hull records that "Twenty persons, or about such a number, did agree to raise a stock to procure a house and materials to improve the children and youth of the town of Boston (which want employment) in the several manufactures." It was considered a public duty in Massachusetts to provide for the training of children in learning and in "labor and other employments which may bee profitable to the commonwealth." It was probably scarcity of clothing that led to the law "that all hands not necessarily imployed on other occasions as women, girls, and boyes, shall . . . spin according to their skill and ability, and that the selectmen in every town, do consider the condition and capacity of every family, and accordingly do assess them at one or more spinners." The town of Boston in 1672 notified a number of persons to "dispose of their severall children . . . abroad for servants, to serve by indentures according to their ages and capacities," and if they neglect so to do "the selectmen will take their said children from them and place them with such masters as they shall provide according as the law directs." The children are both girls and boys from eight years up. The records of many towns go to show that the practice of binding out the children of the poor was wide-spread.

In Boston, 1682, a workhouse was ordered built to employ children who "shamefully spend their time in the streets." Gabriel Harris died in 1684, leaving four looms; his six children took part in the work. Boston in 1720 appointed a committee which recommended that twenty spinning-wheels be provided for such children as should be sent from the almshouse and a Massachusetts act of the same year provided that all children of the poor whose parents, whether receiving alms or not, were unable to maintain them were to be set to work or bound out by the selectmen or overseers, the males till twenty-one, the females till eighteen. Fifty years later William Molineux, of Boston, asked the legislature for assistance in his plan for "manufacturing the children's labor into wearing apparel" and "employing young females from eight years old and upward."

The Connecticut system of dealing with the children of the poor was similar to that of Massachusetts.

Probably children were very much overworked in these early days before the factory system. But in domestic industries on isolated farms their condition was less conspicuous than when, later, children came to be massed in great factories. The custom of giving all Saturday as school holiday seems to have grown out of the need of children at home to make Puritanical preparation for Sabbath.

The industries of children were varied and important. Some have been already mentioned. There was much work on the farm even for small children. They sowed seed, weeded flax fields, hetchelled flax, combed wool. Girls of six could spin flax. The boy had to rise early and do chores before he went to school. He must be diligent in study and in the evening do more chores. His whole time out of school was occupied with bringing in fuel, cutting feed, feeding pigs, watering horses, picking berries, gathering vegetables, spooling yarn. There was sawing and wood chopping, and the making of brooms for which he got six cents each. Splitting shoe pegs was another job; setting card teeth, etc. Such work provided a phase of education that modern educators find it hard to replace now that industry has forsaken the home.

In putting the boys early to some useful handicraft the Puritans imitated their favorite model, the Hebrews. In Puritan ethics, idleness was a serious sin. But colonial child labor was fundamentally a response to a condition rather than to a theory. It was a compliance with the exigencies of the case. The rigor of the struggle for existence in early New England made impossible the prolongation of infancy that marks high civilization. Work was abundant; but real wages were low, as prices were comparatively high. Colonial industry was far from being a poor man's paradise. The starvation line and the debtors' prison loomed large. Child labor was, at least seemingly, a colonial necessity, aggravated of course by the existence of an exploiting aristocracy. The introduction of children into the early factories was a natural sequence of the colonial attitude regarding child labor and of the Puritan belief in the sin of idleness.

VII. SEX SIN AND FAMILY FAILURE IN COLONIAL NEW ENGLAND

Sexual irregularities both before and after marriage gave considerable concern. Part of the trouble was associated with bundling, an antique folkway that found new life in the New World.

Bundling[57] prevailed to a very great extent in New England from a very early time. It was originally confined to the lower classes or to those that were under the necessity of strict economy in firewood and candle light. Many of the early dwellings consisted of but one room. The wayfaring friend must be accommodated, if only with half a bed. The Abbé Robin, who was in Connecticut in 1788, says, "The Americans of these parts are very hospitable; they have commonly but one bed in the house, and the chaste spouse, although she were alone, would divide it with her guest, without hesitation or fear." If this remarkable assertion be true it is not strange that careful mothers saw no impropriety in the custom of allowing young men and women to lie together (without undressing). Evidently the usage was distinctly an economic phenomenon. Harsh economic conditions denied leisure for more seemly courtship and afforded but inadequate facilities for keeping houses warm.

Bundling was carried further in Connecticut and

[57] Massachusetts Historical Society *Proceedings*, second ser., vol. vi, 503-510; Low. *The American People*, vol. i: *Planting of a Nation*, 346-349; Fisher. *Men, Women, and Manners in Colonial Times*, vol. i, 284-290; Stiles. *Bundling*.

Massachusetts than elsewhere. In Massachusetts this trustful innocence did not confine itself to the lower classes it would seem. The Connecticut forefathers tolerated it complacently. In early times in New England, if we may believe numerous authorities, bundling brought very few unfortunate results. The advocates of the custom maintained that mishaps in connection with it were rarer than in higher circles with different methods of courtship. But at no time did it win universal approval. It is easy for those in comfortable circumstances to reprobate as vices the makeshifts of penury.

Bundling lingered long in some places. It is described in western Massachusetts as late as 1777. It was said to be in some measure abolished along the sea-coast but there a like usage called "tarrying" was practiced. Charles Francis Adams believes that bundling continued even in eastern Massachusetts and the towns adjoining Boston until after the Revolutionary disturbance and probably till the beginning of the nineteenth century. Mrs. John Adams writes, 1784, of an ocean voyage: "What should I have thought on shore to have laid myself down in common with half a dozen gentlemen? We have curtains it is true, and we only in part undress–about as much as the Yankee bundlers." It is alleged, indeed, that the practice has not altogether passed away yet.

The menace of the old usage became apparent after the French and Indian wars when the young men, habituated in camp and army to vice and recklessness, stripped bundling of its innocence. At last the custom became such a scandal that the church was forced to proceed to its suppression. Jonathan Edwards attacked it in the pulpit and other ministers, who had allowed it to go unnoticed, joined in its suppression. At Dedham, only ten miles from Boston, the reverend Mr. Haven, alarmed at the number of cases of unlawful cohabitation, preached at least as late as 1781 "a long and memorable discourse" in which he dealt with the "growing sin" publicly from his pulpit attributing "the frequent recurrence of the fault to the custom then prevalent of females admitting young men to their beds who sought their company with intentions of marriage."

In 1785 the reformers published in an almanac (then the only method of reaching great numbers of plebeians) some homely verses calculated to influence the lower classes. This campaign made them self-conscious in the matter. They began to think that they were despised for their conduct. Counter verses were not permanently effective. But it is easy to imagine the vividness of the contest from such stanzas as

It shant be so, they rage and storm
And country girls in clusters swarm,
  And fly and buzz like angry bees,
  And vow they'll bundle when they please.
Some mothers, too, will plead their cause,
And give their daughters great applause,
  And tell them, 'tis no sin nor shame,
  For we your mothers did the same.

  If I wont take my sparks to bed
  A laughing stock I shall be made.

But where's the man that fire can
  Into his bosom take,
Or go through coals on his foot soles,
  And not a blister make?

But last of all, up speaks romp Moll
  And pleads to be excused,
For how can she e'er married be
  If bundling be refused?

The decline of bundling is to be attributed largely to the increase of wealth which made possible larger houses and less rigorous conditions of life.

Pre-contract probably tended to fornication. New England betrothal was a solemnity of moment–a half-way marriage. Incontinence of betrothed might be punished as adultery tho if the offence was with each other the penalty was diminished.

The matter of fornication before marriage was given shameful notoriety. Not even matrimony long previous to the discovery of the transgression was considered complete satisfaction. Fear of infant damnation was a stimulus compelling young married people to shameful public confession. Groton church records show that until 1803 whenever a child was born less than seven months after marriage a public confession had to be made before the whole congregation. Thus, at Roxbury, 1678, Hanna Hopkins was censured in the church for fornication with her husband before marriage and for fleeing from justice into Rhode Island. The Braintree *Records* for March 2, 1683 show that

> Temperance, the daughter of brother F——, now the wife of John B——, having been guilty of the sin of fornication with him that is now her husband, was called forth in open congregation, and presented a paper containing a full acknowledgement of her great sin and wickedness, publickly bewailed her disobedience to parents. . . She was solemnly admonished of her great sin.

In 1728

> Joseph P—— and Lydia his wife made a confession before the church which was well accepted, for the sin of fornication committed with each other before marriage.

The cases of premarital fornication by husband and wife were evidently numerous. The experience of Braintree was by no means singular among the Massachusetts towns of the eighteenth century. The records of the Groton church show that of two hundred persons owning the baptismal covenant there from 1761 to 1775, no less than sixty-six confessed to fornication before marriage. From 1789 to 1791 sixteen couples were admitted to full communion; of these nine had confessed to fornication. The greater part of the Braintree confessions of incontinence were between 1726 and 1744, the period of the Great Awakening. Discipline probably stiffened about 1725. Perhaps confession increased with the rise of religious enthusiasm. It may be that sex excitement was concomitant with the religious frenzy.

Every means was employed to check the evil of incontinence which even in the earliest days of the Massachusetts colonies was a grievous trouble. In Rhode Island, according to Weeden, "the hardest municipal task – beyond early theological differences or proprietors' disputes for lands – was in the control of sexual immorality." In that colony,

> Illegitimacy was a not uncommon offence . . . at any time in the first century of our colonial history. . . A young woman's prospect of marrying respectably and of moving thereafter in respectable society, do not seem to have been seriously impaired by her already having shown herself qualified to discharge the functions of a wife and mother.[58]

As regards Rhode Island in 1655 the Lord Protector "hath lately received complaints against us that we abound with whoredom" and steps were taken to check lasciviousness. In 1642 Governor Bradford bewailed conditions at Plymouth, "not only incontinence between persons unmarried, for which many both men and women have been punished sharply enough but some

[58] Field. *State of R. I. and Providence Plantations at the End of the Century*, vol. iii, 397.

maried persons also." A reforming synod at Boston, 1679, laments "hainous breeches of the seventh commandment." Numerous cases of church confession might be cited. At Dedham for twenty-five years before 1781 twenty-five cases of unlawful cohabitation were publicly acknowledged. Between 1756 and 1803 the number of cases increased alarmingly. Apparently the cases of church discipline publicly administered on the ground of sexual immorality were infrequent in Roxbury (as in Dedham and Braintree) before 1725. Lord Dartmouth, secretary for the colonies, referred to the commonness of illegitimate offspring among the young people of New England as a thing of accepted notoriety and Governor Hutchinson did not refute the charge.

Hawthorne says in *The Scarlet Letter*:

> Morally as well as materially there was a coarser fibre in those wives and maidens of old English birth and breeding than in their fair descendants separated from them by a series of six or seven generations.

Charles Francis Adams wrote regarding New England (1883):

> The illegitimate child was more commonly met with in the last than in the present century and bastardy cases furnished a class of business with which country lawyers seem to have been as familiar as they are with liquor cases now.[59]

In these North Atlantic colonies even sodomy was not uncommon and buggery occurred and had to be dealt with.[60]

These manifestations of carnality so alien to the traditional picture of Puritanism demand explanation. Doubtless the bleak barrenness and economic dearth

---

59 Compare Massachusetts Historical Society *Proceedings*, second ser., vol. vi, 477-516.

60 Elliott. *New England History*, vol. i, 392-393.

that oppressed the first settlers helped to reduce life to elemental levels. As Lamb put it, "Poor men's smoky cabins are not always porticoes of moral philosophy." Moreover, where wealth was scant, questions of legitimacy and inheritance were less urgent. Besides, the settlers had brought from England a fund of coarse sensuality, veneered it might be with modish asceticism, yet certainly demanding to be heard. The form of sex indulgence that developed may have been due in part to the stern morality that did not allow for a class of recognized prostitutes. Brownist influences are also suggested. In extenuation of the incontinence of eighteenth century New England it should be remembered that much of it was not promiscuous and it is hard to accept Adams's opinion that "in the matter of sexual morality, vice in the nineteenth century as compared with the seventeenth or the eighteenth has lost some part of its evil in losing much of its grossness." For whatever surface improvement there has been is probably due largely to the development of organized prostitution and the practice of prevention and criminal abortion at which present day society is adept.

It can not be doubted that the publicity accorded to cases of sex errancy was an unwholesome influence that tended to augment the evil by creating a kind of social hysteria. Such sensationalism was of the nature of suggestion. Living under terrible repression – environmental and social – the New Englanders found morbid satisfaction in conscience-prying and soul-display. The detailed descriptions of their offences that adulterers gave in church outwent the wildest flights of modern sensationalism as an enrichment of the service and doubtless brought and held a large audience. The various civil penalties imposed can not have been much more wholesome. Dunton tells us that there hardly passed a court day in Massachusetts without some convictions for fornication and tho the penalty was fine and whipping, the crime was very frequent. At Plymouth in several cases of premature birth the husband was publicly whipped while his wife sat in the stocks as witness. In their zeal for the sanctity of married life several codes prescribed capital punishment for adultery. Plymouth substituted whipping and the scarlet letter. In Rhode Island the penalty was whipping with payment of costs. It is obvious that the punishment of such offences involved an unwholesome publicity. Moreover, with the prevalence of extreme penalties there went reluctance to urge conviction for adultery.

In marked contrast to the abnormal stimulation of the sex function by morbid publicity was the attempt to suppress like stimulation in the way of social amusement. In New England, as in the home country, the Puritans attacked the Maypole. Specific happenings suggest reason for rigor. A Plymouth court record shows that one Mary Rosse exercised an "inthewsiastical power" over a certain married man who pleaded that "he must doo what shee bade him." The charmer was publicly whipped and sent home to her mother. The victim was also whipped. In New Hampshire Margery Riggs for luring George Palmer was ordered severely whipped while her avowedly helpless victim was only pilloried. In New Haven Mrs. Fancies seemed able to captivate nearly every man with whom she chanced in contact. She was a sore perplexity to the magistrates. It were hard to tell how far undue censorship of sex relations plus pathological publicity were responsible for the epidemic of sickly sentimentality that for many years seemed to prevail throughout America with excessive talk on love, matrimony, and "Platonicks" even between comparative strangers.[61]

Moreover, the remedies tried for sex sin proved relatively unavailing. Church discipline was not always efficacious even in respect to the person in question. On one occasion a committee reported that E. M—— owned to them that she had had two bastard children since she confessed fornication. After promising to make satisfaction to the church she failed to come and was sentenced to suspension and admonition.

A more successful case of discipline was that of Captain Underhill. As early as 1638 he was suspected of incontinency with a neighbor's wife. "The woman being young and beautiful and withal of a jovial spirit and behavior, he did daily frequent her house, and was divers times found there alone with her, the door being locked on the inside." He said she was in trouble and temptation and they were praying together. He was accused "by a godly young woman to have solicited her chastity under pretence of Christian love [this smacks of Brownism], and to have confessed to her, that he had his will oftentimes of the cooper's wife, and all out of strength of love." In 1640, Underhill

> Confessed also in the congregation, that tho he was very familiar with that woman, and had gained her affections, etc., yet she withstood him six months against all his sollicitations (which he thought no woman could have resisted) before he could overcome her chastity, but being once overcome, she was wholly at his will. And to make his peace the more sound, he went to her husband . . . and fell upon his knees before him in presence of some of the elders and others, and confessed the wrong he had done him, and besought him to forgive him, which he did very freely, and in testimony thereof he sent the captain's wife a token.

[61] Earle. *Colonial Dames and Goodwives*, 190-191.

Discretion was not always mixed with the sentences. Witness the case of Polly Baker of Connecticut who was seduced and deserted and when her child was born was punished, various times whipped, fined, and imprisoned. Once she spoke to the court:

> I cannot conceive my offence to be of so unpardonable a nature as the law considers it. . . I readily consented to the only offer of marriage that ever was made me. I have deluded no young man, nor seduced away any woman's husband. . . You have already excluded me from the communion! You believe I have offended heaven and shall suffer everlastingly! Why then will you increase my misery by additional fines and whippings? Compel [the bachelors] either to marry, or to pay double fines. What must poor young women do? Custom forbids their making overtures to men; they cannot, however heartily they wish it, marry when they please.

The court discharged her without punishment for that time, the lawyers made her presents, and her seducer afterwards married her.

Women were more sternly dealt with than men. In 1707 a woman was sentenced at Plymouth to be set on the gallows, receive thirty stripes upon her naked back, and forever after to wear the capital A. The man was acquitted with no assignment of reason.[62] We are reminded that the man of the Reformation knew no chivalry when we read of a woman condemned to stand in the market place in Boston and to wear a placard: "Thus I stand for my adulterous and whorish carriage."

It seems from some cases that the offence of unchastity was, after all, a formal one that the civil power might overlook, provided no burden of supporting illegitimate children was imposed on the community.[63]

[62] Howard. *History of Matrimonial Institutions*, vol. ii, 175. Compare Gage, *Woman, Church, and State*, 282.

[63] *Early Records of the Town of Providence*, vol. iv, 41; Field. *State of*

The weight of economic considerations is evident in the law that "the father of a bastard, convict, shall maintain it, or allow the mother what the court thinks fit." The mere oath of the woman makes him liable to this charge tho not to punishment imposed by law for fornication and adultery. If circumstances throw doubt the court may acquit him. Forced marriage was one of the penalties of fornication. In Rhode Island women with children were ordered off, very likely for the reason that the community feared expense, for a woman guilty of bastardy was dismissed on showing her ability to keep her child.

In Connecticut Chastellux noticed what seems to be a cognate phenomenon. In one pleasing family a daughter was confined to her room having been seduced and betrayed. She was kindly treated and the family seemed to have no hesitation in telling her story to travellers. It might be judged, as the English translator who had travelled in America said, that "it was the custom of the country to regard such accidents not as irretrievable ruin, but as misfortunes which could be remedied." The translator further said that such young women lost no social rights; "their mistake was lamented rather than condemned; and they could afterwards marry and take as good a position as ever, although their story was neither unknown nor attempted to be concealed." In the case mentioned the lover returned and all was well.

Later the Frenchman found a similar case in Connecticut. Again he was impressed with the complete innocence and frankness of all concerned and their willingness to support and take care of a young woman

---

Rhode Island and Providence Plantations at the End of the Century, vol. iii, 395.

that had so gone astray. He suggests a possible explanation of the situation, viz. that citizens are so precious in a new country that a girl, by rearing her child, seems to atone for the initial sin. He found such slips among very young people quite common but the repetition of them exceedingly rare.

Financial means evidently served to render unchastity less heinous. Stories of scandal in high society can be found in the histories of all old New England towns. Thus the widow B——, presented for a second offence in having a child born out of wedlock, the father of both being a married man, was sentenced to pay the usual fine of five pounds and also to wear on her cap a paper on which her offence was written, as a warning to others, or else pay fifteen pounds. The man in the case, a Harvard alumnus, a man of wealth, found another man of wealth to go on her bond and later married the widow. The descendants of the bastards are now a prominent family.[64]

Sir Christopher Gardiner seems to have been a source of much trouble through his relations with women. Then there was the notorious case of Sir Harry Frankland which showed that even social prestige can not wipe out all standards. In 1741 he was made collector of the port of Boston. (He had with him an illegitimate son.) After educating and patronizing a handsome scrub girl he took her as his concubine in spite of her religious instructor, the president of Harvard. The resultant outburst in Boston society drove them to move to another town. Later on he was caught in the Lisbon earthquake and vowed to marry her. After doing so he returned with her to Boston.

A common offence was for an immigrant that had

[64] Giddings. *Natural History of American Morals*, 34.

left a spouse in England to attempt a new alliance in the colonies. A letter dated Bristol, last of August, 1632 tells of a man with two wives who had gone off to New England with a harlot and lived there. Later, fearing trouble when news of his doings reached America he tried to escape to the Dutch but was apprehended and brought back. Later a man married "this Gardner's wench." Massachusetts in 1647 passed a law as follows:

> Whereas divers persons both men and women, living within this jurisdiction, whose wives and husbands are in England, or elsewhere, by means whereof they live under great temptation here, and some of them committing lewdness and filthiness here among us, others make love to women and attempt marriage and some have attained it, some of them live under suspicion of uncleanness and all to the great dishonor of God. . . All such married persons . . . shall repaire to their said relatives by the first opportunity of shipping, upon paine or penalty of £20, except they can show just cause to the contrary to the [court] . . . provided this order doe not extend to such as are come over to make way for their families, or are [transient].

New Haven ordered spouses to repair to their partners in England or elsewhere with similar exception. Winthrop tells of William Schooler, an adulterer, who had left his wife "a handsome, neat woman" in England. Strictness of marriage law seems to have been aimed partly at such cases. Thus the Earl of Bellomont writes (1700):

> The truth is, as I have been informed, some loose people have sometimes come from England and married in New England, tho they had left wives behind them in England, and this law was calculated chiefly for prevention of such marriages. If a minister of the church of England will be at the pains of going to any town or place to marry people, nobody will hinder him.

The disposition to illicit cohabitation, which was treated in a former chapter, is further illustrated in the case of Richard Bates who appeared, April 25, 1683, having "a woman abiding with you." Both were ordered off July 25. He with the woman was cited for contempt and obtained an extension till October 21. In December the time was extended to March 31. Thomas Cooper attempted marriage but was forbidden because he had "manifested himself a person infamous in that he hath forsaken a sober woman who is his wife." His intended appears again "entertained by Thos. Cooper." Her time of removal was set; "not to live with Thomas Cooper meanwhile."

In at least one instance the General Court tried to compel husband and wife to stick together. The reverend S. Batchelder of Lynn, at nearly ninety years of age married a third wife. Trouble ensued. In 1650 the general court ordered that

> Mr. Batchelor and his wife shall lyve together as man and wife, as in this court they have publiquely professed to do, and if either desert one another, then hereby the court doth order that ye marshal shall apprehend both and bring them forthwith to Boston, here to be kept till the next quarter court.

But he got away, went to England, and remarried.

Family peace and safety were of conspicuous social interest. A father might be called to account by church or magistrate. Thus a man is fined for beating his daughter with a flail and John Veasey is put under recognizance in the sum of five pounds "for detaining his child from the public worship of God, said child being about eleven years old." A number of cases of court procedure are on record against men that abused their wives. One man was fined for slandering his wife.

In October, 1691 Ephraim Pierce of Rhode Island repeated a warning to all not to have dealings with or to entertain his wife. At town meeting a complaint had been entered "made by Hannah Pierce unto the town that her husband hath locked her out of doors and hath sold his farm shee desireing the town's assistant." It was decided to order Ephraim to appear at next quarter day and answer. The record runs:

> Whereas there hath been and still is a difference fallen out betweene Ephram Pierce and his wife whereby themselves, family and estate is like to fall to ruin and thereby the towne is like to have charge fall upon them . . . therefore [Ephraim contracts with the town not to sell or mortgage within a specified time house or land without consent of certain men, previous acts as to mortgaging to be null.] [65]

It is evident from this as from previous evidence that social control of family relations was in part due to a desire to avoid possible burdens on the community.

The importance attached to public opinion as a family censor is apparent in various advertisements of delinquent spouses published in colonial papers.[66] Some of them were introduced by the awesome admonition: "Cursed be he that parteth man and wife and all the people shall say Amen." It was alleged of some Connecticut wives that they were rude, gay, frivolous, lazy housewives, poor cooks, fond of dancing and worthless conversation, unloving consorts.

These libels were not all prosaic or masculine. Some were in rhyme, and wives presented their grievances. One, owing to the niggardliness of her husband had to use "Indian branne for Jonne bred," and never tasted good food. Another complained that her husband "cruelly pulled my hair, pinched my flesh, kicked me

[65] *Early Records of the Town of Providence*, vol. xvii, 139-140.

[66] Compare Earle, *Customs and Fashions in Old New England*, 66-68.

out of bed, drag'd me by my arms and heels, flung ashes upon me to smother me, flung water from the well till I had not a dry thread on me."

But women were not altogether dependent on law or public opinion for protection. It was even thought necessary to legislate for the protection of husbands. Thus one law provided that no wife dared lift her hand or use "a curst and shrewish tongue" to her husband under pain of stocks or pillory. Cotton Mather, who in March, 1716 wrote in his diary:

> Very much inculcate in the children the lessons of thankfulness to the glorious God, for having provided so marvellously for them, when he had made them orphans, and now bestowing an excellent mother upon them [was compelled to add as a sequel about three years later:] The dreadful distresses which a furious and froward step-mother brings upon my family, as they oblige me to lay upon the children the most solemn charges of all possible dutifulness unto her, so, they furnish me with opportunities, mightily to press all piety upon them. . . Oh! my poor, distressed family.

In Maine and New Hampshire women sometimes smote their husbands. In Plymouth colony Joan Miller was presented for "beating and reviling her husband and egging her children to healp her, bidding them knock him on the head, and wishing his victual might choake him." One shrew for "vncivill carriages to her husband" was pilloried. Dorothy Talbye of Salem was ordered chained to a post. Later she was whipped, and then hanged for killing her child. (Evidently she was insane.) In 1683 Daniel Abbot wrote of his wife:

> Through her maddness of folly and turbulency of her corrupt will destroying me root and branch putting out one of her own eyes to put out both mine. And is since departed takeing away my children without my consent and plots to rifle my house to accomplish her divellish resolution against me.

He forbade bargaining and contracting with her.

It is, of course, impossible to tell what proportion the untoward phenomena bear to the instances of serene domestic life. But making allowance for the probability that sensational incidents, as at present, received more attention than quiet family purity, it seems probable that sexual morality was not appreciably higher in Puritan times than to-day. As for domestic bliss our day can no doubt hold its own in comparison with the colonial centuries.

The harshness of the lines in the colonial family was as much due to social pressure as to individual perversity. Thus domestic enjoyments were supposed to be omitted on the Sabbath. Some ministers refused to baptize children born on the Sabbath, because of a theory that such infants were conceived on Sabbath. One of the ministers most strenuous in this line kept up his rigor till on a Sabbath his wife gave birth to twins.

As compared with Europe the colonial New Englanders were probably relatively free from sex sin. Chastellux was impressed with American freedom from infidelities among married people and the Abbé Robin, who was in Connecticut in 1781, says:

> There is such a confidence in the public virtue that, from Boston to Providence, I have often met young women travelling alone on horseback, or in small riding chaises, through the woods, even when the day was far upon the decline.

The French at Newport undertook intrigues with married women (during the Revolution). The Abbé tells of one husband equal to the occasion.

> He became more assiduous and complaisant to her than ever; with sorrow and despair in his soul, he showed a countenance serene and satisfied. He received at his house with attention and civility the very officer who was the author of his misfortune; but by a friend's aid, so contrived matters as to hinder him from private meetings with her. The repeated disappointments

seemed to the Frenchman mere chance mishaps. But he grew sullen and peevish under the strain, and thus became less attractive to the lady, while her husband became more amiable in her eyes than ever. Thus her lingering virtue recalled her to her allegiance. Such a procedure in so delicate an affair exhibits great knowledge of human nature, and still greater self-control.

New England took the lead in a liberal civil divorce policy.[67] The Puritans brought English law with them but parted from it in respect to divorce by adopting, as they thought, the rules of the New Testament. By following what they construed to be the spirit of the book, rather than the letter, they spread out from adultery and desertion as the only causes of divorce and by analogy included certain kindred offences until their legislation became broadly tolerant. The canonical decree of separation from bed and board was practically tho not entirely, dispensed with. On the other hand dissolution of the marriage bond was freely granted for a variety of causes, such as desertion, cruelty, or breach of the vow. Generally, tho not always, husband and wife received equal treatment at the hands of the law. The disposition of some to ignore legal process and part at will was not favored. Thus Rhode Island had a law that "if any persons in this colonie shall part themselves and marry again without the authority of the Court of Commissioners, or be convicted of carnal copulation with any other, they shall be punished as in case of adultery."

In Massachusetts, 1639, James Luxford, being presented for having two wives, his last marriage was declared void

Or a nullity thereof and to be divorced, not to come to the sight of her whom he last took, and he to be sent away for England

[67] Compare Woolsey, "Divorce," in *New Englander*, vol. xxvii, 519; Howard, *History of Matrimonial Institutions*, vol. ii, 330.

by the first opportunity: and all that he hath is appointed to her whom he last married, for her and her children; he is also fined £100 and to be set in the stocks an hour upon the market day after the lecture.

He was probably one of the recreant husbands that left their legal wives in England.

In 1661 in Plymouth Elizabeth Burge was divorced from Thomas on scriptural grounds. He was severely whipped twice and soon left the colony.

In 1665 in Rhode Island Peter Tollman applied for a divorce from his wife on the ground of adultery. She confessed. The petition was at once granted and she was arraigned for sentence. The penalty was a fine and whipping. She was condemned to pay ten pounds and to receive fifteen stripes at Portsmouth on the following Monday and the next week fifteen more at Newport. On her petition for mercy the court, strangely enough, examined her as to whether she would return to her husband. She refused and was accordingly remanded for punishment.

At Plymouth, 1668, Goodwife Tubbs had eloped from the colony. The court gave her husband a divorce. On one occasion a certain W. Tubbs sought a divorce and, after patriarchal style, W. Peabody gave him a writing of divorcement with two witnesses. The General Court treated the document as a nullity and fined Peabody five pounds and each witness three pounds. In 1670 in Connecticut Hannah Huitt "having declared that she had not heard from her late husband, Thomas Huitt, for eight years and better, was declared to be at liberty to marry again as God shall grant her opportunity." In Plymouth colony, 1675, a peculiar decision was rendered. Edward Jenkins had petitioned for a divorce for his daughter because her husband had been out of the colony and made no provision for her during seven years or more. The decision was: The court "sees no cause to grant a divorce, yet they do apprehend her to be no longer bound, but do leave her to her liberty to marry if she please."

In one of the colonies in 1676, Elizabeth Rogers obtained a divorce from John. She was also "permetted to have her two children with her, because the said John R. had renounced all visible worship of New England, and declared against the Christian Sabbath." Some property that he owned was appropriated to the benefit of his children. In 1678 Hope Ambrose obtained a divorce from Daniel Ambrose for desertion, non-support of herself and children, and keeping a woman in Jamaica. Ambrose's mistresses appear in the record in unminced terms. When James Shiff's wife went off with another man, tho the deserted husband was not in Plymouth jurisdiction, the general court of that colony certified to his having a divorce from his own court. In 1683 John Warner, a deputy from Warwick, was divorced on petition of his wife for adultery and criminal violence to her and expelled from the Rhode Island Assembly.

When Sara Knight made her journey between Boston and New York in 1704 she found divorces plentiful in Connecticut. She writes:

> These uncomely standaways are too much in vogue among the English in this indulgent colony as their records plentifully prove, and that on very trivial matters of which some have been told me but are not proper to be related by a female pen.

Various conditions contributed to liberal divorce in the colonies: rejection of the sacramental theory of marriage, the establishment of marriage as a civil rite, assimilated to a business contract, the numerous cases of men that had left their wives in the old country, the great difficulty of leading the new life without wives and husbands, probably the feeling that population ought to be increased and family life promoted.

But not all applications for divorce were granted. The civil power aimed also to forestall the necessity for divorce. Thus in Plymouth colony on one occasion the court warned Edward Holman not to frequent the house of Thomas Shrieve and that Goodwife Shrieve should not frequent the house or company of Holman at their peril. This warning proved ineffectual and the next year they were ordered to avoid each other or be whipped. This threat seems to have sufficed. John Robinson, grandson of the Leyden pastor, was bound over once to carry himself properly toward Thomas Crippen's wife.

Sexual irregularity occasioned by slavery was sufficiently noteworthy. A Massachusetts law of 1705 condemns negroes and mulattoes guilty of improper intercourse with whites to be sold out of the province. The presence of the Indian race was also a temptation. Morton, in his "New England Canaan" tells of an Indian infant with gray "eies" whose

> Father shewed him to us and said they were English mens eies, I tould the father that his sonne was . . . bastard, hee replied . . . hee could not tell; his wife might play the whore and this child the father desired might have an English name, because of the likeness of his eies which his father had in admiration, because of novelty amongst their nation.

The servant problem had already begun to be a source of family troubles. All the early travelers note the lack of good servants. Some resorted to Indians. The reverend Peter Thatcher of Milton, Massachusetts bought an Indian girl in 1674. One duty was to care for the baby. "Came home," he writes, "and found my Indian girl had liked to have knocked my Theodorah on the head by letting her fall. Whereupon I took a good walnut stick and beat the Indian to purpose till she promised to do so no more." We find sad accounts of the desertion of aged colonists by their Indian servants. One tells that he took his "Pecod girle" as a "chilld of death" when but two years of age, reared her kindly, cared for her when she was sick, and finally was deserted by her in his time of need. Sewall had a free negro man–a devoted, faithful servant. By 1687 a French refugee wrote: "There is not a house in Boston however small may be its means, that has not one or two" negroes.

Some "help" was early hireable. Children of well-to-do citizens worked in domestic service.[68] Roger Williams writes of his daughter's desiring to spend some time in service. Members of the rich Sewall's family lived out. Sons of Downing and Hooke went with their relative, Governor Winthrop, as servants. Children were bound out at eight, so that people could rear their own servants. The pious colonists felt great responsibility for their servants' souls.

But the problem was vexatious in spite of native, negro, and apprentice service. Downing wrote home to England to try to get good servant girls. Mary Dudley, daughter of Winthrop, writes of a very refractory bad maid. Reverend Ezekiel Rogers wrote in 1657, when extreme Puritanism was fading:

> Hard to get a servant that is glad of catechizing or family duties. I had a rare blessing of servants in Yorkshire, and those that I brought over were a blessing, but the young brood doth much afflict me. Even the children of the godly here, and elsewhere make a woful proof.

[68] Earle. *Customs and Fashions in Old New England*, 86-87.

In Hartford

> Susan Coles for her rebellious cariedge towards her mistres is to be sent to the house of correction, and be kept to hard labour and coarse dyet, to be brought forth the next lecture day to be publicquely corrected and so to be corrected weekly until order be given to the contrary.

There are many like records. The head agent of a London company at a settlement in Maine defended his wife to the powers at home for beating a worthless, idle maid. Thus it is evident that, as now, the servant problem was an apple of discord in family life, as indeed it will continue to be so long as a part of the population demands personal, menial attention from others in the capacity of house servants.

VIII. SEX AND MARRIAGE IN COLONIAL NEW YORK

The middle colonies were startlingly heterogeneous in population. Owing to diversity in respect to nationality and religion each colony possessed an individuality that makes it inadvisable to study them as a unit. Only a few large generalities are in order.

Slighter attention was given there than in New England to the regulation of domestic life. Greater amplitude and fertility of soil and geniality of climate tended to soften the rigor of life and to make family life more kindly. Diversity of population and multiplicity of minor sects tended to clannishness but forced broad tolerance inasmuch as it was hard for any one group to gain unrestrained expression in the form of law. Introduction of continental blood and customs worked toward the softening of the hard lines of life. The Huguenots, for instance, coming from a land more advanced in some ways than Holland or England, established a home life different from that of the other colonists. Their home life was pleasant in contrast to much of the severer life around. Children were instructed with more gentleness and consideration than among the English and Dutch. Warfield notes the "esprit of the Huguenot women." There were Huguenots in both the middle and the northern colonies. They were numerous in New York, where Dutch influence was also strong. The Dutch were a milder species of the genus to which the Puritans belonged.[69]

New York, like New England, recalls the fact that the racial endowment of sex is more than sufficient for race perpetuity when relatively civilized conditions obtain. In Dutch days "improper conduct" with women was a frequent occurrence, ranging from the darkest crimes to words and acts that are not now subjects of law. In the later years of the Old Dutch rule, "sins of sensuality" were frequent. One case was hushed up inasmuch as the woman was an unmarried daughter of Dominie Schaats of Albany. Her paramour was a married man. Stuyvesant wrote bitter words about the affair. In the early English days his half-sister Margriet had a child by a rich bachelor to whom she was affianced but whose sudden demise forestalled the marriage. This incident does not seem to have disgraced her, for she soon found a husband. It may be that a less happy event is indicated in the complaint of a farm wife in 1716 at Court of Sessions at Westchester that "a travelling woman who came out of ye Jerseys who kept school at several places in Rye parish, hath left with her a child eleven months old, for which she desires relief from the parish."

The Dutch custom of long betrothal seems to have had evil results. Some persons had delayed the ceremony even for months after banns. Apparently couples had been living together after banns without marriage. It was accordingly ordered in 1658 that no man and woman should keep house together as man and wife until they were legally married; and a fine was to be the penalty for any violation of the order. The Dutch passed a law requiring the consummation of marriage within a month after publication had been completed

[69] A review of the closing pages of Chapter II will prepare the reader for a study of this colony.

unless there was legal opposition. Bundling was practiced but finally came under prohibition of the authorities. Accounts of scandal in high society can be found in the histories of all old New York towns.[70] Tho strict regulation of marital relations was attempted by the Dutch colonists and severe sentences were provided for adultery, sexual transgressions were not treated with so great rigor as in New England. Neither death nor the scarlet letter was inflicted.

We have noted the custom of civil marriage in the low countries. Marriage by justice of the peace was made lawful by the States General of Holland from 1590. The laws of the Netherlands were, indeed, not uniform and in the Dutch American colony it would seem that the ceremony had to be performed by a minister with religious rites tho there is difference of opinion on this point. An authorized celebrant, at least, was essential: the principle of English common law marriage did not obtain.

In the Netherlands, usually parental consent and often publication of banns was made essential. A majority of the early settlers of New Netherlands hailed from Guilderland and the marriage laws of that province naturally prevailed. There a marriage was void if the express consent of the father, or if he were dead, the mother, had not been obtained before the marriage of a son. With regard to daughters the law was still more rigorous; even marriage with parental consent did not release a girl from parental authority in case her husband died while she was still under age. Governor Stuyvesant of New Netherlands was strict in his application of the law of parental consent and due notice. Proper forms had to be observed.

In violation of the law as to banns, etc., a sheriff of

[70] Giddings. *Natural History of American Morals*, 34.

Flushing married a widower to a girl against her parents' consent and contrary to law. On April 3, 1648, the officer was fined, dismissed from office, and the marriage annulled. The groom was fined and required to have the marriage again solemnized after three proclamations.

In 1654 the court of Gravesend had set up and affixed banns between Johann van Beeck and Maria Verleth of New Amsterdam. The action of Gravesend was thought to prepare

> A way whereby hereafter some sons and daughters unwilling to obey parents and guardians will, contrary to their wishes, secretly go and get married in such villages or elsewhere. . . It is usual according to the custom of our Fatherland, that every one shall have three publications at the place where his domicile is, and then he may go and be married wherever he pleases.

The magistrates of Gravesend appealed to their charter by which they were guaranteed against "molestation from any magistrate or minister that may extend jurisdiction over them." Van Beeck appeared to urge his case. The New Amsterdam council noted

> Who in the beginning instituted marriage; also what the apostle of the Gentiles teaches therein. . . The proper and attained ages of Johannes van Beeck and Marya Verlith. . . The consent of the father and mother on the daughter's side. . . The distance and remoteness of places between this and our fatherland together with the differences between Holland and England. . . The danger that in such circumstances matters by long delay might come to be disclosed between these aforesaid young people, which would bring disgrace on both families. . . We think . . . that by a proper solemnization of marriage (for the Apostle to the Hebrews calls the marriage bed honorable) the lesser and greater sins are prevented.

Accordingly banns should be proclaimed. But some

trouble arose and the young people, eloping to New England, were married by a farmer in Connecticut. This marriage was of course unlawful. Stuyvesant writes:

> Johannes van Beeck had affixed a poster that his marriage contracted contrary to his father's prohibition to marry abroad has been declared lawful and proper by the council of New Amsterdam, we want information.

Finally the marriage was recognized as legal.

In 1674, the year of the Dutch Restoration, Ralph Doxy was indicted for unlawfully entering

> Into the married state with Mary van Harris, making use, for that purpose, of a forged certificate, and that Deft. hath still a wife alive who resides in New England; therefore, [the prosecution] concludes that the Deft. ought to be conveyed to the place where justice is usually executed, severely whipped, and, furthermore, banished the country forever, with costs. Deft. denies ever having been married to a woman before; acknowledges his guilt as regards the forged certificate; says, that through love for Mary Harris he had allowed it to be executed by a certain Englishman now gone to the Barbadoes and therefore prays forgiveness. Whereas parties, on both sides, are expecting further proofs, the Governor General and Council order the case . . . continued.

Later the marriage was declared

> Unlawful, inasmuch as it was solemnized by Jacobus Fabricius, who had no legal power so to act, and without his engagement having been published three several times according to the laws and customs of the government; but finding the charge against him of having a second wife in New England unfounded, he is therefore permitted to confirm himself in wedlock with the above-named Mary, according to the laws of the government; in regard to the forged certificate . . . he is pardoned for this time on his promise of improvement, and request for forgiveness; and finally, they condemn the Deft. in the costs incurred herein.

The celebrant, Fabricius, a "late" Lutheran minister,

was suspended from office of the ministry for one year for performing the ceremony without legal authority.

The same year in case of a man requesting leave of marriage with "Jane Rause, widow of Edward Rause, who died about two and a half years ago at Carolina" it was "ordered: that the magistrates of Rustdorp inquire as to the certainty of said Edward Rause's death and report their conclusions." This incident recalls New England experience with deserting spouses. Bigamists were not uncommon at New Amsterdam.

The English conquest did not much disturb the smooth run of life. Dutch household customs were retained as far as practicable. But contract *de presenti* proved by witnesses and followed by cohabitation now constituted a legal marriage. Ceremonial marriage was at first celebrated by justice of the peace (as allowed by "the Duke's Laws") or clergy, on the governor's license or publication of banns thrice in some place of worship. Clergy of all denominations officiated. In 1678 Governor Andros reported that "ministers have been so scarce and religions so many that no acct. cann be given of children's births or christenings." "Scarcity of ministers and law admitting marriages by justices no acct. cann be given of the number marryed."

In some cases the minister gave a certificate of permission for marriage. Thus at Flatbush:

> Isaac Hasselburg and Elizabeth Baylis have had their proclamation in our church as commonly our manner and custom is, and no opposition or hindrance came against them, so as that they may be confirmed in ye banns of Matrimony, whereto we wish them blessing. . . March 17th, 1689, Rudolph Varrick, minister.

This voucher was probably in order to authorize the performance of the ceremony in another parish. Severe penalties were fixed during the British régime for ministers violating the law requiring license or publication.

Marriage fees in colonial days were not very large and it seems that they were not always kept by the minister. In one pastor's account we find him paying over to the consistory seventy-eight guilders and ten stuyvers for fourteen marriage fees. This was in the Dutch régime.

After the conquest the Church of England tried to gain headway. In numerous governors' commissions we find such instructions as:

> You are to take especial care, that a table of marriages established by ye canons of the Church of England, bee hung up in all orthodox churches and duly observed.

Governor Hunter is urged to try to get a law passed if not already done for the strict observance of said table. An English clergyman writing in 1695 complains of the performance of many marriages by justices. In 1748 through Episcopal influence the wording of the license which previously had run "to all Protestant ministers" was altered to "all Protestant ministers of the gospel." Smith in the *History of New York* says:

> The Episcopal missionaries . . . not many years ago, attempted by a petition to the late governor Clinton, to engross the privilege of solemnizing all marriages. A great clamor ensued and the attempt was abortive. Before that time the ceremony was even performed by justices of the peace, and the judge at law determined such marriages to be legal. The governor's licenses now run to "all Protestant ministers of the gospel." Whether the justices act still when the banns are published in our churches, which is customary only with the poor, I have not been informed. [As a matter of fact, justices no longer meddled except in counties where clergy were scarce.] Marriages in a new country ought to have the highest encouragements, and it is on this account, perhaps, that we have no provincial law against such as are clandestine, tho they

often happen, and in some cases, are attended with consequences equally melancholy and mischievous.

The Quakers had some trouble with marriage regulations and on one occasion petitioned for remission of fine imposed "for suffering our daughters to marrie contrary to their law." Later Quakers were permitted to use their own marriage ceremony.

In 1679 a lamentable irregularity occurred, as recorded in a letter of Luke Wattson against Captain John Avery, a magistrate:

> He tooke upon himselfe to marry the widdow Clament to one Bryant Rowles, without publiquecation notwithstanding she was out aske at least a month to another man, namely Edward Cocke; the which when the said Cocke heard that she was marryed to another man said that it would be his death and presently went home, fell sick, and in fortyeight hours after dyed, he left it on his death that her marrying was the cause of his dyeing. . . Hee took upon him to grant a licence to Marry Daniel Browne to Sussan Garland widdow, without any publiqueation, which marriage was effected, notwithstanding it is generally known or at least the said Daniel confesses that he knows no other but that he have a wife living in England.[71]

As already suggested, license from the governor was an aristocratic resort for people that could afford thus to purchase exemption from publication of banns. It offered a convenient loophole for corruption. The Earl of Bellomont wrote in 1700 to the Secretary of the Board that during his absence in Boston

> Mr. Smith the chaplain . . . comes to the lieutenant governor and desires him to sign a blank licence, pretending the persons to be married were desirous to have their names concealed. The lieutenant governor suspecting Smith's knavery refuses to sign the blank licence. Afterward Smith brings a licence filled up with the names of Adam Ball and the maiden name of a

[71] *Documents relating to Colonial History of the State of New York*, vol. xii, 624-625.

> married woman; he afterwards adds a sillable to the mans name in the licence (after the lieutenant governor had signed it) and then it was Baldridge the pirate. . . and the woman was the wife of Buckmaster a pirate. . . Being askt why he married Baldridge to another man's wife, he answered she had made oath to him that she was never married to Buckmaster. . . It appears Buckmaster was married to the woman by a justice of the peace in one of the Jerseys which is their way of marrying there.[72]

It is easy to see the possibilities of evil in the administrations of the less scrupulous governors.

During the century between the British conquest and the war of the Revolution most marriages of genteel folks were performed by executive license. It was considered very plebeian, almost vulgar, to be married under publication or posting of banns as was done in New England without violence to fashionable standards. An item from a New York paper of 1765 shows the prevalence of aversion to the publication of banns:

> We are creditly informed that there was married on last Sunday evening . . . a very respectable couple that had published three different times in Trinity church. A laudable example and worthy to be followed. If this decent and for many reasons proper method of publication was once generally to take place, we should have no more of clandestine marriages; and save the expense of licenses, no inconsiderable sum these hard and depressing times.

A copy of the *New York Gazette and Postboy* of about the same time contains this item:

> As no licenses for marriage could be obtained since the first of November for want of stamped paper, we can assure the public several genteel couples were published in the different churches of this city last week; and we hear that the young ladies of this place are determined to join hands with none but such as will to the utmost endeavor to abolish the custom of marriage with license which amounts to many hundred per annum which might be saved.

---

[72] *Documents relating to Colonial History of the State of New York*, vol. iv, 766.

It will be remembered also that the governor's income from this source made the colonial expedient of withholding the salary of refractory governors less potent in New York.

The marriage ceremony in old New York usually took place at the home of the bride's parents. Weddings were great events. They furnished occasions to take collections or subscriptions for worthy purposes.[73] In some towns the pastor required written consent of the parents on both sides before the words were said. A riotous charivari followed the wedding. On Long Island the groom's parents often kept open house on the day after the bride's. There was no bridal tour but sometimes the bridal party was entertained successive days by friends for miles around. In New York the groom's friends called for several days to drink punch. It was customary in this colony, as in New England, for the new couple to appear in church on the Sabbath following the marriage. Often they entered late for display.

Such ostentatious recognitions of the importance of marriage as these customs furnish seem normal to us. They are a survival of the struggle for tribal existence which puts such a premium on fecundity. An almost grewsomely contrasting relic, outlandish to us, betokens more vividly the importance of every man as a sire in the hazardous days of tribal struggle. The episode recalling this primitive urgency occurred in New York in 1784. A condemned malefactor about to be executed was reprieved and set free by his marriage on the gallows to a woman clad only in a shift.[74]

The same conditions as furthered marriage and fecundity in New England were operative in this

---

[73] Earle. *Colonial Days in Old New York*, 63-64.

[74] Earle. *Customs and Fashions in Old New England*, 79.

neighbor colony. Men and women married early and remarried promptly and repeatedly. The great lack of hired service that rendered a fatherless or motherless home well-nigh impossible magnified the marital relation. Family life was honored as the only fit condition. Second and third marriages were sufficiently common among the early New Netherlanders. At Gravesend a desolate widower became enamored of a milkmaid on first sight as she milked her father's cows. He proposed on the spot, posted to town for a license, and carried off the fair Grietje. The first of the New York Livingstons came in obscure poverty to the bedside of a Rensellaer in Albany to prepare his will. "Send him away," said the dying man to his beautiful wife, "he will be your second husband." And the prophecy was fulfilled.[75] One man, a German, appears in the chronicles as the fourth husband of his first wife and the third husband of his second wife who had been previously married to a Dane and to a Dutchman.[76]

Nearly all the first settlers at New Amsterdam were young married people. Their children grew up to marriageable years and in the latter part of the Dutch régime the place was celebrated for its marriageable folk and its betrothals. Early mating was facilitated by the innocent simplicity of society that dispensed with chaperons. Travelers sought good wives here and found them.

Emigrant wives brought with them maids to serve three years for their passage. The numerous girls of marriageable age that came over were soon appropriated by young Dutchmen and housewives had to bewail the maids snatched away before their time was up. In 1642 the patroon of Staten Island sued the parents of a

[75] Earle. *Colonial Days in Old New York*, 61.

[76] Van Rensellaer. *History of the City of New York*, vol. ii, 142.

girl for the loss of her services through her marriage. The bride told the magistrates that her first acquaintance with the young man was when her mother and another person brought him to see her. After rejecting him several times she had eloped with him in a boat. She offered to render as compensation the handkerchief that her husband had presented as wedding gift. In 1656 Hans Fromer demanded that Madame Van der Douck "give lawful reason why she forbid the bond of matrimony between him and Maeyken Huybertson." The defendant's son showed the maid's service contract, but the authorities released the girl and let her marry, which laxity encouraged all maids to rebel. Service contracts proved less sacred than the social need of increase in population. Madame Judith Varlith next had to release her maid and pay her much wampum and linen. The wives of the councillors rebelled at such outrage; so arrangements had to be made to import cargoes of young women from Holland under rigid contracts which the dignitaries had pledged themselves in private to hold sacred.[77]

Breach of promise cases sometimes marred the calm of Old New York. Stuyvesant himself intervened in the case of a maid deceived by promise of marriage. In 1654 Grietje Waemans produced a marriage ring and letters promising marriage as grounds on which Daniel de Silla be "condemned to legally marry her." It was vain for him to plead intoxication as defense. François Soleil swore he would rather cast in his lot with the Indians than marry his abandoned Rose. Pieter Koch and Anna van Voorst were unwilling to carry out an agreement to marry. The burgomasters and schepens

[77] Van Rensellaer. *The Goede Vrouw of Mana-ha-ta*, 16-17; Earle. *Colonial Days in Old New York*, 52-53.

decided that the promise held and forbade either to marry another person without permission of the betrothed and the court. Anna flagrantly married another man without asking any one's leave. A young widow, plaintiff in a breach of promise suit, offered as proof a shilling, her second lover's gift. (Untying the marriage knot in which a piece of money was tied and presented signified consent to speedy marriage.)

In New York the economic element in marriage received due attention. As the Dutch women were as keen traders as the men the bargaining was on a more equal footing than in other colonies, where ladies usually got the worst of the deal. This equality of bargaining power between the sexes in New York may have covered some of the sordidness of economic marriage.

Bachelors were not in good standing among the Dutch, at least in Albany. The colony had no laws, as in New England, to regulate these misfits and they shared in the benefit of Dutch tolerance toward misguided folk. But where marriage was so spontaneous, bachelors were almost pariahs. They did manage to find shelter but not home. Mrs. Grant describes them as passing in and out like silent ghosts and seeming to feel themselves superior to the world. Their association was almost exclusively with one another tho sometimes one took part in the affairs of the family with which he lived. Fisher is reminded by them of rogue elephants. "In colonial times," he says, "we often find the people living such a simple life that they instinctively followed some of the primitive laws which have peopled the earth."

The different strains of continental blood blended by marriage into one predominantly Dutch. Then intermarriage preserved such racial integrity that many rural families and many notable city families continued till recent times with little or no infusion of British blood.[78]

> At the beginning of the 18th century the little isolated community of New Harlem consisted of half a hundred homes. . . "Intermarriage," says Riker, "among the resident families was the rule, and he was thought a bold swain truly who ventured beyond the pale of the community to woo a mate." . . Fifty years after the village was settled, or about the end of the first quarter of the eighteenth century, there was scarcely one of the families of the patentees that was not related to every other of the twenty-five or thirty families that first settled the village.[79]

Doctor Douglass, in colonial days, had a visionary scheme for affiliation with the Indians. He said:

> Our young missionaries may procure a perpetual alliance and commercial advantage with the Indians, which the Roman Catholic clergy cannot do, because they are forbid to marry. I mean our missionaries may intermarry with the daughters of the sachems and other considerable Indians, and their progeny will forever be a certain cement between us and the Indians.

William Johnson married a German girl by whom he had several children. After her death he had several mistresses of whom the favorite was a beautiful Indian girl, Molly Brant, sister of Joseph Brant. She bore him eight children and he lived with her until his death.[80]

The presence of the negroes also suggested miscegenation. But in some regions at least this practice must have been tabooed by the colonists if we are to believe the assertion that after the Revolution the path of the British army could be traced by the presence of mulattoes.[81]

---

78 Van Rensellaer. *History of the City of New York*, vol. ii, 142.

79 Pierce. *New Harlem Past and Present*, 313.

80 Fisher. *Men, Women, and Manners in Colonial Times*, vol. ii, 96.

81 — *Idem*, 118.

IX. FAMILY LIFE AND PROBLEMS IN COLONIAL NEW YORK

The marriage ritual among the Dutch was full of realism. The groom was told to lead, instruct, comfort, protect, and love his wife and maintain his home honestly. The bride was warned against lording it over her spouse. Domestic life in the colony was in the main quiet and commonplace. Family troubles seldom came to court. Mrs. Grant testifies to the happiness of marital life in Albany:

> Inconstancy or even indifference among married couples was unheard of. . . The extreme affection they bore their mutual offspring was a bond that forever endeared them to each other. Marriage in this colony was always early, very often happy, and very seldom, indeed "interested."

The Dutch women were strongly influential, active in affairs, and respected by their husbands. In Dutch neither party is married *to* the other: bride or groom marries *with* the other. In New Netherlands both sexes received education and men and women were more equal than later under the English fashion. (In New York, 1780, the men monopolized the seats on the mall. leaving the ladies to stand.)[82] To the end of the colonial period the enjoyment by women of greater independence than in communities of English origin attested the Dutch sources of New York.[83] The wife was her husband's equal in the eyes of the law which rec-

[82] Earle. *Colonial Dames and Goodwives*, 200.

[83] Van Rensellaer. *History of the City of New York*, vol. ii, 157.

ognized a community in possessions if there was no ante-nuptial contract.[84] Such a contract often provided that the wife and husband should inherit absolutely from each other. Often joint wills of like tenor were made. This was a distinctively Dutch usage. Such wills are significant of the mutuality that characterized married life in the New York colony. But in church the seats of husband and wife were ordinarily separate.

Women's high ambition was to be able housewives. Married women were distinguished from maidens by their dress. They stayed at home, read their Bibles and managed. Every good housewife made the apparel of her family. The wife was the head of the household, the sovereign of domestic affairs. Smith, writing after nearly a century of the English régime, says:

> The ladies . . . are comely and dress well, and scarce any of them have distorted shapes. Tinctured with a Dutch education, they manage their families with becoming parsimony, good providence, and singular neatness.

Marriage had a sedative effect on men. In Albany when a man married he was supposed to lose two pleasures, coasting and pig- and turkey-stealing. Nothing was allowed to disturb the serenity of Dutch housekeeping or the spotless order of the parlor. For a time New Netherlands experienced lack of servants; so wife and daughters performed the work of house and dairy. Mrs. Grant says: "A woman in very easy circumstances, and abundantly gentle in form and manners, would sow, and plant, and rake incessantly." Home was home. Irving says: "Dinner was invariably a private meal, and the fat old burghers showed incontestable signs of disapprobation and uneasiness at being

[84] *Van Rensellaer. History of the City of New York,* vol. i, 480.

surprised by a visit from a neighbor on such occasions." Especially did wives resent the visits of fire-prevention inspectors to their homes, and abuse these men. Soldiers, often billeted in private homes, were a nuisance. One citizen wrote that "they made him weary."

It was in the home and in business that woman shone rather than in intellectual affairs. Women teachers and girl-scholars were not eminent in New York in early days. But women were active as shop-keepers, merchants, ship-owners, Indian traders. It was common for a wife to hold her husband's power of attorney in his absence, to help him in business, or to carry on the business after his death. It is said that widows in New Amsterdam often assumed the management of considerable estates. Widow DeVries carried on her deceased husband's Dutch trade making repeated trips to Holland as supercargo on her own ships. She married Frederick Phillipse and by her keenness, thrift, and profitable business helped to make him the richest man in the colony. Widow Provoost enjoyed equal success at the beginning of the eighteenth century. She had a huge business correspondence. New York records other noteworthy examples of woman's ability. Jane Colden was a distinguished botanist and "She makes the best cheese I ever ate in America."[85] Several women in New Amsterdam were tavern-keepers and tapsters.

The court records of Brooklyn contain a scandalous instance of female militancy: Mistress Jonica Schampf and Widow Rachel Luguer assaulted Peter Praa, the captain of the militia, when he was at the head of his troops on training day in 1690. They pulled his hair and beat him and their "Ivill Inormities" brought him

[85] Earle. *Colonial Dames and Goodwives*, 86-87.

within an inch of his life.[86] Among the Dutch, people were brought before the court for saying of another such uncomplimentary things as "He hath not half a wife." One couple sued a woman for saying that the wife in crossing a muddy street raised her petticoats too high.

Pioneer conditions – the emptiness of the country and the shortage of hands – put a premium on large families. Besides in 1650 the West India Company offered one year's exemption from tenths for each child conveyed to or born in New Netherlands. There was no "race suicide" among the colonists tho children seem to have been less numerous than in New England. We are told that in New Harlem at the beginning of the eighteenth century "the small two-story Dutch homes generally sheltered each a half-score or more of sturdy youngsters." But this was a small isolated community. At Albany the Dutch had fewer children than had the people in Massachusetts and Connecticut. The Dutch kept a record of births in the family Bible and also a church register. But by the time of the English régime the heterogeneity of the population left gaps in the record. In 1712, Governor Hunter reported to the Lords of Trade: "As to births and burials has never been any register kept that I can hear of."

It may be that the absence of Puritan rigor allowed a larger proportion of children to survive and that accordingly the Dutch had settled to a lower fecundity. But the repeated marriages guaranteed a sufficient posterity. Dongan had heard of one woman "yet alive" who had "upwards of 360 living descendants." Small families were rare. Mothers nursed their offspring and they flourished. Irving says:

[86] Fisher. *Men, Women, and Manners in Colonial Times*, vol. ii, 57.

To have seen a numerous household assembled around the fire, one would have imagined that he was transported back to happy days of primeval simplicity. The fire places were of a truly patriarchal magnitude.

The midwife's calling was much respected. The New Amsterdam midwife had a house provided by the government. The profession was licensed. Some of the less capable had been refusing to aid the poor; so in Albany one good woman who helped the poor free of charge was appointed along with one other to have a monopoly save in emergency.[87] Births were announced by hanging pincushions on the door-knockers. These cushions were generally handsome ones and handed on as heirlooms. As soon as the mother was strong enough there was a grand reception to women friends.

The sources from which we may learn of the life of children in colonial New York are meager tho children were an important factor in colonial calculations and life. In the plan for the colonization of New Netherlands we read:

Permission should be obtained from the magistrates of some province and cities, to take from the almshouses or orphan asylums 300 @ 400 boys and girls of 10, 12, to 15 years of age with their consent, however. . . It must be, further, declared that said children shall not remain bound to their masters for a longer term than 6 or 7 years, unless being girls, they come, meanwhile, to marry, in which event they should have the option of hiring again with their masters or mistresses, or of remaining wholly at liberty and of settling there, on condition that they be allowed so much land as the director shall consider it proper each should have for the support of [a family] free from all rents and exemptions for the term of 10 years after entering on such land.

In Stuyvesant's time several cargoes of children from the Dutch almshouses were sent to America to enter

[87] Earle. *Colonial Days in Old New York*, 91.

service.[88] The official correspondence shows much kindly thought and interest in them. Vice-director Alricks wrote to the commissioners of the colony on the Delaware River:

> The children sent over from the almshouses have safely arrived and were in sufficient request, so that all are bound out with one and the other; the oldest for two years, the others, and the major portion for three years, and the youngest for four years, earning 40, 60, and 80 guilders during the above period, and at the end of the term will be fitted out in the same manner as they are at present. . . Please to continue sending others from time to time; but, if possible, none ought to come less than fifteen years of age and somewhat strong, as little profit is to be expected here without labor; but from people with large families or many small children, little is to be expected. When the men die they do not leave a stiver behind. The public must provide the coffin, pay all the debts, and feed, or maintain, those who survive.

In New Netherlands servitude was not considered demeaning. The servant was often from a family of station equal to that of the mistress.[89] In case of indenture the chief parental rights passed to the employer but if the children were mistreated, parents or guardians would take the matter to court. If the child absented himself without leave from the master, even to visit home, the act constituted a breach of the engagement.

There was much binding out of children and youth in old New York. Children of paupers were sold as apprentices. That the ruling class wanted hands rather than souls is suggested by the slowness to provide care for orphans and schools for youth. In a remonstrance by people of New Netherlands *Of the Reason and Cause of the Great Decay of New Netherlands* we find

[88] Earle. *Colonial Days in Old New York,* 84.

[89] Singleton. *Dutch New York,* 143-147.

complaint that there is no asylum for aged and orphans. And there ought to be a public school

> So that the youth, in so wild a country, where there are so many dissolute people, may, first of all, be well instructed and indoctrinated not only in reading and writing, but also in the knowledge and fear of the Lord. . . There ought to be, likewise, Asylums for aged men, for orphans, and similar institutions.

The next year the West India Company directed that the governor and council should have jurisdiction of matters pertaining to minors, widows, and orphans. Secretary Van Tienhoven wrote in answer to the *Remonstrance*:

> 'Tis also denied and cannot be proved, that any of the inhabitants of New Netherlands have, either voluntarily nor when requested, contributed or given anything for the building of an asylum for orphans, or for the aged. . . If the people require institutions as above stated, they must contribute towards them as is the custom in this country.

New Netherlands was no more than other colonies in the interest of the general welfare. It is of interest to note the assertion that the slave children of the negroes emancipated by the company in return for long service were "treated the same as Christians." Colonial days witnessed the practice of binding children, without parent's consent into a servitude that made them the cattle of their owners. Such was the fate of the Palatines. Whether the Dutch had in mind any such practices when they explained the case of the negro children is hard to say. Perhaps such rigors belong exclusively to the degenerate English days. In at least one of the settlements nearly every Dutch family of any means had negro house-servants, who were treated kindly, brought up in the family religion, and often as attached to their masters as sons or daughters were. When the negro child was three years old it was given to one of the children of the family. This child presented it a coin and a pair of shoes and thereafter they were master and servant. Every member of a respectable family was supposed to have a personal servant.

As early as 1585 Holland had schools for children of all classes. The charter of New Netherlands patroons, 1630-1635, provided for education. In 1642 marriage contracts included the promise "to bring up their children decently, according to their ability, to keep them at school, and to let them learn reading, writing, and a good trade." For a while the establishment of public schools lagged. Then came a forward movement and before the end of Dutch rule common schools flourished, supported by the towns and state aid. Under English rule these non-conformist agencies were suffered to decline. A Church of England school started in New York City (1704) did not appeal to the Dutch, who clung to the mother tongue and their own rude schools. Just before the Revolution Burnaby found in New York "a very handsome charity school for sixty poor boys and girls."

In spite of artificial restrictions and curtailment of opportunity new-world conditions afforded opportunities for children to rise above their parents' social level. Lieutenant-governor Colden wrote in 1765 here "the most opulent families, in our own memory have risen from the lowest rank of the people."

The tradition of paternal authority was as strong as in New England. Dutch children were respectful and subdued in their manner toward their parents and filial obedience was impressed by ministers and magistrates. In English days came the New England sternness of law. But the Dutch were less stringent than the New

Englanders in the matter of paternal sovereignty. In Holland, as Bradford tells us, the "great licentiousness of youth" was one of the things that led to the Pilgrim migration, and, as Blok, writing of the middle years of the century, notes, all foreign observers were amazed at the freedom of children and servants. In the new world the Dutch retained the old ways in large measure. The ordinances of Stuyvesant's and of early English days show that on Manhattan children were not subject to stricter discipline than in Holland. Children in Dutch New York were not held under such stern restraint as among the Puritans. They were on more familiar terms with their parents and had ample amusement. Schoolmasters complained of youthful insubordination and of maternal complicity in the children's mischief; also that boys were taken from school too soon in order to learn an occupation.

The magistrates found it necessary to censor youthful sports. In New Orange in 1673,

> If any children be caught in the street playing, racing, and shouting previous to the termination of the last preaching, the officers of justice may take their hat or upper garment, which shall not be restored to the parents until they have paid a fine of two guilders.

In New Amsterdam the boys plagued the patrol at night, setting dogs on him, etc. In 1713 the Albany legislators passed this act:

> Whereas ye children of ye sd city do very unorderly to ye shame and scandall of their parents ryde down ye hills in ye streets of the sd city with small and great slees on the lord day and in the week by which many accidents may come, now for pventing ye same it is hereby published and declard yt it shall and may be lawful for any constable in this city or any other person or persons to take any slee or slees from all and every such boys and girls rydeing or offering to ryde down any hill within ye sd city and breake any slee or slees in pieces.

In 1728 Albany children were still pestered and fined for sliding down on "sleds, small boards, or otherwise."

Mrs. Grant tells of a peculiar usage in Albany. The children were divided into groups, each containing as many boys as girls and obeying a boy and a girl as "heads." Brothers and sisters of different ages belonged to different groups. The function of these companies was social amusement. Each child had the privilege of entertaining his group on his birthday and one other day. The parents went away and left them under the eye of some old servant. Good things to eat were abundant and the children amused themselves as they pleased. Albany seems to have been unique among the towns in this grant of freedom.

The Dutch did not recognize the rights of primogeniture and daughters inherited equally with sons. Says Irving: Around the fire

> The whole family, old and young, master and servant, black and white . . . enjoyed a community of privilege. [But at tea-parties] the young ladies seated themselves demurely in their rush bottom chairs and knit their own woolen stockings; nor ever opened their lips except to say "yah Mynheer" or "yah yah Vrow" . . . behaving in all things like decent well-educated damsels.

Chatteldom of women still prevailed in spite of Dutch liberalism. The old Dutch wills seem distrustful of a widow with regard to second marriage. Usually, in this colony, attempts were made to restrain wives by wills ordering forfeiture of property in case of remarriage. Nearly all the wills are more favorable to the children than to the wife. Restraints placed by wills on remarriage were commonly in behalf of children of the first marriage. Even in a joint will one husband enjoined loss of property if his wife married again. Perhaps he had reason for this precaution as she had had three husbands, a Dane, a Frieslander, and a German. His first wife had had four. John Burrows in a will of 1678 expressed the general feeling of husbands: "If my wife marry again, then her husband must provide for her as I have." One old Dutchman who died in 1726 left his estate to his wife with the proviso that

> If she happen to marry again, then I geff her nothing of my estate. . . . But my wife can be master of all by bringing up to good learning my two children. But if she come to marry again, then her husband can take her away from the farm.

In 1674 a woman of Hempstead represented that her deceased husband had made over his entire estate to children by a former marriage and that these left nothing for her necessary support. In response to her request for relief it was ordered "That the Magistrates of the town of Hempstead be recommended strictly to examine . . . and on finding it founded, to extend good right and justice to her." Thus the living of widows was safeguarded. But for some strange reason a hundred years later a bill providing for inheritance by posthumous children was held up by Governor Tryon.

A strange feature of the Dutch law of inheritance, established in New York, was that a widow's own property was liable for her husband's debts (tho she could escape liability by renouncing her dower). Perhaps this fact is a mark of the great equalization of men and women, the wife being assigned burdens as well as privileges.

The settlements in New Netherlands and early New York seem to have had a reasonable share of domestic troubles but not many cases occurred of absolute divorce or even of permanent separation. There was a system of friendly arbitration and the kindly paternalism of the Dutch magistrates tended to ward off serious issues. In 1665 a difference was patched up between a New Amsterdammer, Lantsman, and his wife. A curious feature of the case is that while he was so anxious to keep his wife he had been tardy in marrying her. His only excuse for not appearing on the appointed day was that his clothes were not ready. One woman asked a court order for her husband to vacate her home with a view to final separation. The arbitrators decided that no legal steps should be taken but that the two should "comport themselves as they ought, in order that they win back each other's affections, leaving each other in meanwhile unmolested."

A most interesting case showing the reluctance to sanction final separation developed in 1665 and ran for years. L. Pos tried to secure a separation for his daughter on the ground of insufferable treatment, stating that it was their third appearance in court. The husband denied that he had treated her improperly and blamed the trouble on his wife's father, who claimed that the husband had promised each time amendment but never fulfilled his promise. The council postponed decision, "and meanwhile their worships shall authorize some honorable and fitting person to reconcile if possible, the parties to love and friendship." The quarrel was referred to two ministers for reconciliation. If either husband or wife would not give in "then proceedings may be expected according to the style and custom of law as an example to other evil housekeepers." The wife's parents would not listen to the ministers, the husband claimed and requested the court to order his wife to return to him "as he could not any longer live without his wife, promising again to live with her as an honest man ought to do;" but she refused to go with him. The council considered the parents the chief cause of the trouble, and ordered them not to detain her over fourteen days within which time the pair were to be reconciled, or make joint application again. If any more complaints were made against the husband, he was to be delivered over for punishment. Later it was reported that the wife still held off; also that her father was entertaining her contrary to order. The jury decided that she should return to her husband.

In 1667 the father of the woman complained that his son-in-law had severely beaten his wife contrary to promise. He asked leave to take his daughter under his protection. The court ordered the husband to give security for good behavior and the father was allowed to keep his daughter under his care until further order. Later the sheriff complained against the man for wife-beating. It was ordered that if they again agreed to separation the court would permit it, the husband to pay four guilders weekly to his wife for the maintenance of the children. He wished, however, to live with her again, stating that she was inclined thereto, and he promised to be more considerate.

In 1669 complaint was again made of his bad treatment of his wife "so that the neighbors suffer great disturbance by the noise and uproar." The court ordered him to behave himself properly. In 1671 complaints arose anew. The court, in hope of amendment, once more pardoned the man, for the last time, warning him to let his wife be unmolested, that if another complaint came, he was to be banished. In 1673 the husband petitioned that his wife be ordered to live again with him or else that a divorce be granted. "Petitioner is notified to conduct himself in future . . . so civilly, peaceably, and friendly toward his wife, that by his good behavior his wife may be induced to dwell again with him as she ought." Thus the case had dragged out eight years.

In 1681, there was trouble in Fort Orange about the preacher's daughter Anneke who refused to go to New York to her husband. The man, however, promised to treat her rightly, and to support the family duly; so they were reconciled, "and for better assurance of his real intention and good resolution to observe the same, he requests that two good men be named to oversee his conduct . . . subjecting himself willingly to the rule and censure of the sd. men." She agreed to conduct herself well and to be a true wife and asked that bygones be bygones. The appointment of "two good men" as arbitrators or supervisors of conduct in such cases was a means of obviating the necessity for settlement in open court and helps to explain why family troubles of a violent sort were relatively inconspicuous or rare among the Dutch. Even the complaint of a man whose father-in-law refused to give him what he had promised was referred by the council to arbitration.

Loving parents, as we have noted, could not unduly shelter their daughter if she left her husband. In 1697 a certain man petitioned that his wife be "ordyred to go and live with him, where he thinks convenient." The magistrates promptly notified her father that he was "discharged to shelter her in his home or elsewhere, upon penalty as he will answer at his perill." She returned to her husband. Such episodes show how largely the conception of the wife as a chattel lingered even amid the liberality of this colony. The husband was entitled to a court order for the return of his wife, as if she were a thing rather than a person. The court had a strong bias toward the husband's side in such cases.

In regard to divorce the middle colonies were much nearer to the extreme conservatism of the South than to the broad and liberal policy of New England.[90] The civil courts possessed in New Netherlands "full power to dissolve the nuptial bond." As early as 1655 John Hicks by reason of his wife's adultery obtained a divorce with leave to remarry. In 1659 Nicholas Vellhuyzen was called to account for turning his wife out of doors and was asked why he would not live with her. He answered that he had not done as charged but had given her a blow because she had taken his money that he had laid in his chest; and that she had removed her bed and goods while he was away. The wife denied having taken the money. He said that "she gave her child money to buy one thing or another to eat, as the child would not eat of what was cooked and served up to table." He wished separation, and agreed to maintain the child that was to be born. The wife declared he struck her with the tongs in the presence of Thomas Wandel and that burgher Jones was by when he said "Bride for the Devil!" and "Get out the house." Nicholas was asked whether he could not resolve to live again in love with her, but was not so disposed. The court decided that he should supply her with certain goods according to his offer and further disposition was made for maintenance of her and her child.

The same year Nicasius de Sille requested divorce on account of his wife's unbecoming and careless life, wasting property without his knowledge, and her public habitual drunkenness. Eleven years later all efforts to reconcile Mr. Sille and his wife had failed and the

[90] Howard. *History of Matrimonial Institutions*, vol. ii, 376 ff.

commissioners saw no hope of reconciling them. The commission feared that even should they agree to live together, to which he seemed more inclined than she, it would not last long. The matter was finally settled by paying the bills and dividing the property equally between them.

In 1664 a woman was released from her husband on the ground of bigamy. A couple was divorced in Albany in 1670 "because strife and difference hath arisen between them." Daniel Denton was divorced from his wife, and she was allowed to remarry, under the new provincial divorce law, in 1672. A few other cases occur from 1670 to 1672. In 1674 under the restored Dutch régime

> Catrina Lane, requesting by petition, letters of divorce and separation from her husband, Daniel Lane, as her said husband has been accused of, and arrested for having committed and perpetrated incest with his own daughter, and without clearing himself thereof, hath broken jail and absconded; which being taken into consideration by the Governor-general and the council of New Netherland, they have ordered as follows: In case Daniel Lane . . . do not present himself in court within the space of six months from the date hereof and purge himself of the crime of incest with which he is accused, letters of divorce shall be granted to the petitioner.

The same year, "Abigail Mersenjer, the deserted wife of Richard Darlin, requesting by petition an act of divorce . . . with permission to remarry, on account that her husband, according to his own acknowledgement, hath broken the marriage ties by committing adultery, and . . . has absconded . . . ordered" that the case be postponed six months. If the man in that time did not come and clear himself the petitioner had the right to prosecute her suit. It should be noted that the population of the province at this time was only about seven thousand.

Chancellor Kent says: "For more than one hundred years preceding the Revolution no divorce took place in the colony of New York" and the only way to dissolve marriage was by special act of the legislature. In 1773, royal instructions were issued as follows:

> We have thought fit . . . to disallow certain laws passed in some of our colonies . . . in America . . . for diversing persons who have been legally joined together in holy marriage. . . It is our expressed will . . . that you do not upon any pretense whatever give your assent to any bill for the divorce of persons joined together in holy matrimony.

Thus the intruding feudal spirit of the English church and the English monarchy seem to have checked the freedom that tended to assimilate New York to New England in the matter of divorce.

Tho on the whole the New York family does not appear basally different from that of New England, the reader must have noted the liberalizing influence of bourgeois Holland as contrasted with the sharper lines in English life where Tory feudalism and bourgeois radicalism by their feud injected extremism into affairs. The more genial spirit of Dutch Protestantism as contrasted with the harsh lines of British Calvinism appears to the advantage of women and children. If one were to trace this contrast back, the source could doubtless be found in the narrowness of Dutch territories, which insured the early preponderance of commercialism and the feebleness of landlordism, as a political power. In addition to the resulting placidity of Dutch life, the better soil and less rigorous climate of the Hudson Valley contributed to make life smoother and more genial in New York than in New England.

X. COLONIAL NEW JERSEY AND DELAWARE

In New Jersey the great mass of the people were Scotch Presbyterians and New England Congregationalists, so that family laws give marked evidence of Puritan influence. Circumstances, however, encouraged liberality and New Jersey matrimonial institutions developed along the broader lines of New York.

Tho neither Calvinist nor Quaker regarded marriage as a divine sacrament yet both insisted that so important a civil contract should not be lightly entered and that the record should be carefully preserved. An East Jersey legislative act of 1668 directed that "no person or persons, son, daughter, maid, or servant" should be married without consent of parents or masters. Banns had to be published. Ministers, justices, etc. were authorized to perform the ceremony. The Quakers wanted a liberal law. The "Constitutions" of 1683 made concession to Quaker conscience by providing that all marriages not forbidden in scripture should be counted lawful when solemnized before credible witnesses by taking one another as husband and wife, a certificate being properly registered. Others than Quakers claimed to be exempt from prescribed forms. An act of 1693 imposed a penalty of ten pounds upon ministers and justices who joined parties without publication of banns or governor's license.

By far the most important statute regulating marriages in New Jersey was one of March, 1719, which stood unchanged for over eighty years. It was due to the fact that "young persons have been . . . enticed, inveigled, led away and clandestinely married" to the ruin of the parties and sorrow of parents and relatives. The act provided that no person under the age of twenty-one should be married without the written consent of parents or guardians. Heavy penalties were fixed for non-observance of the act. These penalties restrained men from taking away young girls, a practice which, owing to the proximity of the Hudson and the Delaware, had early become common.

It was a Friends' rule to marry in meeting; *i.e.*, the union of a Quaker with an outsider was forbidden to the extent of religious and social ostracism. West Jersey, owing to the taking up of large tracts, the consolidation of interests through the intermarriage of Friends, and the general observance of primogeniture, passed into the control of comparatively few families.

In 1668 East Jersey decreed divorce, whipping, or banishment as the penalty for adultery. In 1683 adultery was specified as disqualification for membership in the Great Council. In 1682 in one of the Jerseys a man and woman, paramours, were ordered "whipd on their naked bodies," the man to receive thirty stripes and the woman to receive thirty-five and to be sent home; he was to be kept in jail one day after she left and to pay costs.

It is not certain whether divorces were actually granted in New Jersey. If they were, it must have been by the authority of the legislature or of the governor. West Jersey, largely Quaker, had small need of legislation. The courts there sought to unite the couple at variance rather than to effect a permanent separation. Some time before 1694 Thomas Peaches and Mary his wife had agreed upon separation. Quaker justices summoned them into court and asked if they were not willing to live together. Both agreed, Thomas stipulating that Mary "will acknowledge shee hath scandalized him wrongfully." She consents "but saith shee will not owne that she hath told lies of him to her knowledge." This answer brought things to a standstill

> But after some good admonitions from the bench, they both promise they will forget and never mention what unkind speeches or actions they have formerly passed between them or concerning each other. . . Hee . . . p'mises shee behaving herself, with tenderness and love to him, hee will remain as a loveing and a carefull husband to her and make ye best p'vision for her and ye child that hee can.

In East Jersey the right of complaining against a child that smote or cursed father or mother belonged to both parents and the prescribed penalty was death. Among the Friends in Jersey many sons of wealthy plantation owners were indentured owing to an economic aspect of their religious teachings, which was to the effect that every man should have and follow a trade or other occupation. It is not surprising, therefore, to find that bond servitude was no stigma, and under some circumstances a bound boy or girl became one of the family, and sometimes redemptioners' sons married daughters of the former masters.[91]

The education of women was distinctly domestic. Now and then a girl had to be disciplined because she preferred to be an independent old maid (which she became at twenty-five) rather than marry at sixteen or seventeen.[92] In newspapers of the middle of the eighteenth century we find a letter now and then in which a Jersey farmer complains that the young women go

[91] Lee. *New Jersey*, vol. i, 201.

[92] — *Idem*, 196-198.

after fashion and ease to the neglect of butter-making, weaving, spinning, and cooking. Some even were actually negligent in the matter of preparing with their own hands the sheets, blankets, and spreads necessary to marriage.

> The sentiment was abroad that too much education was not beneficial for women, that a knowledge of books weaned them from the domestic circle, and that their place was in the kitchen caring for the children. The selfishness of this view, and the generally subordinate place occupied by women, according to the custom of the time, retarded any great intellectual development. Only among the society of Friends, were women given public position – and then only as approved ministers.[93]

In view of such facts it is a surprise to learn that the early New Jersey constitution was so carelessly framed as to allow women to vote. The clause "all inhabitants of this colony of full age" gave the ballot to women[94] and aliens. Women were allowed to vote, or were rejected, according to the views of the election officers. Griffith in a tract published 1799 says that

> Women, generally, are neither by nature, nor habit, nor education, nor by their necessary condition in society fitted to perform this duty with credit to themselves or advantage to the public. . . It is perfectly disgusting to witness the manner in which women are polled at our elections. Nothing can be a greater mockery of this invaluable and sacred right than to suffer it to be exercised by persons who do not even pretend to any judgment on the subject.

Early Delaware wrestled with clandestine and irregular marriage. A prominent Swede had an altercation with the authorities on this score, "because," says the magistrate, "I suspected him that he, without being authorized, had arrogated to himself to qualify the priest to marry a young couple without the *usual proclamation*

[93] Lee. *New Jersey*, vol. i, 358-359.

[94] On woman suffrage, see *idem*, vol. iii, 266-267.

and against the will of the parents, on which I condemned the priest in a fine of fifty guilders."

Old Swede church ruled in 1714 "that betrothals and marriage proceed in an orderly manner according to the ordinances of our church." Also that espousals and marriages are not allowable according to church law before mature age, and not without consent of parents, and must be without compulsion or secrecy, and not before being well instructed in Christian doctrines.

William Beckett, a missionary, wrote in 1737:

> Our government is under the influence of the Quakers. . . Our president has taken it upon him to grant marriage licenses (and) contrary to former usage lodged them in the hands of laymen of his own kidney or under his immediate influence, to whom we are obliged to apply with much ceremony and no small charge to our parishioners to obtain a marriage license.

In 1750 the pastor of Old Swede tells that

> A woman once came to me asking to wed her anew, or as it is termed here, wed her over again with her husband, altho she had been living with him for seven years. The reason for this was that they were married by a Catholic priest, and therefore the marriage was not so lawful, but I dismissed her with a severe reprimand.

In 1790, Delaware abolished civil marriage.

Intermarriage tended to produce homogeneity in Delaware. Among the Swedes there seems to have been an excess of women. At least there were many marriages of Swedish women with men of other nationalities. Thus the Swedish blood spread through the old families of Wilmington, except (principally) the Quakers, tho occasionally a Friend so far forgot the faith as to marry a Swede. Such blending of the younger elements operated to allay antipathies among the older people. In 1693, thirty-eight years after the surrender of the Swedes, we find in a census list of their families several of the parents bearing Dutch names. (Dutchmen, however, had been in the Swedish enterprise from the start.) By the beginning of the eighteenth century the welding of Swedes, Dutch, and English was under way. The fusion of blood opened the door, of course, to fusion of customs. Thus, the agricultural population of Sweden had no surnames at the time of emigration.[95] After mingling with other nationalities in America they adopted the father's name as family name.

By the middle of the eighteenth century the pastor of Old Swede thought it necessary "to show the Swedish wives of English husbands that they must hereafter do their duty if they expect to remain members." In 1759 some of the congregation complained because their children married to strangers had to pay as strangers for burial places in the churchyard. It was resolved that if they retained membership they were entitled to a place, but not for husband or children without payment. Thus occurred the tragedy so often repeated since–a dwindling handful in the midst of engulfing alien ways.

The Delaware country presented at first the usual difficulties in the way of family settlement. In 1659 Alricks wrote to Holland regarding the settlers at New Amstel among whom was a preponderance of women and children. He desired that "the women and children be omitted for the present, as agriculture could not be advanced without good farmers and strong laboring men." Even in later days family support was not always a simple problem. Citizens of "the lower counties" importing infants and lunatics were to assume responsibility for these visitors. The reverend Mr. Ross

[95] *Records of Holy Trinity*, 1697-1773, 4.

wrote in 1708: "New Castle is a place where everything is extraordinary dear, and a man that has a family can not subsist upon the society's bounty of £50 per annum." He moved to Upland in the hope of getting a better living for his family by keeping a boarding-school. In such emergencies clan loyalty was a valuable asset. In 1706, the pastor of Old Swede complains that paucity of support makes him an incumbrance on his wife's relatives.

There was a decided disposition to develop a sort of familism on an economic basis. Thus in the pew assignment at Old Swede (1699)

> The heads of families, and they that have now paid the first cost, and have worked for them, are to have their room, and if there be room to spare in a pew, or some of the parents are absent, the unmarried children may take seats, but otherwise take the room farther down in the church, and the small children stand in the aisle in front of their parents pews, and after the death of a parent, only the children who remain attached to the home and land which have now contributed to the building, but they who have married away must look out for other places as opportunity may offer.

This identification of family with land is akin to the attempt to establish manorial estates, as for instance Bohemia Manor. The inheritance of a given name as well as surname comes in the same category.

> Oftentimes a child of each succeeding generation has received the name of its father or grandfather, and so it has been handed down, until many of our citizens bear the same name as their first ancestor, who emigrated here more than 200 years ago.[96]

Delaware enjoyed something of the serene Dutch influence that tempered the life of this middle group of colonies and made it more to our modern liking than the colder ways of New England. The Dutch cared

---

[96] Vincent. *History of Delaware*, vol. i, 460.

less for education than did the New Englanders but they introduced comforts and amenities into life without neglecting family protection.

The Swedes likewise gave due attention to family welfare. The church was very insistent on prompt baptism of infants. Thus a church ruling in 1714 says that parents should not, as often happens, let their babes remain at home a whole month or many months, yes even half a year. Most of the children were baptized before they were a week old, many by the third day, and if a child was growing up unchristened it became a matter of public concern. The pastor of Old Swede kept a record of baptisms.

Swedish women seem to have enjoyed something of the same eminence as was accorded to the Dutch vrows. Thus about 1750 the pastor of Old Swede, being under necessity of raising money, wrote:

> I found it best to avail myself of some Sunday when . . . there was a full congregation, to request that all should remain in their seats, so that the women folk, who in many houses rule more than the men, might have opportunity to hear what was presented, and thereafter for their part both agree and direct for the best.

That Delaware was not ungenial to prolific increase is suggested by the following item:

> Died in peace in 1771, at Wilmington, Delaware, a pious, elderly matron, who had been mother of 16 children, all married and comfortable; 68 grandchildren, 166 great-grandchildren, and 4 great-great-grandchildren – in all 238 living offspring survived her. The generation of the just shall be blessed.

With the first body of immigrants from Amsterdam to New Amstel, in 1656, came Evert Pietersen. August 19, 1657, he wrote:

> We arrived here at the South River on the 25th of April and found twenty families there, mostly Swedes, not more than five

> or six families belonging to our nation. . . I already begin to keep school and have twenty five children, etc.

In the Dutch settlements, as in Holland, education reached the youth through the church and the clergyman, a rather unreliable route.

Schools were encouraged by the Swedish government. But Biork writes: "We hardly found here a Swedish book but they were so anxious for the improvement of their children that they lent them to one another, so that they can all read tolerably well." He complained also that the ministers were too old and infirm to "pay proper attention to the education of youth." After the coming of the English in 1682 it became customary for Swedish children first to learn to read English and then their mother tongue. The records of Old Swede church show interest in the starting of school. On one occasion the record tells of the employment of a school-master "and agree to gather for him 18 or 20 children." In 1700 occurs this entry:

> Early in May the schoolkeeping in Boktin was discontinued, partly on account of the above mentioned sickness and some other causes, particularly that some inconsiderate persons neglected to keep their children steadily at school, tho they were diligently and thoroly taught.

House instruction by the pastor was the last glimmer of Swedish education.

Among the laws of the Duke of York in 1676 was one to this effect:

> The constable and overseers are strictly required frequently to admonish the inhabitants of instructing their children and servants, in matters of religion and the lawes of the country, and that the parents and masters do bring up their children and apprentices in some honest lawfull calling labour or employment. And if any children or servants become rude, stuborne, or unruly refusing to hearken to the voice of their parents or mas-

ters, the constables and overseers (where no justice of the peace shall happen to dwell within ten miles of the said town or parish) have power upon the complaint of their parents or masters to call before them such an offender and to inflict such corporal punishment as the merit of their fact in their judgment shall deserve, not excepting ten stripes, provided that such children and servants be of sixteen years of age.

The provisions of Penn's frame of government may be found in the following chapter on Pennsylvania.

Mr. Ross in a sketch of the church at New Castle describes education in 1727:

There are some private schools within my reputed district which are put very often into the hands of those who are brought into the country and sold for servants. Some schoolmasters are hired by the year, by a knot of families who, in their turn entertain him monthly and the poor man lives in their houses like one that begged an alms, more than like a person in credit and authority. When a ship arrives in the river it is a common expression among them who stand in need of an instructor for their children *Let us go and buy a Schoolmaster.* The truth is, the office and character of such a person is generally very mean and contemptible here, and it cannot be otherways 'til the public takes the education of children into their mature consideration.

A letter by Beckett, a missionary, in 1728 says:

There is no public school in all the county, the general custom being, for what they call a neighborhood (which lies sometimes four or five miles distant) to hire a person . . . to teach their children to read and write English, for whose accommodation they meet together at a place agreed upon, cut down . . . trees and build a log house in a few hours . . . whither they send their children every day during the term for it ought to be observed by way of commendation of the American planters nowadays, that whatever pains or charge it may cost, they seldom omit to have their children instructed in reading and writing the English tongue.

The Presbyterians came in the years from 1718 to

1740. The *Shorter Catechism* was learned in their homes and recited at school. Psalms were the lullabies. On Sabbath parents, children, and servants went through the catechism. Sermons were read and points of doctrine compared with the Bible.

The reverend Mr. Hacket writes of Delaware in 1732:

> The people . . . frequently bring negroe children to church, and after being instructed, their Masters become their sureties.

Education in Delaware was obviously very imperfect. Even late in the eighteenth century children were exposed to the influence of immoral teachers. Nor was family morality always high.

In 1660

> Among the Finns is a married couple who live together in constant strife. The wife receives daily a severe drubbing, and is expelled from the house as a dog. This treatment she suffered a number of years; not a word is said in blame of the wife, whereas he, on the contrary, is an adulterer. On all which the priest, the neighbors, the sheriff appeal to [an official] at the solicitation of man and wife, that a divorce might take place, and the small property and stock be divided between them.

The official asked for orders. This is the first mention of a divorce case in Delaware.

In 1661 the South River folk were stirred by the first recorded elopement. The wife of a Finnish priest ran off with another man and the couple eluded arrest. The husband was indignant but not inconsolable, for in less than a month he applied for permission to marry a young girl. The answer was deferred till Stuyvesant could be heard from. Two months after the bereavement the priest again asked permission to marry, as the situation of his family, he said, imperiously required it. A month later he received a divorce, and a few weeks after this release, married himself, "a transaction in my opinion, under execution, entirely unlawful," wrote the local official in quest of orders from higher authority. The marriage was shortly declared void. Conditions in Delaware corresponded to the account of Maryland by an Episcopal rector (1676): "All notorious vices are committed; so that it is become a Sodom of uncleanness, and a pest house of iniquity."[97]

Fabritius, a Lutheran minister, came to New Castle in 1671 having gotten into hot water in Albany for not baptizing several children on application, etc. Soon he was suspended from the ministry for one year for having performed a marriage "without having any lawful authority thereto, and without publication of banns." His wife remained at Albany, and he managed to keep in trouble at both places.

Tienhoven, at one time secretary of the colony on South River, seduced in Holland on promise of marriage a girl of Amsterdam. She came and found him already married and took her case into court. In 1709 Thomas Crawford, a missionary, wrote of uncleanness:

> [Mr. Middleton, a vile man, sent me word of the disappearance of Elizabeth Watson. Some] believed it was done by a fellow that was in the house with her whom all say she admitted to her embraces. But what I have to say of her uncleanness, that on earth I can get proved, and other villany to obtain her lust, and gratify her unclean desires as also a certificate of her former husband's death whom she trapanned and sent to sea, and then removed under the name of a maid to a strange place, and things worse than that I shall not mention. . . . With all the last money I sent Elizabeth Watson, she laid it out to pay the boarding of a gentleman's children, to whom she had been valet de chambre many a night till all

[97] Holcomb. *Sketch of Early Ecclesiastical Affairs in New Castle, Delaware, and History of Immanuel Church*, 29.

the world took notice of her base carriage with him, and then when she had lost her fame she came after me.

The records of the Welsh Tract Baptist Meeting contain numerous records of church censorship of sex morals. In 1714 Evan Edmunds and Catherine Edwards were excommunicated for conducting themselves scandalously and unseemly and withstanding the advice of the church not to keep company till they cleared themselves of the scandal. In 1717 Richard Lewis was turned out for keeping unseemly company with his neighbor's wife and withstanding the counsel of the church. Mary Rees was "dismembered" in 1723 for withstanding the advice of the church and marrying a man against the warning of the brethren and of her father. Besides there was no proof of her former husband's death. The sentence was to stand so long as both parties were alive. In the previous cases the sentences were really only suspension until satisfaction should be given. Thomas Jones and wife were excommunicated for improper conduct with regard to the obligation of the marriage vow, etc., and for disregard of the call of the church. Numerous others cases of excommunication, etc., occured for such causes as bastardy, bigamy, disorderly marriage – without advising with the church and without parental consent – fornication, excessive drinking to the hurt of the culprit's family, adultery. These cases, however, are spread over half a century, namely from 1736-1786. The church undertook also to adjust differences between husband and wife.

In the eighteenth century the Delaware assembly made sodomy, buggery, and rape capital offences. Death without benefit of clergy was fixed as the penalty for the killing of bastards.

Perhaps the most outstanding fact in the history of the New Jersey and Delaware colonial families is the unsettling influence of heterogeneity of population. This factor is visible in the liberalization of the New Jersey marriage law, in irregularities of marriage in Delaware, in family division due to cross-marriages, and in the variety of petty groups, each censoring the affairs of its members.

XI. THE FAMILY IN COLONIAL PENNSYLVANIA

Pennsylvania was cosmopolitan, hence tended to breadth and tolerance. Here we must study varied influences, particularly Quaker, German, and Scotch-Irish.

In the early days the Quaker element was dominant. They always held marriage and the family in great esteem. The records of the colonial Pennsylvania Quaker meetings are full of instances of discipline administered to young people for fornication. Penn claims that wedlock should grow only out of reciprocal inclination. "Never marry but for love," he says, "but see that thou lovest what is lovely."

Tho holding, like the Puritans, that the regulation of marriage belongs to the civil power, the Quakers,[98] as a sect, imposed restrictions of their own. The Meeting exercised constant surveillance over family discipline and private life. As it was impossible properly to discipline the family of a mixed marriage a Quaker marrying one of another sect was dismissed from the society even tho their numbers were thus greatly depleted. If a Friend sought a wife elsewhere than in his home community he carried a letter from the Meeting.

In the first half of the eighteenth century perplexing questions were rife as to forbidden degrees, marriage by justice of the peace, mixed marriages, young couples' keeping company without parental consent. Adverse

---

[98] See Index for Quakers in England.

decisions were rendered on every question. A tendency to recognize the validity of common law marriages appears. The following are illustrations of the problems that confronted the Friends in Pennsylvania: many young Friends, impatient of the slow and troublesome process of passing meeting, would hasten off to the priest or to a magistrate and be married without delay or formality. Refusal to confess fault meant expulsion. At Warrington, 1767, Sarah Delap acknowledged "keeping company with a young man not of our society and attempting marriage with him by a priest to the great grief of my tender parents." She was reinstated.

While Quaker discipline was, on the whole, rather Puritanlike the home life was charming. The families were often large. The Friends were especially appreciative of the aged. Hospitality was a genial virtue. In American Quaker homes there were spare rooms, and Quaker visitors, no matter how numerous, never went to a hotel.

The *Diary* of Christopher Marshall, a well-to-do Quaker of Philadelphia, kept during the year 1778, describes his wife's activities: "From early . . . morning till late at night she is constantly employed in the affairs of the family, which for four months has been very large. . . It is a constant resort of comers and goers." Moreover she did the baking and cooking; made twenty large cheeses from one cow; was gardener and butter-maker; kept the house clean; cut and dried apples; made cider without tools "for the constant drink of the family;" attended to the washing and ironing. She also sewed, knit, etc. "I think she hath not been above four times since her residence here to visit her neighbors." In sickness furthermore he stated that she was a faithful nurse day and night. She was ever ready to supply poor neighbors with milk, always had cream to spare for her dairy. She rose at daybreak, tho aged, and went to the wharves to buy wood. Her hearty old husband records complacently that the horse would have died had not the energetic woman skirmished for hay in the barren city. Besides she endured Poll, a pestiferous bound girl. Such was the life of the Revolutionary housewife. Yet the Quakers went far toward a recognition of woman's equality.

Penn's frame of government contains provision for education in the New World:

> The governor and provincial council shall erect and order all publick schools and encourage and reward the authors of useful sciences and laudable inventions. . . And [there shall be] a committee of manners, education and arts, that all wicked and scandalous living may be prevented, and that youth may be successively trained up in virtue and useful knowledge and arts. . . All children within the province of the age of twelve years shall be taught some useful trade or skill, to the end none may be idle, but the poor may work to live, and the rich, if they become poor, may not want.

The first General Assembly (Chester, 1682) accepted the provisions. The Assembly of the next year ordered that "persons having charge of children should have them instructed in reading and writing before they were twelve years of age, or pay a fine of five pounds for every sound child." Children were to be taught "some useful trade or skill." Force, if necessary, was to be used to execute the law. The insistence on industrial training recalls Puritan devotion to child labor.

Penn did away with the old laws that gave to the state the estates of murderers and suicides. He also abolished primogeniture. But a huge estate became vested in the Penn family thus producing a strange contrast to his liberalism. This estate was the source of great mischief. Penn's heirs, or proprietaries, made claim to all the soil within the bounds of the original charter. In 1779 the Pennsylvania legislature denounced the manner in which the Penn family had perverted and abused the terms of Penn's charter. Thus the opportunity to ground a family aristocracy in landlordism reversed the characteristic trend of Quakerism toward "democratic" capitalism.

From Maine to Georgia the Germans were hinterlanders occupying the best farm acreage. They were numerous in the middle states and have left their imprint on that section. In the fatherland marriage was held to be of divine appointment. Some of the immigrants did, indeed, form communities with sex segregation but the bulk of the German immigrants settled by families.

The Germans are a domestic people. The middle-class German is fond of home life and joins with his family in the pursuit of simple pleasures. The Germans gave to America a domestic type of woman. To this fact can be attributed much of the vigor of the population and the solid quality that comes from home training. They laid great emphasis on the household arts, excelling in thoroness and efficiency. A writer of the eighteenth century says:

> When a young man asks the consent of his father to marry a girl of his choice, the latter does not so much inquire whether she be rich or poor, but whether she is industrious and acquainted with the duties of a good housewife.[99]

The pioneer, of course, did not care for an intellectual wife but preferred a woman of sound industry. The industry of the German women was indeed marvelous. The men loved their homes; they were home-makers–

[99] In Kuhns, *German and Swiss Settlements of Pennsylvania*, 101.

industrious and frugal. The children were trained to industry. The Pennsylvania Germans had very few slaves. Often their farms descended from father to son for more than a hundred years, in many cases without a mortgage.

Pastors' baptismal records and the entries in family Bibles show that Pennsylvania Germans often had numerous children. The pioneer did not murmur when his family grew. Penn found the kindred race, the Swedes, on the Delaware likewise fertile.

> They have fine children, and almost every house full: rare to find one of them without three or four boys and as many girls; some six, seven, and eight sons. And I must do them that right, I see few young men more sober and laborious.

Rush writes in 1789:

> The favorable influence of agriculture, as conducted by the Germans . . . is manifested by the joy they express upon the birth of a child. No dread of poverty or distrust of Providence, from an increasing family, depresses the spirits of these industrious and frugal people. Upon the birth of a son, they exult in the gift of a plowman or a waggoner; and upon the birth of a daughter they rejoice in the addition of another spinster or milkmaid to the family.

Home discipline was rigid. When necessary the rod was used. Children received diligent home-training. They were taught early in life to work. The practice of binding children out to service so that they might learn trades or because the home family was so large as to render their services superfluous was followed quite generally in old Germantown. The Pennsylvania Germans thought it no disgrace for a daughter to work in another family, where she might add to her knowledge of good housekeeping. Servants ate with the family on ordinary occasions and were well cared for. The servant and the master and mistress frequently were to each other as child and parents. Parents loved their home and their children and made the home attractive with proper games and privileges. Children also loved home and parents and other members of the family. Part of the home, sometimes a separate dwelling, was provided for aged parents or grandparents. Often an unmarried daughter held it her duty to remain with the aged parents to the end of their days.

The old church records are honest in mentioning the illegitimate birth of children. But the smallness of this unfortunate number as compared with the number born in wedlock shows the esteem of matrimony. Adultery was a grievous sin to the pioneers. Divorces were viewed with abhorrence. Parents counselled their children to live in purity and gave good advice regarding the choice of husband or wife.

Many German immigrants met with unfortunate experiences. A letter dated March 16, 1684, says: "If any one come here in this land at his own expense, and reaches here in good health, he will be rich enough, especially if he can bring his family or some man servants, because servants are here dear." For the man that could not come at his own expense, the outlook was not so good. "It often happens that whole families, husband, wife, and children are separated by being sold to different purchasers." Ships brought hordes of Germans to America. Children seldom survived the journey. "Many a time parents are compelled to see their children die of hunger, thirst, or sickness, and then see them cast into the water. Few women in confinement escaped with their lives; many a mother is cast into the water with her child." When the ships reached Philadelphia unmarried people of both sexes found ready sale. Old married people, widows, and the feeble, were a drug on the market unless they had children to assume the debts of the parents, thereby extending their own period of servitude. "Parents must sell and trade away their children like so many cattle." Thus the exploiting element that dominated here as in all the colonies subordinated moral considerations, as always, to profits.[100]

An important continental sect, the Moravians, were not unlike the Quakers. They had their system of censorship and administration of discipline over families. Tho tending to communal life (for they were successors to the revolutionary Taborite communists of Bohemia), they did not believe in celibacy. Marriage they elevated into a very sacred duty. All souls were in essence feminine and the male was a mere temporary function for the probation period on earth.[101] It might be supposed that this feministic theory would give supremacy to woman, but not so. Man's duties were exalted, clear, and positive. As Christ was the true husband of each woman so the man was his representative and the wife's Savior. Thus marriage was highly idealized and, naturally, subject to very strict regulation. The church often acted as match-maker, helping in the choice of a wife and conveying the proposal. Divorce is said to have been practically unknown among them.

Their communal tendency took shape at Bethlehem, where the land belonged to the church, which took into its treasury the fruits of the joint labor of the community and gave to each member the necessaries of life, instruction for his children, and care in sickness and

[100] On slavery of whites in the colonies see Oneal, *Workers in American History*, chapters iii and iv. A rather amateurish work, but, to the ordinary reader, indispensable.

[101] On the sect see Fisher, *The Making of Pennsylvania*, 138.

old age. Separate quarters were provided for bachelors as also for widows and for single women.

The cohesion of the Pennsylvania Moravians outlasted the colonial period. A historian in 1819 writes thus of them:

> The young man who has an inclination to marry makes application to the priest, who presents a young woman designated by the superintendent as the next in rotation for marriage. Having left the parties together for an hour, the priest returns, and if they mutually consent to live together, they are married the next day; if otherwise, each is put at the bottom of the list, containing perhaps sixty or seventy names, and on the part of the girl there is no chance of marriage, unless the same young man should again feel disposed for matrimony. When united, a neat habitation, with a pleasant garden, is provided, and their children, at the age of six, are placed in the seminary. If either of the parents die, the other returns to the apartment of the single people.[102]

The Dunkers, also, are worthy of special mention. The Brethren church has distinctly stood for the exaltation of the home and family life. Among the early settlers of this sect was found a high type of Christian home. The typical home was a sanctuary for the preaching of the word: for forty-seven years the Brethren had no church nor meeting-house. The Dunkers developed sex-segregation. In 1819 we are told that "the women live separate from the men, and never associate except for the purpose of public worship or public business."[103]

The Schwenkfelders were also noteworthy. Among them mixed marriages were discouraged. During the period before marriage the minister met the young people several times and gave them instruction in Christian

[102] Mackenzie. *Historical Topographical and Descriptive View of the United States*, 379.

[103] — *Idem*, 380.

doctrine and especially in the duties of married life. Entrance into the marriage relation was a most sacred step. The bride had, perhaps for years, been getting things ready in preparation for her duties as wife and mistress of a home. Children were objects of pious solicitude. They were not allowed to frequent places of public resort.

In 1720-1740 thousands of Ulster Scots came to America and peopled the hills and valleys of the Pennsylvania frontier. Clannish by nature and tradition they held together in small communities of forty or more families, a majority of them akin by blood or by marriage. The Scotch-Irish are comparable to the Puritans but coming from a less central people were of freer and less sombre type. Their matrimonial customs were simple as befits a frontier people. Men seldom went far afield for wives. In the preliminaries of a marriage there was great deliberation and thoroness. The girl's outfit had been prepared from her birth. On two successive Sabbaths before the wedding after the benediction one of the clerks would announce the banns. Marriage took place at the bride's home. On the following Sabbath they made their appearance in state at church. The race was marked by family loyalty. The women led hard lives but were patient and submissive. (The person familiar with the back country of western Pennsylvania to-day will note apparent survivals of the last two primitive features.) Divorce was practically unknown.

Pennsylvania presented the usual pioneer hardships, in juxtaposition with city luxury. For instance John and Rebecca Head arrived in Philadelphia early in the eighteenth century with a flock of children and various household utensils. In default of other means of transportation they put the two younger girls in a tub and each parent took a handle. The older children, aged three and four, walked in front carrying as much as they could. A surprising counter item is found in the correspondence of Mrs. John Adams:

> Philadelphia must be an infertile soil or it would not produce so many unfruitful women. I always conceive of these persons as wanting one addition to their happiness; but in these perilous times, I know not whether it ought to be considered as an infelicity.

Children in Pennsylvania schools were sometimes the victims of "drunken, dirty, careless, and cruel teachers." Slight attempt was made by the English in early Pennsylvania toward popular education outside the capital. Penn Charter School, opened at Philadelphia in 1698, was for fifty years the only public school in the province. The Germans and Moravians had some good private schools in the larger towns but educational facilities in the country were usually wretched or lacking. A Pennsylvania pedagog of 1765 advertising for pupils urges young ladies not to be discouraged on account of age or through fear of not obtaining a spouse, as he has had "the honour to give the finishing stroke in education to several of the reputed fine accomplished ladies in New York, some of which were married within two, three, and four years afterwards."[104]

Pennsylvania had notable women. In the days of settlement one woman took up a tract of twenty-five hundred acres in what is now Lancaster County. There are instances of prominent business women in the colony. Benjamin Franklin both respected and admired his wife. But the subordination of woman was still manifest. One old law in Pennsylvania (1690) pro-

[104] Wharton. *Colonial Days and Dames*, 126.

vided that a widow could not marry till a year after her husband's death.

Pennsylvania was not staidly Puritan. In 1741 a Grand Jury notes that whites in markets, etc., strive "to excell in all lewdness and obsenity which must produce a generall corruption of such youth (apprentices, etc.) if not timely remedied." Stories of scandal in high society can be found in histories of all old Pennsylvania towns.[105] Sarah Eve writes of unrestrained kissing of girls by men in Philadelphia (1722). In Philadelphia the groom's friends called for several days after a wedding to drink punch.

Quakers and Moravians did not legislate about divorce and the Scotch-Irish had no use for it. The Great Law of 1682 for Pennsylvania permits divorce for the scriptural cause. A penalty was prescribed for adultery.

> [One convicted] shall for the first offence be publicly whipped and suffer one whole year's imprisonment in the house of correction at hard labor, to the behoof of the publick and longer if the magistrate see meet. And both he and the woman shall be liable to a Bill of Divorcement, if required by the grieved husband or wife within the said term of one whole year after conviction.

For a second offence the penalty is "imprisonment in manner aforesaid during life." Gordon in a summary of the laws of the colony says that these "made no general provision for the dissolution of marriage; and divorce from bed and board was allowed in case of bigamy only, on request of first wife or husband, made in one year after conviction."[106] Legislative authority, however, granted absolute divorces. But there is no

[105] Giddings. *Natural History of American Morals*, 34.

[106] Howard. *History of Matrimonial Institutions*, vol. ii, 386-387.

evidence to show that divorces either absolute or partial were at all common in Pennsylvania.

Servitude and slavery marred morality in this as in the other colonies.[107] Reference has already been made to the dissolution of families by white servitude. The pathos of such a system was brought home to a Philadelphia gentleman who wanted an old couple for house servants. After purchasing an old couple and their daughter he found that he had bought his own father, mother, and sister.[108] If members of a family died on the ocean the survivors were held responsible.

Servants were not allowed to marry without master's consent and a severe penalty was attached to this infringement of property rights. Women having illegitimate children (and thereby, of course, impairing the value of their services) were punished by a prolongation of their term of bondage.

Miscegenation doubtless took place from the first. In 1677 a white servant was indicted for intercourse with a negro. In 1698 the Chester County Court asserted the principle that mingling of the races was to be tabooed. Court records run as follows:

> For that hee . . . contrary to the lawes of the government and contrary to his masters consent hath . . . got with child a certain molato wooman called swart Anna. . .
>
> David Lewis Constable of Haverford returned a negro man of his and a white woman for haveing a baster childe . . . the negro said she intised him and promised him to marry him; she being examined, confest the same . . . the court ordered that she shall receive twenty-one lashes on her beare backe . . . and the court ordered the negroe man never to meddle with any white woman more uppon paine of his life.

A law of 1700, for negroes, provided that buggery or

107 See Turner, *History of Slavery in Pennsylvania.*

108 Oneal. *Workers in American History*, 67.

rape of a white woman was to incur the penalty of death. The penalty for attempted rape was to be castration.

In 1722 a woman was punished for complicity in a clandestine marriage of a white woman to a negro. Shortly after a petition came up to the Assembly attacking the wicked and scandalous practice of negroes' cohabiting with white people. The Assembly proceeded to the framing of a law. The law of 1725-1726 provided that no negro was to be married to any white person on any pretense whatever. A white person violating this law was to forfeit thirty pounds or be sold as a servant for a period not over seven years. A clergyman abetting such a union was to be fined one hundred pounds. The law was not able to check cohabitation tho there is almost no record of marriages of slaves with white people.

Advertisements for runaway slaves indicate that mulattoes were very numerous. The Chester County slave register for 1780 shows that they made up twenty per cent of the slave population in that locality. It would seem that it was not, in general, the masters that were guilty of illicit intercourse but rather servants, outcasts, and the lower class of whites[109] The records of 1766 contain an instance of a white woman prostitute to negroes and those of the following decade give evidence as to mulatto bastards by pauper white women. One case was noted in 1715 where the guilty white man was probably not a servant. Benjamin Franklin was openly accused of having colored mistresses.[110]

Children of negro slaves became, of course, the master's property. Owners considered the rearing of slave

[109] Turner. *History of Slavery in Pennsylvania*, 31.
[110] — *Idem.*

children a burden. One writer affirmed that in Pennsylvania "negros just born are considered an incumbrance only, and if humanity did not forbid it, they would be instantly given away" (1780). A likely wench was sold because of her fecundity. In 1732 the Philadelphia Court of Common Pleas ordered a man to take back a negress that he had sold that proved to be with child. He was to return the price and pay the money spent "for phisic and attendance of the said negroe in her miserable condition." In the Pennsylvania *Gazette* occurs an advertisement of an exemplary young negress for sale. "She has . . . a fine, hearty young child, not quite a year old, which is the only reason for selling her, because her mistress is very sickly, and cant bear the trouble of it." The child of a free mother and a slave father was a servant for a term of years.

Slavery in Pennsylvania was mild. The chattels generally lived in the master's house. Some had cabins for their families. Negroes were often allowed to visit members of their families living in other households. Something was done toward the maintenance of slave family life. Penn's conscientious attempt in 1700 to secure a law for the regulation of slave marriage was defeated. One writer attributes this result to the waning of Quaker influence, the lower tone of the later influx, and temporary hostility to the executive. But the universal incompatibility of property rights in men with stable marriage is sufficient to account for the vote.

Slaves came under the law forbidding servants to marry without the master's consent. It is said that many masters permitted their human cattle to marry as they pleased save that the owner would try to prevent marriage off the place. (In conflict with the alleged unprofitableness of slave raising, Kalm adds that it was considered an advantage to own negro women, since otherwise the offspring of one's negroes belonged to another master.) The marriage ceremony was frequently performed as for white people. The records of Christ Church show many such instances. Among the Friends there are very few records of such marriages. But Joshua Brown's *Journal* kept during the year 1774 contains this item:

> I rode to Philadelphia . . . and lodged that night at Wm. Browns and fifth day of the Moth I spent in town and was at a negro wedding in the eving when several per mett and had a setting with them, and they took each other and the love of God seemd to be extended to them.

A negro marriage in Friends' fashion is recorded for West Chester. Mittleberger said: "The blacks are likewise married in the English fashion." But Benezet wrote: "They are suffered, with impunity, to cohabit together, without being married and to part, when solemnly engaged to one another as man and wife." It would be absurd to attribute to the negroes all the blame for family laxity. But in Pennsylvania there was no active trade in negroes and when they were bought or sold there was some attempt to keep families together.

It is said that negro children were taught submission to their parents and that these were suffered to train, cherish, and chasten them. Many slaves were treated like members of the master's family: nursed and cared for in sickness, provided for when past work, and in some instances remembered in the master's will. Often members of a negro family bought freedom for other members.[111]

Opposition to slavery took into account its influence

[111] Turner. *History of Slavery in Pennsylvania*, 46, 51, 62.

on family relations. The Quakers of Germantown in 1688 indicted slavery as follows: "Some do commit adultery in others, separating wives from their husbands and giving them to others . . . and some sell the children of these poor creatures to other men." In 1780 an act for gradual abolition was passed. It provided that no child thereafter born in Pennsylvania should be a slave; but it held in servitude till the age of twenty-eight children born of a slave mother.

After the passage of this act some masters sent negro children into other states there to be sold. Others sent their pregnant women into another state that the children might not be free. An act of 1788 provided that births of children of slaves should be registered; that husband and wife were not to be separated more than ten miles without their consent; that pregnant females were not to be sent out of the state pending delivery. In 1816 it was decided that in certain cases if a fugitive slave bore a child in Pennsylvania the child was free.

XII. THE FAMILY MOTIVE IN SOUTHERN COLONIZATION

In the first settlement of Virginia no regard was given to family and no appeal was made to the family motive. The settlement was a camp rather than a colony. The early voyagers did not expect to tarry long in the new country and did not bring their families or establish their homes. Their intention was to make a fortune and then return to England. It is natural, therefore, that the settlement did not thrive. Byrd thinks it a pity that the adventurers looked askance at marriage with the Indians. Intermarriage, he thought, would have been a good means for the conversion of the natives and for the reconciliation of them to the loss of lands.[112] The natives were not averse to such unions[113] but it is to be feared that the Indian damsels would not have been adept at scouring dishes, darning hose, and the like.

A Spanish representative in England wrote in 1609 to Philip III. informing him that the English were about to send a few women to Virginia. He enclosed an advertisement inviting men and women of occupation "who wish to go out in the voyage for colonizing the country with people." In Virginia they would have houses, gardens, orchards, food, and clothing, a share of products, and a share in the division of the land for themselves and their heirs forever.

---

[112] Goodwin. *The Colonial Cavalier*, 45-46.

[113] *Letters from Virginia*, 167.

A letter of Gabriel Archer, on a voyage to Virginia in 1609, says: "We had twenty women and children." A minute of a letter of Philip III. to Don Gaspar de Pereda, from Madrid, February 20, 1611 indicates that the Ambassador in England had written the previous December that ships with three hundred men and a few women were to leave for Virginia. Toward the end of May, 1611 Sir Thomas Gates was sent with three ships and three caravels containing in all two hundred eighty men and two hundred women. The minutes of the meeting of the directors of the Virginia Company, November 3, 1619 record the need

> That a fitt hundreth might be sent of woemen, maids young and vncorrupt to make wives to the inhabitants and by that means to make the men there more settled and lesse moueable who by defect thereof (as is credibly reported) stay there but to get something and then to return for England, wch will breed a dissoluc̃on, and so an overthrow of the Plantac̃on. These woemen if they marry to the publiq ffarmers, to be transported at the charges of the company; if otherwise, then those that takes them to wife to pay the said company their charges of transportac̃on, and it was never fitter time to send them then nowe.

The "liberals," the business class, with business sense, had by this time captured the corporation; hence the saner economic judgment displayed. Sir Edwin Sandys of the company was able to see that the possibility of business success depended on making Virginia a country of homes. It was clear to him that the best way to make it a place of homes was to provide wives for the men. If they had wives and children depending on them they would work with better cheer and not pine for England when they should be giving all their energies to the work. With wife and children, home in Virginia would replace the English home in the affections of the emigrants. He arranged, accordingly, the plan of sending out young women as companions to the Virginia adventurers. Ninety came in the first installment. They were girls of good character, willing to become new-world wives. The would-be husbands each had to pay one hundred twenty pounds of tobacco which was the price of the passage over (about ninety dollars).

The purity of the imported wives was carefully guarded. Two transgressors were deported. Every precaution was taken to secure the happiness of the new wives.[114] It was ordered that

> In case they cannot be presently married, we desire that they may be put with several householders that have wives until they can be supplied with husbands. . . We desire that the marriages be free, according to nature and we would not have these maids deceived and married to servants, but only such freemen or tenants as have means to maintain them . . . not enforcing them to marry against their wills.

The results were most happy. So kindly were the maidens received that they wrote back and induced sixty more "young, handsome, and chaste" to come over for the same purpose. It was in connection with such a shipment that the company minutes note that if any died the charge was to be added to the rest.

Regarding the girls shipped over as wives old writers alleged that some were seized by fraud, trapanned in England; that unprincipled spirits "took up rich yeomans' daughters to serve his Majesty as breeders in Virginia unless they paid money for their release."[115] This is scarcely probable so far as the company's cargoes above mentioned are concerned. Those invoiced maidens seem to have had a square deal and the company was not interested in the prosperity of his Majesty.

[114] Cooke. *Virginia*, 120-122.

[115] Earle. *Colonial Dames and Goodwives*, 4.

Yet Bacon (a member of the royal council for the Virginia Company) did recognize the worth of such a move as the company made. In his *Essay on Plantations* (seemingly revised between 1620 and 1624, tho probably written earlier) he says: "When the plantation grows to strength, then it is time to plant with women as well as with men, that the plantation may spread into generations, and not be ever priced from without."

The scarcity of women naturally hastened the marriage of any that were available. Some families invited female relatives from England. These, of course, were soon married. The company discriminated in favor of married men. As an incentive to marriage married men were given preference in the selection of officers for the colony. Men with families began to come out from England. Their advent together with the shipment of wives and the previous abolition of communist living served to establish Virginia as a land of homes. The colony became settled and well-ordered. The careless adventurers were metamorphosed into responsible fathers of families anxious for the prosperity of a country that now seemed their own.

It was not necessary to continue permanently the importation of wives. It seems that a number of women of "the better class" came to Virginia with their husbands between 1617 and 1624. Immigrants presently sought marriage into the families of the older colonists. The English patrons encouraged this intermarriage as well as family migration as means of increasing the importance of the colony and thus enlarging dividends. Men of later generations wooed and won their wives in conventional fashion. By 1688 children, grandchildren, and great-grandchildren called Virginia their home and looked to England as the motherland.

The great bulk of the population of early Virginia was pure English. Almost always, persons of foreign origin took partners of Virginian or English birth. Thus the foreign blood was lost. The majority of the Virginia settlers were from the humbler ranks of life, including numbers of the stalwart yeomanry. Few men of rank ever came to the "wilderness of Virginia" and the planters were generally of bourgeois stock. Even cavaliers were not necessarily of noble blood. The leading families of Virginia had exactly the same origin as those of New England. The Virginia middle class sprang from free families of immigrants of humble means and origin, which migration began early and continued through the seventeenth century. The law allowing settlers fifty acres of land for each member of the family was an inducement. Many men barely able to pay their way came. The number of small grants in the first half of the seventeenth century was large. After the execution of Charles a host of royalists sought shelter in America and the immigration of this class continued even after the Restoration. The influx of well-to-do is marked by a sudden rise in the size of land grants and in the number of slaves.[116]

Enthusiasts in eugenics catch eagerly at this straw. For the eddies of chaff that swirled to Virginia were considerable. We find the council of Virginia early complaining that

> It hurteth to suffer parents to disburden themselves of lascivious sonnes, masters of bad servants and wives of ill husbands, and so clogge the business with such an idle crue, as did thrust them-

[116] See Bruce, *Social Life of Virginia in the Seventeenth Century*, 250-251; Wertenbaker, *Patrician and Plebeian in Virginia*, vol. v, 4-5, 28, 143, 160; Yonge, *Site of Old "James Towne,"* 139; Ross, *Origins of the American People*, 712-713.

selves in the last voiage, that will rather starve for hunger than lay their hands to labor.[117]

In 1618 Bridget Gray informed the Privy Council that her grandson, John Throckmorton, was in Newgate for stealing and begged that he might be delivered to Sir Thomas Smith and be deported beyond the seas. In 1637 the collector of the port of London affirmed that "most of those that go thither [to Virginia] ordinarily have no habitation . . . and are better out than within the kingdom."[118] From the beginning of the plantation in Virginia, it had been the policy of the company to send thither poor children. For fifty years indentured servants came – from one thousand to sixteen hundred a year. Slum and alley sewage fertilized the plantations. Men sold dependent kindred to the colonies. Boys and girls were spirited from English streets for "the plantations can not be maintained without a considerable number of white servants." And America was a convenient dump for criminals.

Sponsors of Virginia's aristocracy console themselves with the thought that a large proportion of these seemingly "undesirable citizens" were unfortunate rather than depraved, and with the belief that natural selection eliminated or reduced the worst strains. The scarcity of women "made it impossible for the degraded laborer, even tho he ultimately secured his freedom, to leave descendants to perpetuate his lowly instincts."[119] The wilder spirits took to the woods where death-rate was high. Thus the alleged blue-blood had an easier task in its breeding of "a germ plasm which easily developed such traits as good manners, high culture and the ability to lead in all social affairs – traits combined

117 Ross, *op. cit.*, 712.

118 — Idem.

119 Wertenbaker. *Patrician and Plebeian in Virginia*, 176.

in a remarkable degree in the first families of Virginia."[120]

The dearth of careers in England, especially for younger sons, contributed to the peopling of Virginia and also of Maryland. The settlers of Maryland were for a long time of a sort very desirable in a new colony. Able and industrious young men whose purpose was to work, to secure homesteads, and to rear families strengthened the colony. There were also men of means, who came with wives and children. The colony encouraged family migration. A man bringing over his wife and children was allowed one hundred acres each for self and wife and fifty for each child. A woman coming with children received land for herself and them. For every woman servant brought, the master could claim sixty acres.

There was opportunity in Maryland. The young fellow that came penniless in 1634 might by 1660 be a prosperous country gentleman surrounded by broad acres belonging to himself and sons, their farms girdling his, and his family related by marriage with the neighbors for miles around.

The author of *Leah and Rachel* [Virginia and Maryland], (1655) gives this advice to prospective immigrants:

> [It it better for any one going over free, but poor, to hire for wages the first year if he strikes an honest home] where the mistresse is noted for a good housewife, of which there are very many (notwithstanding the cry to the contrary) for by that means he will live free of disbursement, have something to help him the next year and be carefully looked to in [sickness]. Now for those that carry over families and estates with a determination to inhabit, my advice is that they neither sojourn, for that will be chargeable; nor on the sudden purchase . . .

[120] Davenport. *Heredity in Relation to Eugenics*, 207.

but that they for the first year hire a house (for seats are always to be hired) and by that means they will not only find content and learn the worth and goodness of the plantation they mean to purchase.

The Carolina project made direct appeal to the family motive. Robert Horne writing in 1664 of the Cape Fear country says that younger brothers can come over there and found families. Among the privileges granted to Carolina settlers in 1666 were the following:

Every free man and free woman, that transport themselves and servants by the 25th of March . . . 1667, shall have for himself, wife, children, and men-servants, for each 100 acres of land for him and his heirs forever, and for every woman servant and slave, 50 acres paying at most ½d. per acre per annum in lieu of all demands, to the lords proprietors.

After 1667 in South Carolina the allotment to immigrants was: to each free person fifty acres; to every man servant and marriageable woman servant whom he brought, the same. In 1671 an allowance of land was made for every person in each family settling on a certain creek. Again there was promised to every freeman settler before March 25, 1672, one hundred acres, one hundred for every man servant, seventy for a woman servant or a man under sixteen, and seventy to every servant when his time was up. Families in groups of eight might settle in such places as they chose. Thomas Ashe, clerk on the ship Richmond, 1682, wrote:

His majesty to improve so hopeful a design [wine culture] gave the French we carried over, their passage free for themselves, their wives, children, goods, and servants.

The moderate allowances made to real family settlers were insufficient to suit would-be exploiters. In 1755 there came before the king a representation from Governor Dobbs of North Carolina to the effect that wealthy settlers wanted to come but were not satisfied with the one hundred acres for master or mistress and fifty for each child. It was thought desirable that not over six hundred forty acres should be given to each person able to cultivate the same. Doubtless this recommendation was too meager to satisfy the prospective plutocrats.

South Carolina, in her zeal for population, offered bounties that must have been very attractive to persons with families. Milligan in 1763 gave the schedule as follows: For children under two years, one pound; two to twelve years, two pounds; persons over twelve years, four pounds. Royal land offers were still in force.

Carolina drew a motley population – English, Scotch, Scotch-Irish, German, Irish, Swiss, Huguenot. All these strains merged into one in the process of time. The Huguenots for a time were treated meanly, doubtless from envy of their superior economic qualities. In South Carolina in 1693 they were threatened with the loss of their estates at death because they were foreigners.[121] The proprietors reassured them on this point. The Huguenots wished to forget France. In Charleston the children of the refugees were not appreciably different from the English. Successful Huguenots tended to intermarry in English families for the sake of social prestige. Moreover Huguenot names were anglicized thus obscuring the history of families. For a long while the Santee Huguenots intermarried mainly among themselves. Not before the end of the second generation did the French on the Santee merge with the English. Even then the blending was not complete. At the end of the colonial period the Carolinas con-

[121] Huguenot Society of South Carolina, *Transactions*, 61-62, 67-68.

tained many villages whose inhabitants were all Huguenots or all Highlanders.

In Georgia, as elsewhere, the strongest appeals were made to the family interest. Oglethorpe in 1732 set forth that a family of father, mother, and child over seven, able to earn in England say ten pounds per year, all told, while it cost them twenty pounds to live, could in Georgia produce a gross value (including land yield) of sixty pounds per year. This beautiful prospect for a man with only one-fourth of normal earning power is figured out thus: He will be assigned a lot of about fifty acres. The usual wage of common labor in Carolina is three shillings per day.

> Our poor man . . . at about 9d. per day earns about £12 per annum, his care of stock on his land in his hours of resting from labor (amount to ½ of each day) is worth also £12 per annum. His wife and eldest child may easily between them earn as much as the man.

Provisions will be cheap.

Benjamin Martyn wrote booming the Georgia settlement and picturing the Georgia that was to be: "Women and children feeding and nursing the silkworms, winding off the silk, or gathering the olives;" men "in content and affluence, and masters of little possessions which they can leave their children." The picture is an attractive contrast to their condition in England, a prey to want and "hunger, and seeing their wives and children in the same distress."

In addition to very liberal food allowances, provision was made for sending to Georgia on charity "such as have numerous families of children, if assisted by their respective parishes, and recommended by the minister, church-warden, and overseers thereof." On the voyage to America the German dissenters were given spaces according to families. The single men were located by themselves. The women were given thread, worsted, and knitting needles, and they were required to employ their "leisure time in making stockings and caps for their family, or in mending their cloaths and linnen."

"The difficulties of the southern settlement" were considered "almost insuperable to women and children." But new settlers, after consulting their wives and families, resolved to go on to Frederica, as brothers, sons, and servants were gone before and it would be base to forsake them.

The *True Narration of Georgia* published at Charleston in 1741 purports to expose the fraudulence of claims made for the new colony. The author quotes the calculation as to the "poor man's" magnified earning powers in Georgia and asserts that very soon after the settlement numbers of people left the province being unable to support their families there. Among the causes of the "Ruin of Georgia" he cites the restricting of land tenure so as to cut off daughters and other relatives from succession in default of male heirs. In that case land reverted to the trustees. It was urged also that "the extent of possessions" was too much restricted, "it being impossible that fifty acres of good land, much less pine barren, could maintain a white family." Finding it hard to support their families settlers hesitated to remain in the colony. Alarmed at the prospect of depopulation the magistrates joined the free-holders in and about Savannah in petitioning the trustees for title in fee simple and the use of negroes.[122] Right of inheritance in lieu of male heirs was presently granted to

[122] Arthur and Carpenter. *History of Georgia*, 41, 47.

daughters as will appear in a later chapter; moreover provision was made for grants larger than fifty acres.

The trustees showed a willingness to make concessions to the family interest. The minutes of the trustees for July 26, 1742, show a petition of Christian Steinharrel, Theobald Keifer, etc., in behalf of the German servants in Savannah indented to the trustees. Their term was about to expire but their sons were bound to serve till twenty-five, and the girls till eighteen. The parents wanted to settle in Georgia and had some cattle but "they must unavoidably labor under great difficulties by being deprived of the freedom of their children, without whose assistance it will be impossible for them to make any progress in cultivating the land, being most of them advanced in years." They prayed for the freedom of their children to take effect at the time when their own indentures should expire. The trustees resolved to recommend to the council to grant the petition.

As previously observed English primogeniture drove younger sons across the ocean. In Georgia gentle stock and serf lineage dressed alike, married and intermarried.

As indicated in the account of Virginia the failure of the family interest was a factor also in the peopling of the South. Recreant husbands and wives could escape justice by coming to America. The Mayor of Bristol in 1662 said: "Among these who repair to Bristol" for America "some are husbands that have forsaken their wives, others wives who have abandoned their husbands, some are children and apprentices run away from their parents and masters." Bishop Spangenberg (Moravian) in his *Journal of Travels in North Carolina* (1752) noted that some of the people "have left a wife and children elsewhere." Some involuntary immigrants to America were persons whose marital partners or other relatives, for reasons of their own, contrived to have them deported.[123] New World settlers removed thus from all restraints of family were exposed to divers temptations. Yet such cases as these do not obscure the eminence of the family motive in American colonization.

The family interest was prominent in migration to the frontier. At the beginning of the eighteenth century as inducement to settlers to migrate to Western Virginia every male or female coming into the frontier colony was to have fifty acres. Families were to have fifty for each member. Villages did not spring up as had been expected. Presbyterians and others did come as settlers. The Presbyterian congregations in Virginia sought wilderness homes "where every man's cabin might stand upon his own acres." Pioneer families moved in companies or fixed their abodes in neighborhoods for defence and for social and religious privileges. In some places intermarriage merged groups of different sects. Thus the family appears as the shaper of the new people.

As the hunter penetrated the western wilds and found game abundant he thought to himself, "Well now, if I had the old woman and babies here, I should be fixed." Special inducements were offered to draw population westward. In 1776 Virginia offered each family settling vacant lands on waters of the Mississippi four hundred acres and to families who, for greater safety, had settled together and worked the land in common a town site of six hundred forty acres was given and a further grant of four hundred acres contiguous to town to each family on consideration of such settlement.

[123] Morton. *History of Highland County*, 44-45.

XIII. FAMILISM AND HOME LIFE IN THE COLONIAL SOUTH

The life of the Southern family, at least on the coastal plain, was very different from that of the North Atlantic section. Especially in Maryland and tidewater Virginia did plantation life prevail. The plantations tended to isolation and self-support. They were isolated because tobacco soon sapped the fertility of the soil and made it necessary to seek fresh fields. Old grounds were left to revert to wilderness. Thus plantations were often separated by belts of forest. The estates had to be independent, for roads were poor and communication was often directly with England by means of vessels coming up the streams to the plantation docks.

Domestic industry was a matter of course. In old Virginia female slaves and white servants wove coarse cloth and fashioned it into suits. Cotton spinning was a home industry. Artisans were to be found among the indentured servants. Washington's plantation at Mt. Vernon was a specimen of the self-sufficing estate. He had a smithy, charcoal-burners, brickmakers, carpenters, masons, a flour-mill, coopers, and a vessel to carry produce to market. He also employed shoemakers and operated a weaving establishment.

The importation of white slaves was promoted by the fact that the immigrant to the South might secure for himself additional land for every servant brought over.

The condition and treatment of bond-servants was variable. Redemptioners were often separated from their family. Alsop, a redemptioner who came in 1658, paints the position of a servant in Maryland in the brightest colors as far better than that of an apprentice or young craftsman in London. He argues in favor of the indenture of children as a means of giving them a place in the world. It has been suggested that his work is perhaps a paid-for puff of Maryland in the interest of the proprietor and merchant adventurers. Opinion differs on this point.

The author of *Leah and Rachel* reports that in Virginia

> The women are not (as is reported) put into the ground to worke, but occupie such domestique imployments and housewifery as in England, that is dressing victuals, righting up the house, milking, imployed about dayries, washing, sewing, etc., and both men and women have times of recreation, as much or more than in any part of the world besides, yet some wenches that are nasty, beastly, and not fit to be so imployed are put into the ground, for reason tells us, they must not at charge be transported and then maintained for nothing, but those that prove so aukward are rather burdensome then servants desirable or useful.

In Maryland of 1679,

> The servants and negros, after they have worn themselves down the whole day . . . have yet to grind and pound the grain . . . for their masters and all their families, as well as themselves and all the negros.

A letter from Savannah dated 1741 reads:

> The trustees German servants in general behave well and are industrious: of these, eight or ten families are more remarkably so, and have this last year purchased a good stock of cattle, some having six cows, the least two; and each having a garden, where they raise some corn, peas, pumpkins, potatoes, etc., which with the milk of their cows is the chief part of their food; they are at little expense for clothing.

On the St. Johns River in Florida was placed, during the English régime following 1763, a colony of people from the Mediterranean. They were "obliged to indent themselves, their wives and children for many years." They were given

> A pitiful portion of land for ten years . . . this being improved and just rendered fit for cultivation, at the end of that time it reverts to the original grantor, and the grantee may, if he chooses, begin a new state of vassalage for ten years more. Many were denied even such grants as these, and were obliged to work in the manner of negroes, a task in the field . . . instead of allowing each family to do with their homely fare as they pleased, they were forced to join altogether in one mess, and at the beat of a vile drum, to come to one common copper, from whence their hominy was ladled out to them.

In Virginia all servants and apprentices were to be taught along with their master's children every Sunday "just before evening prayer" by the minister of the parish. In view of the shady character of many servants in the South such a measure was perhaps appropriate. The shortage of good servants constituted a Southern household problem.

Geniality of climate worked against frugality. The appearance of opulence on the large plantation is illustrated in the following entry in 1772 by a southern gentleman:

> This day I went to see my plantations under John E. Beale. . . Jack lives well; but I was sorry to see his wife act the part of a fine lady in all her wearing aparell, with at least two maids besides her own girl to get the dinner and wait upon her; but this I do suppose she did to show her respect; however, I had rather have seen the diligent, industrious woman.

It was intended to make Georgia a colony of home industry.

> A man with his son, or a servant, may, without much trouble, gather leaves sufficient for as many worms as he can keep. His wife and daughter or a servant maid may feed and attend the worms as they are within doors.

The southern planter could turn only to his family for regular companionship. Conditions promoted that patriarchal régime with strong feeling for family ties so typical of Maryland and tidal Virginia and indeed of the plantation South in general.

The "family" might assume large proportions. An act of the Virginia Assembly, 1640, held every master of family responsible for the military service of each of its members, the "family" including servants but not blacks. Of North Carolina in 1752 Bishop Spangenberg wrote:

> If a man of family . . . does not appear before a justice . . . once a year, and render an account of all taxable property . . . also the names and ages of all persons of his household who are taxable, be they white or black, shall pay a fine of forty shillings, and for every month that it is neglected, twenty shillings more.

A Georgia letter of 1740 runs thus:

> I have this day . . . inquired at Mr. Whitefields (who has by far the largest family of any in this colony consisting of nearly 150 persons) and received the following account . . . that their family consists of 60 persons, including bond servants, 61 orphans and other poor children, 25 working tradesmen, and others, in all 146, exclusive of many others, who have remained at their house a month, two or three months at a time (and have been accounted to be of their family) and that all the family are in good health.

The influence of family connection was strong in all the old colonies. Virginia saw the rise of families of gentry who intermarried for generations and built up a landed aristocracy. Family life and ties reached strong development in Virginia. Every person desired to found a family or spread the influence of the one he had. Relationship was noted to a degree that made the term "Virginia cousin" a symbol for remote kinship. A strong caste spirit grew up. The leading

Virginians of a later day were proud to trace their pedigree. Coats of arms were esteemed. The vastness of available lands held in abeyance during the seventeenth century the disposition to magnify the social standing of a family by the cult of primogeniture but there was a potent desire to promote family distinction by monopoly of as many public offices as possible. From 1670 to 1691 every official position in Henrico County was filled by a member of the Randolph family or of two other families. Four families got most of the military offices of the county. Similar conditions prevailed in all the older counties where certain families had been long enough to establish powerful social and political connections. Thus colonial Virginia developed a privileged hereditary bureaucracy so that offices were handed from father to son and the social system became fossilized with the impedimenta of lineage.

It was inevitable that as soon as untaken land began to be relatively scarce, a tendency toward soil engrossment within the family would develop. This trend was not altogether due to direct economic considerations. It was in some degree an inheritance of the English idea that the ownership of large lands was the surest foundation of family aristocracy. Jefferson in his *Memoirs* wrote:

> At the time of the first settlement of the English in Virginia, when land was had for little or nothing, some provident persons having obtained large grants of it, and being desirous of maintaining the splendor of their families, entailed their property on their descendants. The transmission of these estates from generation to generation, to men who bore the same name, had the effect of raising up a distinct class of families, who, possessing by law the privilege of perpetuating their wealth, formed by these means a sort of patrician order, distinguished by the grandeur and luxury of their establishments.

Nearly all the extensive Virginia estates were obtained by corrupt means. On one occasion Fairfax as proprietor made a grant of three hundred thousand acres to his nephew who promptly and fraudulently reconveyed it to Fairfax as his own. Thus was laid in fraud the basis of family prestige and fortunes in the colonies – a factor of great influence on later American affairs.[124]

English primogeniture does not appear to have been in general operation in the seventeenth century. Real estate was not yet sufficiently valuable to constitute a rare distinction and there was a dearth of mechanical trades for younger sons. Generally sons shared equally. Often the oldest son was allowed first voice in the division of the estate.[125] Among the early Eastern-Shoremen the practice of dividing estates among children before decease was common. They did not greatly favor the doctrine of primogeniture. The first entail mentioned as occurring in that region took place in 1653 and entails were relatively rare.[126]

But the illiberal spirit took strong hold of Virginia. A York County man in 1688 bequeathed all lands and tenements to his eldest son *in ventre*, the living children being daughters. In England the courts could cut off entails; but an old Virginia law of 1705 forbade this course except by express act of the legislature.[127] Thus Virginia feudalism outdistanced that of England. Virginia in the eighteenth century continued patriarchal. No creditor could touch the great estate. It was entailed on the eldest son. This system of artificial aristocracy prevailed until the American Revolution. But

---

124 Myers. *History of the Supreme Court*, 22-27.

125 Bruce. *Social Life of Virginia in the Seventeenth Century*, 126-127

126 Wise. *Ye Kingdom of Accawmacke*, 319.

127 Cooke. *Virginia*, 445.

in case of intestates the law in force at the middle of the eighteenth century gave one third to the widow and divided the rest equally among the children with special privilege to the heir-at-law. Moreover most of the distinguished families of the colony degenerated.[128]

In Maryland from the first settlement until American independence lands followed, in case of intestacy, the English law of primogeniture but parents commonly devised tracts of land to their younger sons and often to their daughters. Men of large estate not infrequently gave property to a "beloved son-in-law," thus bestowing a marriage portion on a daughter. But generally fathers bequeathed the home plantation to the oldest son. In the absence of a will he inherited everything. The widow received one third of the land and a dower house which she occupied when the heir came of age or married and took possession of the mansion. English entail kept lands for many generations in the straight male line inalienable save by payment of a fine to the proprietary.

The homestead of the small Maryland farmer was, in its way, what his rich neighbor's plantation was on a larger scale. It too was largely independent – a little community. On both, interest and devotion centered in the family. The children grew up and spread the area of cultivation and when they married settled on the land. But the manors were soon divided among the different descendants of the original proprietors. The last one was broken up by the death of Charles Carroll of Carrollton at the end of the first third of the nineteenth century. Thus schemes for medieval aristocracy came to naught.

The failure of feudal principles in Maryland and

[128] Wertenbaker. *Patrician and Plebeian in Virginia*, 139-141.

Virginia and the noteworthy collapse of the medieval project for feudalism in the Carolinas illustrate the futility of dreaming the establishment of social structures without the requisite economic base or their perpetuation after that base is gone. One can not create feudalism with a sparse population in a limitless land; nor can primogeniture persist when land is too plentiful to be a great prize, and when there is lack of soft openings for younger sons.

North Carolina developed on more uncouth lines than its neighbors. The people lived in isolated independence, each family apart on its small farm in the midst of dense swamps and wilds, responsible only to itself. The living came largely from hunting, with a little agriculture, a large part of which was performed by the women. German settlers began settling western North Carolina about 1750. Among them the paternal abode generally passed to one child; other children built near by. Land seldom passed from family to family. In many instances the descendants of the pioneers continued on the ancestral homesteads at least until recent times.

In none of the southern colonies was city life important save in South Carolina. At Charleston lived the wealthiest planters. They were more prosperous and independent than those in the colonies farther north, who in spite of their apparent wealth were generally deep in debt and frequently fell into bankruptcy due to wasteful agricultural methods, speculative disposition, reckless habits, and expensive tastes.[129] The unhealthful climate in the rice lands of South Carolina forced the planters to live in town. Even then exposure to disease and hard living killed off the men so rapidly

[129] Thwaites. *The Colonies*, 98, 107.

that it was common for a woman to have several successive husbands.

Fraud was present in the acquisition of great Carolina and Georgia estates. Governor Wright wrote from Savannah to the Lords of Trade, 1763, referring to the "very extraordinary procedure of the Governor of South Carolina" in allowing a few to monopolize the most valuable areas.

> I say, my lords, this procedure has struck a general damp and dispirited the whole province. . . . An extension of the limits to the southward, if the lands were properly parcelled out to people who would really cultivate and improve them, would draw some thousand inhabitants here; whereas, by this step taken in Carolina, great part of the lands, my lords, are ordered in large tracts to some wealthy settlers in Carolina, who probably will never see it themselves, and some of whom, it is said, have already more lands in that province than they can cultivate or improve. This, my lords, is pretty well known on this side of the water; and who, having a great number of slaves, claim what they call their family right, that is, fifty acres of land for each slave, although it is highly probable that their ancestors had land for those very slaves, and it is well understood here that many of those persons, especially those who have the largest tracts, have no intention to remove here or settle them; but probably some years hence, when it begins to get valuable, will sell it, and in the meantime those vast tracts of land are to lie waste and unimproved, as very great bodies yet do in Carolina, and if they should do anything at all with those lands, it is expected that it will only be by sending an overseer and a few negros [as a technical occupation of the land].

The problem of family interest in land tenure and the question of primogeniture caused great concern in the Georgia colony, especially as it was a military outpost against Spain. Four of the colonists before going asked that daughters might inherit as well as sons and that widows' dower be considered. It was

> Agreed that the persons who now go over, and desire the same,

> shall have the priviledge of naming a successor to the lands granted them, who in case they die without issue male, shall enjoy the same to them and their heirs male for ever. Agreed that the widows shall have their thirds as in England.

The Trustees in a later account of the colony give as the reason for first "making it tail *male*" the need of soldiers.

Moore in his *Voyage to Georgia* (his trip began in 1735 and he published his account in 1744), wrote:

> All lots are granted in tail male, and descend to the heirs male of their bodies forever. . . [In default of male heirs, lands revert to the Trust to be granted as seems best.] They will have a special regard to the daughters of freeholders who have made improvements on their lots, not already provided for, by having married, or marrying persons in possessions, or entitled to lands in the province of Georgia, in possession or remainder. . . The wives of the freeholders, in case they should survive their husbands, are, during their lives, entitled to the mansion house, and one half of the lands improved by their husbands. . . In order to maintain many people, it was proper that the land should be divided into small portions, and to prevent uniting them by marriage or purchase. . . They suffered the moiety of the lots to descend to the widows during their lives: those who remarried to men who had lots of their own by uniting two lots made one to be neglected. . . These uncleared lots are a nuisance to their neighbors. . . The quantity of land by experience seems rather too much (50 acres) since it is impossible that one poor family can tend so much land. . . The trustees grant the land in tail male, that on the expiring of a male line they may regrant it to such man, having no other lot, as shall be married to the next female heir of the deceased, as is of good character.

The restrictions, as noted previously, aroused resentment. In a letter to Oglethorpe, "the Plain-dealer" wrote:

> I shall suppose that, were full and ample rights given, that some idle persons, who had no judgment to value, or inclina-

> tion to improve their properties, no affections for their families or relations, might dispose of their rights for a glass of rum; but I absolutely deny, that the colony could lose by such an exchange. I own such persons were much safer if bound than at liberty; but where the affection of the parent and the reason of the man die, the person is a fitter inhabitant for Moorfields than Georgia. I must notice further, that not only are parents incapable for want of credit, to provide for themselves, being necessitated to dispose of their servants for want of provisions; but if they could, only their eldest son could reap the benefit; their younger children, however numerous, are left to be fed by Him who feeds the ravens; and if they have no children, their labor and substance descends to strangers. How, sir, could you, or indeed any free-born spirit, brook such a tenor? Are not our younger children and daughters equally entitled to our bowels and affections? And does human nature end with our first, and not extend itself to the rest of our progeny and more distant relations? And is it not inverting the order of nature, that the eldest son should not only enjoy a double portion, but exclude all the younger children? and having an interest independent of the parents', how natural is it he should withdraw that obedience and subjection which proceeds from paternal authority and filial dependence!

This remonstrance was included in the *True and Historical Narration* by several landholders in Georgia printed in Charleston, 1741.

In 1739 the trustees had revised the law so as to allow the widow to enjoy, if there were children, a moiety of the property during her life and, if no children, all of it. This grant was to be void if she remarried, unless the new husband would give security to keep the property in good condition, and then it was to go to her heirs. Further if any tenant died without male heirs, any daughter might hold all (in tail male), if not over eighty acres, and if there was more than that amount, it might be held by one or more daughters designated by will. In default of such apportionment the eldest daughter was to hold in tail male. If there was no issue the man might will the land in tail. In case of intestacy the property went to the heir at law. No devise was to be made of over eighty acres or less than fifty to one person. No person could enjoy a devise if it increased his estate to over five hundred acres. Martyn in the *Impartial Inquiry*, written in 1741, said:

> The daughter of a freeholder, or any other person, is made capable of enjoying by inheritance a devise of lands, provided that it does not increase her or his possessions to more than 2000 acres.

These changes had not come about without considerable agitation. When concessions were made they were alleged to be too complex to be understood. The animus of the campaign can be gathered from the complaint that "several of the houses which were built by freeholders, for want of heirs male, are fallen to the trustees."

The scope and influence of family relationship was great in the South. Sometimes several brothers came together to America. In many cases men of wealth brought over their young kinsmen and friends, for each of whom, in Maryland, they received fifty acres of land. (There the larger the family group the better. Poor kinsfolk were welcome assets.) There it was customary for such a "servant" to receive the fifty acres on reaching freedom. Redemptioners signed in Europe contracts that surviving members of a family must make good the loss of ones dying *en voyage*. So a wife that lost her husband or her children would be sold for five years for her own voyage and additional years for the fare of her dead husband or children tho they had died at the very start of the voyage.

Ties persisted between English and American branches of families. In seventeenth century Virginia there were numerous bequests from the colonial branch of a family to the English. Often Virginia children were commended to the care of their kindred oversea while pursuing education at an English school. These trans-oceanic relations were hard to maintain in that day of slow transit. In Maryland false claims to property were frequently made in the absence of the rightful heirs abroad.

The dominance of familism in the colonial South was promoted by rural isolation as has been seen. Landed gentry had family burying-grounds on their own estates. Hugh Jones wrote regretfully of this individualism: "It is customary to bury in garden, or orchards, where whole families lye interred together . . . the graves kept decently." Some of the German settlers in western North Carolina had family graveyards. It could scarcely be expected that plantation dwellers on widely separated estates and remote pioneers would observe the institution of burial in church grounds.

Early Virginia legislation showed a disposition to promote familism. By acts of 1623-1624

> All the old planters that were here before or came in at the last coming of Sir Thomas Gates they and their posterity shall be exempted from their personal service to the warrs and any public charge (church duties excepted) that belong particularly to their persons (not exempting their families) except such as shall be employed to command in chief.

In 1631 the phrase "they and their posterity" was struck out.

About the time that Puritanism was getting hold in Massachusetts, Virginia enacted blue laws: Men were to dress according to rank and the law of 1619 provided

> Against excesse in apparell that every man be cessed in the

church for all publique contributions, if he be unmarried according to his owne apparell, if he be married according to his owne and his wives, or either of their apparell.

We read of charming family relations in the colonial South. Life at the South was grander, shabbier, and more genial than in the Puritan commonwealths. Home rather than church was the shrine of the colonial cavalier, notwithstanding his nominal reverence for "mother church." It was at home that most christenings and funerals occurred and Hugh Jones complained that "in houses they most commonly marry."

The Virginia planter on his manor surrounded by his family and retainers was a feudal lord. At the great Christmas festival around the huge log fires gathered the family clan. It was a time of joy for high and low. This plantation life in a mild climate and cut off from the great world gave rise to the greater geniality of southern family relations and to the deep attachment to the soil, so proverbial in those regions. Coaches of four rolled from the doors of the aristocracy. Profusion of gold and silver plate shone on the boards even while the Declaration of Independence in high-sounding phrase voiced the stage-play theories of make-believe "democracy." More than a hundred years earlier the English people had been informed:

Your ordinary houses in England are not so handsome [as the houses in Virginia] for usually the rooms are large, daubed and white-washed, glazed and flowered, and if not glazed windows, shutters which are made very pretty and convenient.

Soil engrossment was a means to that isolation of dwelling that has always appealed to the Englishman. No hedge or walls were needed in Virginia. Hill and grove furnished natural screens. The secluded life intensified hospitality as well as family affection. As houses were small and families large, bed-rooms were overcrowded in early colonial days.[130] Governor Berkeley's home at Green Spring had only six rooms and a hall. The planters found it necessary to put beds in every room save the kitchen. In the parlor might be found not only beds but chests of clothing and linen. An account of the eastern shore of Virginia (seventeenth century) says that there seem to have been few homes at that time without musical instruments. The James River mansions and others that survive were erected in the eighteenth century.

Rude tenant huts about the southern mansions formed sharp contrast to the relative grandeur of aristocratic life. But for many years in Virginia wages were high; so that laborers could accumulate means to buy a farm.[131] Squatters were sometimes driven from homes and farms.

Colonial Virginia was well supplied with taverns, or grog shops. The use of liquor was general. The development of high class hotels was retarded by the fact that the presence of strangers was a welcome break in the montony of plantation life and hence the traveler need not pay for accommodations. A Virginia act of 1663 throws interesting side-light on the entertainment of strangers:

> Whereas it is frequent with divers inhabitants of this country to entertain strangers into their home without making any agreement with the party what he shall pay for his accomodations, which (if the party live) causes many litigous suites, and if the stranger dye lays a gap open to many avaricious persons to injure the estate of the person deceased, ffor remedy whereof for the future, be it enacted that noe person not making a positive agreement with any one he shall entertayne into his home for diet or storeage shall recover anything against any

[130] Wertenbaker. *Patrician and Plebeian in Virginia*, 113; Yonge. *Site of Old "James Towne,"* 141.

[131] Wertenbaker, *op. cit.*, 183-184.

one soe entertayned. or against his estate, but that every one shall be reputed to entertayne those of curtesie with whom they make not a certain agreement.

Early Maryland did not differ from Virginia in pride of birth and family. There are strong proofs of family affection. Deeds of gift of large lands to sons and daughters for "natural love and affection" show us the human side of remote forbears. Sons were not expected to wait till their parents' death before having a home of their own. Fathers encouraged sons to marry early; this was easy with a good plantation. Daughters were endowed with land at the time of marriage. Many homes originating thus are still the foundation of family pride after nine generations. Hospitality to friends ran high. Home life was fuller in those early days, the days on which ideals of home life ground. Yet no modern town could equal Annapolis in the proportion of club life.[132]

The Huguenots embellished society with the courtesies and graces of domestic life. J. A. Johnson says:

When the writer on the South wants characters for a story of domestic joy and content, and that cause life to run smoothly into a green old age – an age crowned with the glory of children's children – he can turn to old Huguenot life at Bordeaux in Abbeville County.

In the later eighteenth century wealthy families of Charleston kept open house. One merchant had "guests almost every day at one or more of the four meals." He had to entertain ship captains and the like. Perhaps Huguenot influence cherishing French usage had something to do with society standards. On the eve of the Revolution marriages were formal affairs requiring consultation of parents and guardians, and approbation of the family.

---

[132] Fisher. *Men, Women, and Manners in Colonial Times*, vol. ii, 207.

XIV. SOUTHERN COLONIAL COURTSHIP AND MARRIAGE AS SOCIAL INSTITUTIONS

As commonly in new countries so in the American South marriage was highly esteemed. The foundation was early laid for that conservatism that even yet characterizes southern marriage.

The exigencies and opportunities of pioneer life operated to produce universal, early, and repeated marriage. The colonial maiden came into society and married with astonishing precocity. In seventeenth century Virginia if the father made a gift to his daughter it was customary to insert a proviso in case she married before sixteen. In one clandestine marriage in Northhampton County the wife was not past her twelfth year. Chief Justice Marshall met and fell in love with his wife when she was fourteen and married her at sixteen. In North Carolina cheap lands and large families promoted early marriage of the children. Marriage at thirteen was not very unusual and at fifteen was most common. Doctor Brickell, who practised in North Carolina at Edenton about 1731, wrote: "They marry generally very young, some at thirteen or fourteen, and she that continues unmarried until twenty, is reckoned a stale maid, which is a very indifferent character in that country." A colonial spinster of over twenty-five was regarded as a hopeless and confirmed old maid.

Men also married at an early age. But marriage was

less essential to a man and some males began to see advantages in single life. Colonial Maryland was marked by the number of adult unmarried sons living at home. Bachelors, along with light wines and billiard tables, were taxed for the French war. There were many to pay the tax. Between 1755 and 1763 there were in the parish of St. Thomas thirty-nine recorded bachelors. St. Anne's parish vestry books show thirty-four bachelors subject to the colony tax on unmarried men over twenty-five. The tax was scarcely heavy enough to promote marriage: five shillings on estates under three hundred pounds sterling and twenty shillings on larger estates. This burden was a small one compared to the cares of a household.

It may be that celibacy indicated inability to meet the growing demands of luxury. The Abbé Robin at a later date says of Annapolis: "Female luxury here exceeds what is known in the provinces of France. A French hair-dresser is a man of importance, it is said a certain dame here, hires one of that craft at a thousand crowns a year salary." George Grieve, an Englishman, writing of the Revolutionary period, said:

> The rage for dress amongst the women in America, in the very height of the miseries of the war, was beyond all bounds; nor was it confined to the great towns, it prevailed equally on the sea-coasts, and in the woods and solitudes of the vast extent of country from Florida to New Hampshire. . . In travelling into the interior parts of Virginia I spent a delicious day at an inn, at the ferry of the Shenandoah . . . with the most engaging, accomplished and voluptuous girls, the daughters of the landlord, a native of Boston transplanted thither; who with all the gifts of nature possessed the arts of dress not unworthy of Parisian milliners, and went regularly three times a week . . . seven miles, to attend the lessons of one De Grace, a French dancing master, who was making a fortune in the country.

There is a suggestion that women, as well as men were supposed to be in danger of perverse neglect to marry. It must have been a feeling that unmarried females were anomalous that led to the early Maryland law:

> That it may be prevented that noe woman here vow chastity in the world, unless she marry within seven years after land fall to her, she must either dispose away of hir land, or else she shall forfeite it to the next of kinne, and if she have but one mannor, whereas she cannot alienate it, it is gonne unless she git a husband.

Thomas Copley wrote to Lord Baltimore:

> To what purpose this ole law is maid your lorpe perhaps will see better than I for my part I see great difficultys in it, but to what purpose I well see not.

He must have been very obtuse in view of the fact that celibacy was out of place in a new country needing people. In 1642 there were four female householders numbered among taxable citizens.

The precocity of colonial marriage allowed time for repetitions of the act. Many of the Virginia girls that married in childhood and assumed the burdens of family at so immature an age became broken in health and after bearing a dozen children died leaving their husbands to marry again and beget new broods perhaps as large as the first. On the eastern shore of Virginia in the seventeenth century it was not remarkable for a man to have three or four successive wives. There were instances of Virginians married six times. It is not unusual to find a colonial dame that was married four times. Few conspicuous colonial men in Virginia, at least, lived beyond middle life; most died short of it. The malarial climate, exposure, and reckless habits cut them off. The young and attractive widows need not remain long forlorn in a country with a preponderance of males, at least if the feminine charms were supplemented by a fine plantation. Sometimes the relay was so close that the second husband was granted the probate of the will of the first. In one case funeral baked meats furnished the marriage table. One husband left all the estate to his wife's children by her next marriage. Quickness of remarriage does not indicate callousness but rather the woman's need of protection on the plantation and of an overseer for the work.[133]

A noticeable feature of colonial Virginia was the belleship of widows.[134] Maidens seem not to have been "in it." As we come toward the Revolution the widows still reign supreme. It may be that the larger social experience of the widows magnified their charms or made them more adept at handling bashful lovers. Washington belonged in this class if we may trust the sentimental poems that he wrote to the unknown maiden that he loved when he was fifteen. After several unsuccessful affairs he probably was sufficiently experienced not to dally in his wooing of Mrs. Custis. Patrick Henry's father married a widow; so did Jefferson and James Madison.

The charms of a widow were likely to be largely economic. The second husband counted himself the real successor of the first, entitled to demand whatever was due to his predecessor. In 1692 the governor and council of Maryland were thus petitioned:

> James Brown of St. Mary's who married the widow . . . of Thomas Pew . . . by his petition humbly prays allow-

---

133 On remarriage, see Wise, *Ye Kingdom of Accawmacke*, 319; Bruce, *Social Life of Virginia in the Seventeenth Century*, 224, 226; Barton, *Virginia Colonial Decisions*, vol. i, 226.

134 Goodwin. *The Colonial Cavalier*, 51; Earle. *Colonial Dames and Goodwives*, 34-39.

> ance for two years sallary due to his predecessor as publick post . . . as also for the use of a horse, and the loss of a servant wholly, by the said Pew deputed in his sickness to officiate; and ran clear away with his horse, some clothes, etc., and for several months after not heard of.

Often seemingly insoluble tangles arose from the repeated marriages of widows, often to widowers. Sometimes, especially when three or more sets of children were involved, the labyrinth of property rights was a puzzle.

The colonists were naturally delighted with the high marriage rate. The South Carolina *Gazette* of March 2, 1734 remarks:

> We have by the last advice from Purrysburg an account of the noble effects the climate of that colony has produced: there is six couples embarked thence for Savannah in Georgia to be joyned in the holy state of matrimony, and half a dozen pair more are preparing themselves for the same.

In the early plantation of Maryland there was no official wife market. Yet the trade was as brisk as in Virginia. Many of the women that came as servants to Maryland between 1634 and 1670 married well and gained wealth and distinction. Thus "Helenor Stephenson, who came out from England with Sir Edmund Plouden as his servant, was lawfully joined in matrimony with Mr. Wm. Braithwaite of St. Marie's." Anne Bolton of St. Martin in the Fields was sold to Mr. Francis Brooke for his wife. These servants were often innocent country girls that had been kidnapped. Women that went to Maryland as servants had "the best luck in the world," they were courted as soon as they landed. "As for women," says Alsop (a redemptioner of 1658), "they no sooner arrive than they are besieged with offers of matrimony, husbands being ready soon for those whom nature had apparently marked out and predestined for lives of single blessedness."

One of the most notable of the female immigrants was a niece of Daniel Defoe, who, crossed in love in England, ran away to America as a redemptioner. She afterwards married her owner's son. Governor Charles Calvert wrote to Lord Baltimore in 1672: "Before William Brooks died, he had a great inclination for a young woman here who is my servant to whom upon his death-bed he gave 3000li of Tobacco." In the *Sotweed Factor* the author narrates a quarrel over cards, in which the planters' wives abuse each other. One says:

> Tho now so brave
> I knew you late a four years' slave,
> What if for planter's wife you go,
> Nature designed you for the hoe.

A maid is represented as saying:

> Kidnapt and fooled, I hither fled,
> To shun a hated nuptial bed.

To which is attached this note: "These are the general excuses made by *English* Women, which are sold, or sell themselves to Maryland."

In numbers of cases sisters that came to Maryland as housekeepers for brothers soon found husbands. An act for pillory and ducking-stools exempted Baltimore and Talbot Counties "because they are not sufficiently settled." One wonders whether this exemption was designed to attract women. But men, also, found in Maryland matches above their station. Many transported persons and some servants had married within a few years, perhaps the daughters of councillors.

Bullock advises English fathers to send daughters rather than sons to Virginia and promises that they

> Will receive instead of give portions for them. . . Maid servants of good honest stock may choose their husbands out

of the better sort of people. Have sent over many but never could keep one at my plantation three months except a poor filly wench made fit to foille to set of beauty and yet a proper young fellow served twelve months for her. [He tells men servants how they may prosper and lay up a competence] and then if he look to God, he may see himself fit to wed a good man's daughter.

The author of *Leah and Rachel* says:

If they are women that go . . . paying their own passages, I advise them to sojourn in a house of honest repute, for by their good carriage, they may advance themselves in marriage, by their ill, overthrow their fortunes; and altho loose persons seldom live long unmarried if free, yet they match with as dissolute as themselves, and never live handsomely or are ever respected.

The agent for Carolina wrote:

Most of the West India settlements will not receive women convicts. If you resolve to send them to Carolina, I have a ship bound thither that will carry them at the usual rate. . . What reception they will find there I cannot say, tho it will be better than elsewhere.

The agent of Massachusetts said that criminals would be willingly accepted in Virginia, Maryland, etc. Many of the women that came to America as servants had a shady past. But the continent had no very warm welcome for women convicts. As an inducement to migration to Carolina the following was written in 1666:

If any maid or single woman have a desire to go over, they will think themselves in the golden age, when men paid a dowry for their wives; for if they be but civil, and under fifty years of age, some honest man or other, will purchase them for their wives.

The significance of the official stimulation of female migration is strikingly portrayed in the words of a Catawba chief who begged for the life of a white woman that had incited Cherokees to steal horses in Virginia. The chief said he was "always sorry to lose a woman; that the loss of one woman might be the loss of many lives, because one woman might be the mother of many children."

In 1738 a minister in Georgia wrote that it was a good time to send some unmarried women to Ebenezer. A letter of the Salzburgers at Ebenezer confirms the assertion. They would like to have

> Some unmarried Christian Salzburger women or other honest members of the female sex who it is hoped would not regret to marry here and likewise to establish an orderly household. Hitherto the young bachelors have endured much disorder in their dwellings rather than marry such persons in whom they did not discern the token of a genuine fear of God and an exceptionally honest life.

Of a supply of German servants it was stated:

> Those delivered Mr. Bolzins were families in which there were many unmarried young women, the congregation of Salzburgers desired they might be left there, there being many unmarried men and no unmarried women. They believed that several would take them for wives.

Again Oglethorpe wrote:

> The first measures for us as trustees to take is after supporting religion to encourage marriage and the rearing up of children. Here are a great number of married people and yet their is now in this place only above 700 men more than there are women most of these would marry if they could get wives. The sending over single women without familys that could protect them might be attended with indecencys but the giving passage to the wives, sisters, and daughters of recruits, and a small maintenance till they go on board would be a remedy to this and much the cheapest way of peopling the country since after their arrival they are no further expense, for their husbands can maintain them. We have found out also that the married soldiers live easiest many of them having turned out very industrious planters.

Of the city of the South, Charleston, on the eve of

the Revolution, it is told that mesalliances sometimes occurred but were regarded with horror. One young lady wedded the coachman. An old servant stabbed the fellow to death. The unfortunate girl (said to have been weak-minded) and her child fell to a lower social level.

The family pride of the South early grew into economic marriages or marriages determined by other social considerations. As early as 1655 while Virginia and Maryland were the only southern colonies fathers were giving portions with their daughters, "so that many coming out of England have raised themselves to good fortunes there merely by matching with maidens born in the country."

In Maryland, 1679, Sara Ford, a Quakeress widow, leased land to a man on condition that "he provide and allow for her three children . . . lodging and washing, housing, apparel, meat and drink, for . . . seven whole years from date, and . . . that he will teach or cause to be taught, her said children to read and write according and so far as their capacitys will attain within the time and term aforesaid." He was so far in loco parentis that he probably thought he might as well go all the way. At any rate he married the widow.

That Virginia was familiar with economic marriage is suggested by one wedding effusion with the verse "Here no sordid interest binds." The marriage settlement is illustrated in the following letters from Virginia.

May 27, 1764

Dear Sir: My son, Mr. John Walker, having informed me of his intention to pay his addresses to your daughter Elizabeth, if he should be agreeable to yourself, lady, and daughter, it may not be amiss to inform you what I think myself able to afford for their support in case of an union. My affairs are in an uncertain state; but I will promise one thousand pounds, to be paid in the year 1765, and one thousand pounds to be paid in the year 1766; and the further sum of two thousand pounds I promise to give him, but the uncertainty of my present affairs prevents my fixing on a time of payment – the above sums are all to be in money or lands and other effects at the option of my said son, John Walker. I am, Sir, your humble servant,

JOHN WALKER.

Col. Bernard Moore esq., in King William.

May 28, 1764.

DEAR SIR: Your son, Mr. John Walker, applied to me for leave to make his addresses to my daughter Elizabeth. I gave him leave, and told him at the same time that my affairs were in such a state that it was not in my power to pay him all the money this year that I intended to give my daughter, provided he succeeded; but would give him five hundred pounds next spring, and five hundred pounds more as soon as I could raise or get the money; which sums, you may depend, I will most punctually pay to him. I am, sir, your obedient servant,

BERNARD MOORE.

George Washington had given thought to marriage conventionalities for he wrote:

I have always considered marriage as the most interesting event of one's life, the foundation of happiness or misery. To be instrumental therefore in bringing two people together, who are indifferent to each other, and may soon become objects of disgust, or to prevent a union which is prompted by affection of the mind, is what I never could reconcile with reason.

A North Carolina illustration of the mercenary interest in marriage is contained in a letter written in 1762 by a gentleman in that colony to a friend in Maryland. The old governor, aged seventy-eight, had fallen in love with a girl of fifteen of good family and fortune. Her parents persuaded her to marry the governor tho she reciprocated the love of a certain youth. But the governor signed away all his property to his son.

The girl's friends found out this calamity and she married the youth. When the governor came he was full of rage.

In South Carolina, eighteenth century marriage notices often mentioned "a large fortune" as one of the lady's qualifications.[135] In Charleston on the eve of the Revolution marriages were preceded by settlements duly drawn. "So-and-so to Miss — —, a most amiable young lady with £10,000 to her fortune" was a very common form of marriage notice. Some notices were more elaborate.

In the southern colonies notwithstanding the economic forces sentiment seems to have figured more largely in marriage alliances than in New York and New England. Women's interests were guarded. In the making of marriages it seems to have been assumed as a matter of course that the widow would be left in possession of everything as the custodian of the children.

The marriage contract was as common in seventeenth century Virginia as it was in England. Some of these agreements reserved to the woman her entire property. Such was perhaps, always the case when the bride-to-be was a widow with children whose first husband had left her his estate in fee simple. In a marriage contract between John Hirsch and Elizabeth Alford, of Lower Norfolk County, 1675, it was provided that the husband should not "meddle" with his wife's property and that she should be fully authorized to manage and sell it. She retained also the right to the proceeds of such goods as she should export. She also reserved the right to bequeath her estate as she chose. In a bond of 1750

[135] Salley. *Marriage Notices in the South Carolina Gazette and its Successors*, 8 ff; Ravenel. *Charleston, the Place and the People*, 165-166.

the groom and his guardian gave security of fifty pounds that the marriage would take place if there was no lawful impediment.

Seventeenth century Virginia records at least one instance where a woman contracted not to marry any one but the other party to the pact tho apparently not pledging herself absolutely to him. Sarah Harrison, after "cordially promising" thus, married another man. And to increase the flagrancy of her wantonness she persistently refused in the marriage service to pledge herself to "obey." She was married without that promise.

Colonial courtship was no simple matter. Alsop said of Maryland in 1666:

> He that intends to court a Maryland girl must have something more than the tautologies of a longwinded speech to carry on his design, or else he may (for ought I know) fall under the contempt of her frown.

One Maryland cavalier that tarried too long making an impression, as he thought, on a fair damsel found that she had thoroly whitewashed his black charger during his stay. One maiden that threw her suitor's hat into the fire saw him fling her bonnet after it and ultimately capitulated. The colonial records of 1657 show a courtship agreement in which a man undertook to leave his stepdaughter at a certain man's house where her expenses were to be paid by a young man who was to have the privilege of courting her there in order to settle a difficulty about a promise of marriage alleged to have been made by her and a rape committed by him on her.

A writer on colonial Culpepper County, Virginia, remarks that young people did not make love till their fathers had arranged the preliminaries. Virginia youths prosecuted their love affairs in fine style. They took up the quest on their good steeds. The poetic souls wrote love verses to their charmers and published them in the Virginia *Gazette*.

The ruffianly Governor Nicholson proceeded otherwise. In a right Oriental manner he demanded the hand of a young girl and finding no favor with her or her parents threatened the lives of father and mother "with mad furious distracted speech." The brother of Commissary Blair was a would-be suitor. His excellency assailed Blair insanely: "Sir, your brother is a villain, and you have betrayed me;" and he swore revenge on the whole family. He vowed that if the girl married any rival he would cut the throat of bridegroom, minister, and justice that issued the license.

A Staunton man in 1764 set about courtship more discreetly. He wrote:

> I intend to call . . . when down that I may no longer worship a shadow but either banish the idol or admire the fair, therefore must request you to let me know by the first conveyance the name of the charmer and whether the elder or the younger of the two sisters that bears the amiable character of being the most worthy of her sex, I shall likewise reconnoitre the fair enthusiast on this side of the stream, and by the assistance of our mutual friend Joel perhaps I may know how far my addresses there would be agreeable.

In South Carolina at the end of the seventeenth century young girls received beaus at three o'clock expecting them to leave about six as many families retired at seven in winter and seldom sat up in summer beyond eight. It is hard to realize how different life must have been when artificial lights were almost negligible and screen wire was unknown. It may be that the usage described belonged as did its narrator in the Puritan group, which was ridiculed by the neighbors.

John Wesley in Georgia became entangled in the

web of love. He was charmed by a designing damsel; but, warned by his friends and the Moravians, broke the engagement. Within eight days she married another man. Then came the famous episode of scandal to which reference will be made later.

A colonial traveler wrote thus:

> Young women are affable with young men in America, and married women are reserved, and their husbands are not as familiar with the girls as they were when bachelors. If a young man were to take it into his head that his betrothed should not be free and gay in her social intercourse, he would run the risk of being discarded, incur the reputation of jealousy, and would find it very difficult to get married. Yet if a single woman were to play the coquette, she would be regarded with contempt. As this innocent freedom between the sexes diminishes in proportion as society loses its purity and simplicity of manners, as is the case in cities, I desire sincerely that our good Virginia ladies may long retain their liberty entire.

XV. REGULATION AND SOLEMNIZATION OF MARRIAGE IN THE SOUTHERN COLONIES

Owing to the presence of various sects and nationalities in the colonial South, marriage came under varying control.

Church of England bigotry is most conspicuous in Virginia, Maryland, and North Carolina. In Virginia throughout the colonial period the ceremonial of the Church of England was prescribed by law. In Maryland Episcopal reaction gradually abrogated optional civil marriage, which had been allowed under the Catholic proprietors, and finally in 1777 saddled upon the people compulsory ecclesiastical marriage which continued to prevail there through the national period. In North Carolina initial tolerance was similarly abrogated during the colonial period. In the two southernmost colonies Episcopal rites were established by law but free civil or religious celebration worked itself in.

The intolerance exhibited by the state church in this particular was directly and indirectly an economic phenomenon. It was due to clerical eagerness for marriage fees and to the desire to fortify the prestige of the established church, that mossy prop of an outworn social order, destined to recede before the non-conformist churches of capitalism. Stalwart non-conformists or Catholics sharply fought or defiantly ignored its marriage requirements even at the risk of illegitimacy.

How crassly material was the spirit that prompted

the ecclesiastical bigotry is evident from the frequently low character of the clergy of the establishment. The Episcopal church in Maryland was a disgrace and "Maryland parson" was an epithet of contempt. "They extorted marriage fees from the poor by breaking off in the middle of the service, and refusing to continue until they were paid." In Virginia there was a penalty for exacting more than the legal fee for marriage or banns.

Ecclesiastical control of the sort described was a temporary anachronism. Save in Maryland, the civil ceremony was recognized, tho with restrictions. Marriage was already a civil contract.

Some idea of the strictness with which the law hedged the entrance to matrimony may be gained from the following excerpts from colonial laws and citations of colonial incidents.

In Maryland in 1638 a couple was married by license under bond that the man was not precontracted and that no lawful impediment existed. Many like bonds have been preserved. The 1640 act on marriage ordained that

> No partie may solemnize marriage with any woman afore the banes three days before published in some chappell or other place of the county where public instnts are used to be notified or else afore oath made and caution entred in the county court that neither partie is apprentice or ward or precontracted or within the forbidden degrees of consanguinity or under govermt, of parents or tutors and certificate of such oath and caution taken from the judge or register of the court upon paine of fine and recompense to the parties aggrieved.

The act of 1658 enforced banns in all cases. In 1662 a new act was aimed against clandestine marriages. The option of governor's or lieutenant-general's license instead of banns is allowed in this act. One hundred pounds of tobacco was fixed as the legal marriage fee. By 1673 Maryland had become the haven for runaway Virginia couples. The Pocomoke boundary lured many eastern shore Virginians for whom love did not run smooth at home. The Virginia assembly of 1673 initiated negotiations with the neighboring government in respect to this evil. A Maryland proclamation of 1685 notes that

> Severall great damages and Inconveniences have and doe daily happen by the private and clandestine marrying of strangers and others comeing into this province from Virginia, and other neighboring parts, to the greate irreparable griefe trouble and disquiett of the parents and guardians, overseers, masters or dames . . . and also to the great dishonor of and reflection upon the government.

Marriage to strangers from Virginia, etc., without Maryland license was accordingly prohibited.

In 1751 a former teacher came to Frederick in the rôle of a minister. His right to the title was disputed and the rector applied for an injunction to prevent him from solemnizing marriage. The court did not grant it but told the person in question to marry none but Germans.[136]

The Maryland colony passed an act requiring the registration of marriages, births, and burials with penalty for infringement. The law was no doubt subject to neglect. In All Saints Parish in 1742 it was ordered that a notice be posted at the church door to inform the parishioners to come forthwith "and have all former and future births, marriages, and burials put on the parish records or they will be prosecuted as the law directs."

Marriage was highly esteemed in Maryland. In one locality after marriage the bridal party was often con-

---

136 Society for History of Germans in Maryland. *Sixth Annual Report*, 20.

veyed from place to place to be entertained by everyone before settling down at home.[137]

In Virginia the earliest statutes show a notable advance over the custom of the motherland. The administration of marriage law was gradually instrusted to lay tribunals. Moreover marriage began to be hedged by statute and was no longer left to the hazards of custom. Banns or license, parental consent, certificate, and registration were presently introduced. Marriage became substantially a civil contract long before the law avowed such a purport.

An act of the Commonwealth period shows that ministers had ignored the law in respect to license or banns and a heavy penalty is attached to such misconduct in the future. The first act of the Restoration requires license or

> Thrice publication according to the prescription of the rubric in the common prayer booke, which injoynes that if the persons to be marryed dwell in severall parishes the banes must be asked in both parishes, and that the curate of one parish shall not solemnize the matrimony untill he have a certificate from the curate of the other parish, that the banes have been there thrice published and noe objection made.

There seems to have been difficulty in enforcing the legal restrictions on marriage. A proclamation was issued in 1672 under which it was declared that the ceremony was to be invalid unless attended by license or banns.

A law of 1661 exhibits the folly of allowing to the governor the perquisite of license granting as a source of income. "Whereas many times lycences are granted and the persons are marryed out of the parishes, which lycences have been usually granted by the governor, whose knowledge of persons cannot possibly extend

[137] Ridgely. *The Old Brick Churches of Maryland*, 109-110.

over the whole country," therefore persons desiring to be married by license must give bond that there is no lawful impediment. The clerk will then write the license which will be signed by a justice or by a deputy of the governor. Marriage bonds were sometimes signed by the bridegroom and a friend but in numerous cases it appears that only the friends signed. This form of marriage must have been a rather aristocratic luxury. Banns were cheaper. Sometimes the would-be bridegroom posted at the court-house door a notice of his purpose of marriage. The act of 1705 requires bond in all cases and requires parental consent only in the case of minors.

In 1662 a prominent citizen eloped with a twelve-year-old heiress from a conspicuous eastern shore family while she was staying at the home of Captain Jones receiving education. The couple fled across the bay in a sailboat to a place where they were not known. In 1696 an "act for the prevention of clandestine marriages" was passed. According to it "many great and grievous mischeifes have arisen and dayly doe arise by clandestine and secret marriages to the utter ruin of many heirs and heiresses" and "the laws now in force . . . do inflict too small a punishment for so heinous and great an offence." A minister ignoring banns or license is hereafter to be imprisoned "for one whole year without bayle or mainprize and shall forfeitt and pay the sume of" five hundred pounds, half of which goes to the informer. A girl between twelve and sixteen contracting irregular marriage forfeits during coverture her inheritance to the next of kin. If widowed she regains the inheritance or it goes to those that should have been entitled to it "in case this act had never been made." The act of 1705 declares that if any minister, contrary to the spirit of the law, leaves the colony and marries Virginians without license or publication, the penalty shall be the same as if the offence had been committed in the province.

The minister of every parish was required to keep a book and in it to register every christening, wedding, and burial. The church wardens and ministers had the duty of making an annual return to the quarter court of all marriages occurring. The act of 1642 required that the report be made to the "commander of every monethly court." The Proclamation of 1672 required the return of licenses (at least in certain cases) to Jamestown for final record. When Williamsburg became the capital returns of registration were to be made thither.

Marriages within the "levitical degrees prohibited by the laws of England" were forbidden. Offenders were subject to separation and the children were illegitimate. Fines might be imposed at discretion of the court. There were cases of proposed or actual marriage contrary to the prohibition. All dispensations of Rome were voided in the colony.[138]

Virginia laws did not attempt to regulate courtship and "sinful dalliance" in New England fashion. But Wyatt, one of the early governors, issued a proclamation aimed chiefly at women forbidding them to contract to two men at once, for

> Women are yet scarce and in much request, and this offence has become very common, whereby great disquiet arose between parties, and no small trouble to the government. . . [Such conduct must cease and] every minister should give notice in his church that what man or woman soever should use any word or speech tending to a contract of marriage to two several persons at one time . . . as might entangle or breed

[138] Barton. *Virginia Colonial Decisions*, vol. i, R 55.

scruples in their consciences, should, for such their offence, either undergo corporal correction, or be punished by fine or otherwise, according to . . . quality of the person so offending.[139]

There is no proof that any maid was ever thus corporally corrected; but a man was whipped for engaging to two women at once.

William and Mary College in colonial days had a regulation on the subject of marriage of faculty members. Certain professors were bent on marrying. Complaint is made that two have "lately married and taken up their residence" out of bounds whereby they are incapacitated for attending to their duties. Accordingly "all professors and masters hereafter to be appointed" are subject to the condition that upon marriage "his professorship be immediately vacated." It was doubtless not with the same intent that the Assembly at the beginning of the Revolution laid a tax of forty shillings on each marriage license. The plebeian banns were still available.

Marriage notices in the Virginia *Gazette* at the time of the Revolution are accompanied by a few verses. Also the papers might be used to prevent marriage. An advertisement of the later eighteenth century warns all ministers from marrying a youth "as he is under age, and this shall indemnify them for so doing."

A Virginia wedding was a notable event involving much ceremony and great preparations and engaging the attention of the neighborhood. The long journeys of guests and the scarcity of social contacts in early days demanded in the wedding a great event. The occasion seems to have been, in the first century of the colony, one of hilarious abandon. In the early days the cere-

---

[139] Cooke. *Virginia*, 149.

mony seems to have been heralded by a lively fusillade but this serious waste of powder was restricted if not forbidden in years when the Indians were menacing. In 1656 we find this item: "Mr. Bushrod what do you mean by suffering your tobacco to run up so high? Why do you not topp itt?" "Because my overseer has gone to a weddinge without my consent, and I know not how to help it." In 1666 when a Dutch man-of-war ravaged the shipping the guard-ship was practically useless because the captain was ashore at a wedding.

Seemingly it was not always customary for the groom to procure the wedding ring. In 1655 Mr. H. Westgate left a hogshead of tobacco to purchase two wedding rings for his daughters. The rings were bought in England. In the later years of the colony when there was a greater supply of clergy the bride had the choice of the officiating priest.

North Carolina made provision for license, banns, and registration. The stipend for licenses was a lucrative perquisite for the governor. Royal instructions in 1730 to the governor declare:

> To the end ecclesiastical jurisdiction of the Bishop of London may take place in that our province so far as may be we do think fit that you give all countenance and encouragement to the exercise of the same excepting only the collating the benefices granting licenses for marriages and probate of wills which we have reserved to you our governor and to the commander in chief of our said province for the time being as far as by law we may.

There is recorded an objection of Governor Tryon to court clerks' issuing of licenses save on his blank. He wanted the emolument.

In 1715 it was enacted that the "inhabitants and freemen of each precinct" are to elect three freeholders, one of whom the governor or commander-in-chief is to choose as register of deeds. Until there be a clerk of the parish church the register is to record betrothals and marriages. Every "master or mistress of a family who shall neglect to register the birth or death of any person born or dying within his or her house or plantation; and every married man who shall neglect to remit to the said register a certificate of his marriage and cause the same to be registered, for longer than one month" must pay a shilling a month for the delay, total not to exceed twenty shillings. One act for the government of Carolina provided that births, christenings, marriages, and burials were to be registered in each parish (except in case of negroes, mulattoes, and Indian slaves). Any person reasonably desiring was to have access to such records. Royal instructions in 1730 required the governor to keep account of births, deaths, and burials. An act of 1748 fixed fees for registry and certificate of births, burials, and marriage and imposed a penalty for refusal to render the service at that price or for charging more.

The following Carolina episode of 1713 savors of New England:

> Whereas we are informed by the Rev. Mr. John Urmston that Mr. Richard French have and doe take upon him to administer ye holy sacrt. of baptisme and to marry persons without being duly qualified for the same, it is ordered by this board that the provost marshall doe sumons ye said Richard French to appeare at ye next councill to be holden at Capt. Hecklefield on the 3d day of the next genll court to answer to ye said complt and that he forbid ye said French to marry or baptize any persons in ye meanwhile.

South Carolina early had provision for registration of marriage. The act of 1704 required registration of births, christenings, marriages, and burials, except those of "negroes, Mullatoes, and Indian slaves" and prescribed a fine for wedding contrary to the table of forbidden degrees.

In Maryland the Quakers were strong and practiced their usual rites. The question of marriage, involving legitimacy and inheritance, early was a serious one for them. They exercised great caution with a view to preventing the union of persons that already had partners in the old country. They required two or three applications to the meetings so as to secure publicity and avoid anything "contrary to the order of truth" or that might bring discredit. A proposal of marriage in 1678 is recorded as follows:

> Obadiah Judkins and Obedience Jenner, acquainted this meeting, and also the women's meeting, with their intentions of coming together as husband and wife, according to the order of truth; now inasmuch as the young woman is but lately come forth of England, and Friends noe certaine knowledge of her, the advice of the men's and women's meeting is that they forbeare, and proceed noe further till certificate be procured out of England from the meeting where she last belonged unto, of her being cleere from others, and as to the manner of her life and conversation, that so the truth may be kept cleere in all things; both the partys being willing to submit to the same, and also to live apart in the mean time.

It was not unusual to appoint a committee to inquire as to the freedom of the parties. Too many immigrants to Maryland had deserted their lawful spouses; hence the precautions of the Friends were quite in order.

A list of queries adopted by the yearly meeting of 1725 to be answered by lower meetings includes the following:

> Is care taken and Friends advised that none too nearly (related) proceed in collateral marriages, and that none marry

> within the third degree of affinity and the fourth degree of consanguinity?

The Friends were especially disquieted by marriages of members with outsiders and by hasty marriage without formal publication of the banns as also by an attendant evil–the marriage of children by priests and magistrates. William Dixon informs the meeting

> That his daughter-in-law [probably stepdaughter] is stole away and married by a priest in the night, contrary to his and his wife's minds; that he has opposed the same and refused to pay her portion, for which he is cited to appear before the commissary general, and now he desires to know whether the meeting would stand by him, if he should sue the priest that married her. The meeting assents.

Nothing seems to have distressed the Friends in Talbot more than "outgoings" in marriage. To be married with a license by a magistrate or by a "hireling priest" was a reprehensible abomination. One Church of England minister was specially obnoxious on account of such services. At a meeting in 1681 a committee appointed to wait on the lord proprietary "concerning Friends children being taken away from them and married by the priest without their consent or knowledge" reported "that they were treated very civilly" by the proprietor, who said "that for the future he would take care in all his counties that the like should be prevented." The evil continued. A quarterly meeting in 1688 recommended the disinheritance of disobedient children. The yearly meeting confirmed this position and recommended that "priests or magistrates that do marry Friends children without their parents or guardians consent should be prosecuted."

The Labadists, who had a colony in Maryland, were in some respects similar to the Friends. They were stringent on the subject of intermarriage with gentiles. A convert to the society was expected to abandon his unregenerate spouse when he entered the fold.[140]

The Virginia Quakers exercised oversight like that of their Maryland brethren. A typical document is as follows:

> This is to certify the truth to all people that A.B. son of R.S., and C.D. daughter of J.S. haveing intentions of marriage according to the ordinance of God and his joyning did lay it before the men and weomans meeting, before whom their marriage was propounded, and then the meeting desired them to waight for a time, and so they enquireing betwixt the time wheather the man was free from all other weomen, and shee free from all other men, so the second time they coming before the man and weomans' meeting, all things being cleare, a meeting of the people of God was appointed for that purpose, wheare they tooke one another in the house of W.L. and in the presence of God and in the presence of us his people according to the law of God and the practis of the holly men of God in the scriptures of truth and they theare promising before God and us his people to live faithfully togeather man and wife as long as they live, according to Gods honorable mariage, they theare setting both their hands unto it the —— day of —— in the yeare —— and wee are witnesses of the same whose names are heareunto subscribed.

Parental consent is certified in the following document:

> This may sattisfie friends that I have given my consent to Moses Hall as concerning marriage with my daughter Margrett Duke as witness my hand this 7 day of the 11 mo 1707. Thomas Duke Senior.

Other records are as follows:

> Margaret Tabbarer states in a paper sent to the meeting that her daughter had been married to a young man by a Priest, and expresses her sorrow that she has married that way.
>
> Tho: Hollowell and Alic his wife desire that their testimony

[140] Howard. *History of Matrimonial Institutions*, vol. ii, 245, *footnote* 2.

be recorded against their childrens unlawful behavior in being married by Priests.

Daniel Sanbourn on behalf of the men's meeting in Chuckatuck signed on "the eight day of the 3 mo in the yeare 1701" a certificate of disownment against "Tho Duke" for "marrying one that was not of us and lickwise goeing to the hireling priest." There are other protests and references to disorderly marriage.

The North Carolina records contain several instances of the control exercised by the Friends over the marriage of their members. In this colony also, Friends gave two notices of intended marriage and we find note of two men appointed "to enquire into his life and conversation and clearness in respect of marriage." In one locality a man's not having paid his debts would lead Quakers to refuse his request of marriage.

In Virginia there was to be no marriage of servants without certificate of master's consent.

> Servants procuring ymselves to be married wthout consent of their Masters shall serve a year and if any being free shall secretly marry wth a servant he or she shall pay ye mr. of ye Servt 1500 lb. tobo, or a years service and ye Servt shall serve ye whole time and a year after.[141]

In Maryland free persons and servants were prohibited from marrying without the express approval of master or mistress. The General Assembly of 1777 passed an act prohibiting ministers, under penalty of fifty pounds, from marrying a free person and a servant without consent of master or mistress.

A North Carolina statute forbade any one, under penalty of five pounds to be paid to the master, to marry servants without the written consent of the master. All

---

[141] Cooke. *Virginia*, 122-123; *Virginia Magazine of History and Biography*, vol. x, "Abridgement of Laws of Virginia, 1694," 145-146.

servants so married were to serve one year extra. Probably many masters used their power to prevent the marriage of servant women. This embargo must have increased the number of unlawful unions. Baptists seem to have considered it a hardship. Just before the Revolution the Kehukee Association declared marriages not made according to law to be binding before God and that it was not lawful to fellowship a member that broke the marriage of servants.

XVI. WOMAN'S PLACE IN THE COLONIAL SOUTH

Southern "chivalry" does not date back to the beginnings of the South. It took time for the softening influences of the genial climate and the feudalizing trend of the broad expanse to prevail. Seventeenth century Virginia was bourgeois rather than knightly. Like their New England compeers, the founders of the Old Dominion were prosaic and practical. The economic interest dominated and left little room for sentiment. Women fared like contemporary English women of the middle class. Their lot was domestic, commonplace, subordinate. The early Virginians prepared the ducking stool for gossiping women. At an early day Betsey Tucker was ducked for making her husband's house and the neighborhood uncomfortable by her violent tongue. In 1662 the Assembly passed an act to the effect that wives that brought judgment on their husbands for slander should be punished by ducking. Bacon captured wives of loyalists and notified their husbands, who were with the governor, that he intended to place the ladies in front of his men in the line of battle. This was no empty threat and the "Apron Brigade" saved him from the fire of the governor's guns. The man that was thus guilty (as Colonel Ludwell put it) of "ravishing of women from their homes and hurrying them about the country in their rude camps" was a wealthy planter. Nor was His Excellency more chivalrous. Governor Berkeley spurned with vile insult a woman begging for her husband's pardon for his part in the insurrection. We find record also of a rude insult to a lady of a leading family from a Virginia colonel, member of another leading family.

Some little feeling for womanhood is indeed manifested in the case of Grace Sherwood who in 1706 on suspicion of witchcraft was examined by a jury of *women* who reported her "neither like them, nor any other woman they knew of." She was fortunate in not coming under the Massachusetts law authorizing examination by a male "witch pricker" but she was ducked as a suspected witch. On the whole her experience is scarcely an exhibit of chivalry.[142]

The accounts that Colonel Byrd gives of his visits to Virginia homes show sufficiently the attitude toward women in the middle of the eighteenth century. "We supped about nine and then prattled with the ladies." "Our conversation with the ladies was like whip-syllabub, very pretty but nothing in it." He jokes rather coarsely about Miss Thekky's lamentable maiden state and refers to Mrs. Chiswell as "one of those absolute rarities, a very good old woman." Another man wrote of the Virginia women:

> Most of the women are quite pretty and insinuating in their manner if they find you so. When you ask them if they would like to have husbands they reply with a good grace that it is just what they desire.

A young Virginia lady writes:

> Hannah and myself were going to take a long walk this evening but were prevented by the two horrid mortals Mr. Pinkard and Mr. Washington, who siezed and kissed me a dozen times in spite of all the resistance I could make. They really think, now they are married, they are prevaliged to do anything. . .

---

[142] See Wertenbaker, *Patrician and Plebeian in Virginia*, 82-87; Forrest, *Historical and Descriptive Sketches of Norfolk, Virginia*, 464-465.

> While we were eating the apple-pye in bed – God bless you, making a great noise – in came Mr. Washington dressed in Hannah's short gown and peticoat, and seazed me and kissed me twenty times in spite of all the resistance I could make; and then Cousin Molly.

Evidently women had reached by this time the status of toys.

It was out of such perspectives as those detailed that "chivalry" arose. By the time of the Revolution there was sufficient recrudescence of feudalism to cause an atavic reversion to chivalric standards.

> The Virginia gentleman [says Wertenbaker] taught by the experience of many years, was beginning to understand aright the reverence due the nobleness, the purity, the gentleness of woman. He was learning to accord to his wife the unstinted and sincere homage that her character deserved.

But as we trace the later history of sex morals in the South it will become glaringly apparent what a veneered mockery was this boasted southern chivalry.

The domestic life of women on the old plantations must have been rather monotonous. According to travelers' descriptions they did not share largely in the diversions of the men. The subordination of woman is illustrated in various ways. Her husband was responsible for her behavior. Thus in a Virginia witch case the husband was under bond on his wife's account and upon her acquittal the bond was cancelled. The minutes of the council at Wilmington, North Carolina, August 31, 1753 contain the following:

> Read the petition of Wm. Barns setting forth that his wife having during his absence retailed liquors contrary to law a bill of indictment had been found against him in the county court of New Hanover and that he being poor as well as innocent of the said crime prayed that a nolle prosequi might be entered in his behalf. . . Attorney general was ordered to enter a nolle prosequi.

The early Baptists in North Carolina met the penalty of too great liberality to women when a regular Baptist preacher in South Carolina refused to assist at an ordination and rebuked them for letting women pray in public. The minutes of one Baptist association for 1771 record that it was not lawful for a woman to vote in conference.

The subjection of women was of course coupled with a legal claim on their part upon the property of the husband and a natural hold on the husband's consideration. The first will in Maryland, dated in the year 1638, is that of William Smith in which he leaves all his goods to his wife. In North Carolina,

> Elizabeth Bateman widdow . . . of . . . Jon. Bateman declining her legacy given in . . . will and craving to have her third of her deceased husband's estate. Ordered that . . . said Elizabeth Bateman have her third.

In Virginia in the case of Brent *vs.* Brent the husband was a terrible fellow. The wife was allowed a separate maintenance, being ill-treated, and he was to be arrested for seditious words. At the general court of Carolina, 1695, "John Wilson acknowledged his assignment of a warrant of right to Wm. Duckenfield Esqr. and Marget his wife relinquisheth her right of dower." In Georgia the wife's consent had to be secured to the alienation of lands in which she had an interest. Thus there was a certain technical protection for woman that did in a measure assure her property rights but from the standpoint of equity no amount of legal standing could offset the cancellation of personality.

Yet tho colonial usage kept woman in retirement, the colonial South had notable women that vied with their assertive sisters of the North in the world of affairs. There was no marked difference between the sections in the extent to which women took up independent careers, or assumed responsibilities beyond housewifery.

Maryland women of the middle of the seventeenth century must have possessed executive ability and intelligence; for the keen pioneers generally appointed their wives, or if unmarried their sisters, as executors of their wills. The Assembly of 1671 decided that in case of intestacy the wife should be administrator if the husband had left no directions.

The first seventeenth century business woman in Maryland, and possibly in America, received a license from the assembly to establish a printing press at Annapolis to print official papers. This lady could not write. Verlinda Stone was a woman of force and courage. She wrote to Lord Baltimore demanding an investigation of a fight in which her husband was wounded. The letter was sufficiently business-like but ends vehemently. Captain Cornwallis refers to the wife of Commissioner Hawley

> Who by her comportment in these difficult affairs of her husband's hath manifested as much virtue and discretion as can be expected from the sex she ones whose industrious housewifery hath so adorned this desert, that should his discouragements force him to withdraw himself and her, it would not a little eclipse the glory of Maryland.

Margaret Brent administered Leonard Calvert's estate. She never married. In 1658 she testified that "Thos. White, lately deceased, out of the tender love and affection he bore the petitioner, intended if he had lived to have married her, and did by his last will and testament" leave her "his whole estate." She asserted her right to vote in official capacity as Calvert's successor and she conducted the colony through a dangerous situation with ability and patience. In colonial Maryland women began to function in public service as keepers of ordinaries and ferries. During the Revolution a woman was postmistress of Baltimore.

In Virginia, also, women showed strength and ability. "Mrs. Procter, a proper civil, modest gentlewoman" defended herself and family for a month after the massacre. "Lady Temperance Yeardly came on November 16, 1627 to . . . Jamestown and confirmed the conveyance made by her late husband . . . late governor . . . to Abraham Percy." James Clayton writing as early as 1688 of "Observables" in Virginia mentions several "acute ingenious gentlewomen" who operated thriving tobacco plantations, draining swamps, raising cattle, buying slaves. One near Jamestown was a fig-grower.

In South Carolina women took an active part in all sorts of affairs and seem to have enjoyed a certain standing not gained by women elsewhere in the colonies. The men often had to be absent and it was not uncommon for a woman to be alone for several months in charge of a great plantation with hundreds of slaves with no white man to assist her save the overseer. Women often taught their own children. Eliza Lucas studied law and while studying it drew up two wills and was made trustee in another. In the Revolution the women were often more stalwart than the men, urging husbands and fathers not to give in in order to save their property and bearing cheerfully hardship and banishment.

In all the southern colonies there were keen gentlewomen that took up tracts of land and cleared and cultivated their estates. Southern women were not outdone by the business women of the North. A traveler who had been through Maryland, Virginia, and Carolina wrote (in the London *Magazine*, 1745-1746): "The women, who have plantations, I have seen mighty busy in examining the limbs, size, and abilities of their intended purchases." There were several women editors in the South.[143]

In general the women of the South were freer from toil than those of the North. Yet even in this milder region pioneer life required a degree of fortitude that tended to strengthen female character as the perils of feudalism had done for the châtelaines of earlier days. A Maryland missionary letter of 1638 remarks that "a noble matron has just died, who coming with the first settlers . . . with more than woman's courage bore all difficulties and inconveniences. . . A perfect example as well in herself as in her domestic concerns." Maryland planters' women lived in the saddle but were none the less "queens of the household" with the grace of those "to the manor born." A writer on Virginia says in 1853:

> Many of the respected females who figured in the earlier period of our history, were very different, in some respects, from the accomplished and esteemed fair ones of the city at this day. They were generally more robust and capable of enduring much greater fatigue. The roseate tints upon the full cheek of health were more frequently to be seen, nor so soon gave place to the pale hues of debility, disease, and premature death. . . They mounted the spirited horse and cantered [before sunrise].[144]

[143] For woman's sphere in the southern colonies see Richardson, *Side-lights on Maryland History*, vol. i, chapter xxxiii; Early, *By-ways of Virginia History*, 155-157; Bruce, *Social Life of Virginia in the Seventeenth Century*, 231; Earle, *Colonial Dames and Goodwives*, chapter ii; Fisher, *Men, Women, and Manners in Colonial Times*, vol. ii, 321-323; Sioussat, *Colonial Women of Maryland*, 214-226.

[144] Forrest. *Historical and Descriptive Sketches of Norfolk, Va.*, 42-43.

Doctor Brickell of North Carolina wrote:

> Both sexes are very dexterous in paddling and managing their canoes, both men, women, boys, and girls, being bred to it from their infancy.

Woman's function as housewife and helpmeet was indeed important. A traveler wrote of Maryland:

> The women are very handsome in general, and most notable housewives; everything wears the mark of cleanliness and industry in their houses; and their behavior to their husbands and families is very edifying. . . I am not writing anything yet of the more refined part of the colony, but what I say now is confined to a tract of about 200 miles; for in some other parts you will find many coquettes and prudes, as well as in other places; nor, perhaps, may the lap-dog or monkey be forgotten.[145]

At all events woman's civic service was mainly in the home.

Concerning Virginia an eighteenth century writer said:

> Of the planters' ladies, I must speak in terms of unqualified praise; they had an easy kindness of manner, as far removed from rudeness as from reserve. . . To the influence of their society, I chiefly attribute their husband's refinement.

A nineteenth century writer on Norfolk, looking back, said:

> [The colonial ladies were] noted for their personal attractions; and many, in the higher walks of life, for great dignity of character, modesty, and politeness of behavior, as well as for their activity and frugality in the management of their household affairs. These commendable qualities left their impress and beneficial influence upon succeeding generations. . . Some spun at the wheel or wove at the hand loom! and cultivated kitchen and flower gardens. They studied the Bible, and other books of sound moral and religious instruction; instilled correct, honorable, virtuous, and patriotic principles into the minds of their children, and presided with dignity and grace at the

[145] *Itinerant Observations in America*, 46.

> social entertainment. . . Of many it might then have been said. . . "She openeth her mouth with wisdom, and in her tongue is the law of kindness. She looketh well to the ways of her household, and eateth not the bread of idleness. Her children arise up and call her blessed; her husband also, and he praiseth her."

James Franklin wrote at the end of the Revolutionary period that except for certain amusements the Virginia ladies

> Chiefly spend their time in sewing and taking care of their families; for they seldom read or endeavor to improve their minds. However they are in general good housewives; and tho they have not perhaps, so much tenderness and sensibility as the English ladies, yet they make as good wives and as good mothers as any in the world.

Brickell wrote further of North Carolina:

> The girls are not only bred to the needle and spinning, but to the dairy and domestic affairs, which many of them manage with a great deal of prudence and conduct, tho they are very young. . . The women are the most industrious in these parts, and many of them by their good housewifery make a great deal of cloath of their own cotton, wool and flax, and some of them weave their own cloath with which they decently apparel their whole family tho large. Others are so ingenious that they make up all the wearing apparel both for husband, sons and daughters. Others are very ready to help and assist their husbands in any servile work, as planting when the season of the year requires expedition: pride seldom banishing housewifery.

Tradition of South Carolina tells us that among the Huguenots "men and their wives worked together in felling trees, building houses, making fences, and grubbing up their grounds . . . and afterwards continued their labors at the whip-saw." One man asserts that his grandfather and grandmother started their handsome fortune by working together at the whip-saw. A writer on South Carolina in 1763 said: The women of the province "are excelled by none in the practice of all the social virtues, necessary for the happiness of the other sex as daughters, wives, or mothers."

There was more grace and charm perhaps in the settled life of the South than in that of New England but it is pretty clear that divergence of life between North and South was less marked in colonial days than since. But even before the Revolution "chivalry" was, as we have seen, under way. Lady Tryon and Esther Wake wrought so successfully with their feminine charms that the North Carolina assembly granted a large appropriation to build a governor's palace. Woman's influence was felt not only in private but in public–in council, in assemblies, in the House of Burgesses.

It must be remembered that when writers eulogize the women of the South and the attitude of the men toward them the picture in mind is likely to be of the women of the "aristocracy." Common people were not very likely to get into books very adequately in the Old South. Side by side with the women of the nobility lived the miserable sisters of toil–the poor, the servants, the slaves–and their lot was by no means roseate. Some conception of the life of the servile class will be gained in a later chapter. In Virginia in order to discourage planters from working women in the fields, female servants so working were made subject to tithe, while all other white women were exempt.[146] A woman in *The Sot-weed Factor; or, a Voyage to Maryland*, contrasts England and America thus:

Not then a slave for twice two year
My cloaths were fashionably new
Nor were my shifts of linnen blue.

[146] Burk. *History of Virginia*, vol. ii, appendix xviii.

> But things are changed; now at the hoe,
> I daily work and barefoot go,
> In weeding corn or feeding swine,
> I spend my melancholy time.

In the valley of Virginia in harvest German women worked in the fields. Females reaped, hoed, plowed. A writer on the valley said: "Some of our now wealthiest citizens frequently boast of their grandmothers, aye mothers too, performing this kind of heavy labor."

North Carolina became a dumping ground for "white trash." If we may believe one sharp writer (seemingly Byrd, whose reliability has been impugned)

> The men . . . just like the Indians, impose all the work upon the poor women. They make their wives rise out of their beds early in the morning, at the same time that they lye and snore, til the sun has run one third of his course. . . They loiter away their lives . . . and at the winding up of the year scarcely have bread to eat.

North Carolina possessed much of the roughness and crudeness of frontier life. The reverend Mr. Urmstone, a missionary, writes numerous querulous letters detailing the hardships of the country and the roughness of the people. A letter, dated February 15, 1719, relates that his wife died in October. She had

> Declared before several of her neighbors that her heart was broken through our ill usage and comfortless way of living; she prest me sore for divers years either to quit this wretched country or give her leave to go home with her children: I wish I had done either it might have pleased God to have continued her to me many years longer.

XVII. CHILDHOOD IN THE COLONIAL SOUTH

Children were of use in the colonial South as in New England. The opportunity for child-labor left unbridled the spontaneous impulse to propagation and fecundity was a social boon in the new country.

The London Company, which settled Virginia, was anxious to utilize child-labor in developing the resources of the colony. In 1619 arrived one hundred children "save such as dyed on the waie" and another hundred, twelve years old or over, was asked for. In 1627 many ships came bringing fourteen or fifteen hundred children kidnapped in Europe. A few years later a request went to London for another supply of "friendless boyes and girles."

How the system of servitude affected family relations may be gathered from the following illustrative material.

A boy six years old was kidnapped in England by a sea-captain and sold to America where he married his master's daughter and became his heir. He never found his parents. Later he bought the sea-captain (now a convict). The latter, probably fearing vengeance, killed himself the first day.

James McAvoy and thirteen other youths were kidnapped from Ireland and brought to Virginia. Several of the boys were recovered by their parents. McAvoy was sold to Mr. R. Carlile and by him resold to a man in the valley. While in service he married but returned to the bull-pasture before his time was out. His owner came and took him back. Presently his wife came to him with her child. The couple soon ran away together and he was not again disturbed.

Banishment to the plantations was the probable fate of a child whose existence menaced the honor or peace of a noble family.

In 1632 the Virginia colony gave John and Anna Layton five hundred acres of land in official recognition of the fact that their child, Virginia, was the first white child born in the colony. By 1634-1639 is noted faster growth due to advance in birth-rate. The writer of *Leah and Rachel* said of Virginia:

> Children increase and thrive so well there that they themselves will sufficiently supply the defect of servants, and in small time become a nation of themselves sufficient to people the country.

Primal fertility appeared. We hear of a family of twelve living in a cabin with only an earth floor and with no beds save bearskins. Some families had eight, ten, or fifteen children. Patrick Henry, born in 1736, was one of nineteen children and John Marshall, born in 1755, was the first of fifteen.

In Maryland thrifty yeomen had large families. Evidence of family magnitude is found in the graveyard Mrs. Richardson remarks in regretful retrospection:

> Manor houses with outstretched wings were built to gather under their sheltering roofs the dozen or more little ones who usually came to break the stillness of the quiet days in that far off time when there was more of maternity than nervous energy in the world.

Families in North Carolina were large. Fecundity

was a family ideal. Pioneer vigor ensured numerous offspring; and as a rule children repaid even before the age of twenty-one the expenses of rearing. Doctor Brickell wrote in 1737:

> The women are very fruitful, most houses being full of little ones, and many women from other places who have been long married and without children, have removed to Carolina and become joyful mothers, as has often been observed. It very seldom happens they miscarry, and they have very easie travail in their child-bearing. . . The Europeans, or Christians of North Carolina are a streight, tall, well-limbed and active people; their children being seldom or never troubled with rickets, and many other distempers that the Europians are afflicted with, and you shall seldom see any of them deformed in body.

Governor Dobbs wrote from Newbern in 1755:

> There are at present 75 families on my lands. I viewed betwixt 30 and 40 of them, and except two there are not less than from five or six to ten children in each family, each going barefooted in their shifts in the warm weather, no woman wearing more than a shift, and one thin petticoat; They are a colony from Ireland removed from Pennsylvania, of what we call Scotch-Irish Presbyterians who with others in the neighboring tracts had settled together in order to have a teacher of their own opinion and choice.

Woodmason's *Account of North Carolina in 1760* informs us that "the necessaries of life are so cheap and so easily acquired and propagation being unrestricted that the increase of people there is inconceivable even to themselves." For the fifty years from 1753 to 1803 the church register of a Moravian group shows more than twice as many births as deaths.

In 1708 Oldmixon wrote of Charlestown:

> There are at least 250 families in this town, most of which are numerous, and many of them have ten or twelve children in each.

He likewise informs us that in Carolina "the children

are set to work at eight years old." Milligan wrote of Charlestown in 1763:

> I have examined a pretty exact register of the births and burials for fifteen years, and find them, except when the small-pox prevailed, nearly equal; the advantage, tho small, is in favor of the births, tho the burials are added all the transient people who die here.

Genealogical registers show the following instances of South Carolina fecundity during the seventeenth and eighteenth centuries: Five persons with nine children each; six with ten children each; three with eleven children each; four with twelve each; two with thirteen each; one with fourteen; one with fifteen; one woman with nineteen children by one husband. There is no reason to suppose that the elect few whose genealogies are available were unique in prolificness.

In Georgia some people settled on the edge of swamps. In one settlement so high was the death-rate among children that they seldom survived till puberty. Those that lived to adulthood possessed feeble constitutions. But a letter from Savannah in 1740 contains this item:

> I have carefully inquired into the account of our births and burials at Savannah, and its districts for one year past, and find the former has exceeded the latter as three to two.

As always in a new country natural conditions imparted a training in activity and responsibility. Thus the author of *Leah and Rachel* says of Virginia:

> This good policy is there used; as the children there born grow to maturity, and capable (as they are generally very capable and apt) they are still preferred and put into authority, and carry themselves therein civilly and discreetly.

Alsop says of Maryland in 1666: There are no ale-houses; "from antient custom . . . the son works as well as the servant; so that before they eat their bread, they are commonly taught how to earn it." By the time sons are ready to receive what the father gives them, which is partly their own earning, "they manage it with such a serious, grave, and watching care, as if they had been masters of families, trained up in that domestick and governing power from their cradles."

The spiritual welfare of the young was an object of solicitude but also subject to vicissitudes. In the Maryland Assembly in 1694, it was ordered that a law be proposed that parents frequently bring their children to be catechized and that the ministers call upon them. In 1696 it was voted that the ministers frequently admonish the children's parents in their parishes to send them to be catechized. A circular letter in 1701 to the clergy of Maryland by the reverend Thomas Bray, a clergyman of the Church of England, urges religious training of children in which there has been remissness. In Virginia an act of 1661-1662 recites that "many schismatical persons . . . refuse to have . . . children baptized." Accordingly parents refusing to carry a child to a lawful minister for baptism were to be fined two thousand pounds of tobacco. The records of the period contain one case, at any rate, of an order against a father under charge of not baptizing children. The reverend Samuel Davis, minister at Hanover, wrote in 1751 that family religion was a rarity. Byrd said that the North Carolina settlers took no trouble to get children baptized and Christianized. It may be that the strictures of this Episcopalian cavalier were unfair. The North Carolina records for 1771-1775 contain an account of an Episcopal minister's charging fifteen shillings for baptizing a sick child.

> I have of my own knowledge seen a man as he passed his door desire him to call in and baptize his child which lay sick and he

has refused and in consequence . . . the child died unbaptized.

In an account of missionaries sent to South Carolina in the early part of the eighteenth century occurs a report, dated in the year 1706, from the reverend Doctor Le Jean that "the parents and masters" were "endued with much good will, and a ready disposition to have their children and servants taught the Christian religion." When he found parents refraining on account of expense from having children baptized he told them he desired nothing.

Scattered residence and aristocratic spirit retarded the planting of schools. Education in the South was very defective. Only the aristocracy could provide for its children according to the best educational standards of the age in England.

With this dearth of formal arrangements for education the training of the young was naturally subject to varying vicissitudes. In seventeenth century Virginia the desire of parents to provide education for their children was indicated in various ways. Often directions were left and provision was made in wills. One of the most ordinary provisions of wills was that the testator's children be taught to read the Bible. Many planters provided surprisingly large amounts for the education of their children. John Custis IV. provided by will that the proceeds of the labor of fourteen slaves should be devoted to the maintenance and tuition of his grandson until he should be sent to England for advanced training for which an additional large amount was provided. John Savage directed in his will that a horse and mare, two steers and two cows, with their increase, should go for the education of his son in England. For the tuition of his two daughters the executors were to hire out three servants. That the desire to have their children educated was not confined to whites is shown by the will of Thomas Carter, a free negro, which directed as to the education of his sons. In early Maryland wills also fathers provide for the education of their sons – "as befits their station," frequently directing that they be sent to college in England.

Maryland children were taught by parents, tutored, or sent to England to school. Many sons of wealthy parents enjoyed the privilege of an education abroad. In Virginia the wealthiest families kept tutors. Sometimes the tutor was a freed servant, as in the Washington family, and sometimes a servant still in bondage. Often the tutor in a great Virginia family was an Episcopal clergyman. When the sons outgrew their master they were sent to New or Old England, or perchance to William and Mary. Before 1770 nearly every South Carolina planter sent his sons to Oxford or Cambridge.

To William and Mary many Maryland boys were sent – a fact that largely accounts for the numerous marriage alliances between the early families of Maryland and those of Virginia. A traveler in the South wrote before the middle of the eighteenth century: "The Williamsburgh college in Virginia is the Resort of all the children, whose parents can afford it." It is inferior to the universities of Massachusetts, "for the youth of these more indulgent settlements, partake pretty much of the petit maitre kind, and are pampered much more in softness and ease than their neighbors more northward." Such a spoiled lad was, perhaps, Thomas Byrd who was sentenced to a whipping on the charge of breaking windows. He refused to submit; his father offered to compel him; but he was expelled from college.

The traveler just quoted says also:

Often a clever servant or convict, that can write and read tolerably, and is of no handicraft business, is indented to some planter, who has a number of children, as a schoolmaster, and then, to be sure, he is a tip-top man in his parts, and the servant is used more indulgently than the generality of them.

The diary of John Hanower (1773-1776) who came to Virginia as a schoolmaster, indented to Colonel Dangerfield, illuminates this phase of pedagogy. His wife seems to have been in England.

[May 27.] This morning about 8 A M the colonel delivered his three sons to my charge to teach them to read, write, and figure. His oldest son Edwin ten years of age, intred into two syllables in the spelling book, Bathourest his second son six years of age in the alphabete and William his third son four years of age does not know the letters. he has likewise a daughter. . . My school houres is from six to eight in the morning, in the forenoon from nine to twelve, and from three to six in the afternoon. . . [June 14] This morning entered to school Wm. Pattie son of John Pattie wright, and Salley Evens daughter to Thos. Evens Planter. . . [Monday, 20th] This morning entred to school Philip and Dorothea Edge's Children of Mr. Benjamin Edge, Planter. . . [Tuesday, 21st] This day Mr. Samuel Edge Planter came to me and begged me to take a son of his to school who was both deaf and dum, and I consented to try what I cou'd do with him. . . Munday, 17th [Apr., 1775] At 8 A M I rode to Town. . . On my aravel in town the first thing I got to do was to dictate and write a love letter from Mr. Anderson to one Peggie Dewar at the howse of Mr. John Mitchel at the Wilderness. . . [Tuesday, April 23d, 1776] Settled with Mr. Porter for teaching his two sons 12 Mos. when he very genteely allowed me £6 for them, besides a present of two silk vests and two pair of nankeen breeches last summer and a gallon of rum at Christenmass, both he and Mrs. Porter being extreamly well satisfied with what I hade don to them.

Not all pedagogy was so amateurish as that suggested

by the diary of this worthy pedagog. Mrs. Pinckney wanted to get her son a toy so that he might learn by play according to Locke's method. His father undertook to contrive a set of toys to teach him his letters by the time he could speak. "You perceive we begin betimes for he is not yet four months old." The infant began to spell before he was two years of age. He became General C. C. Pinckney of Revolutionary fame but he declared that this early teaching nearly made him a stupid fellow. Martha Laurens, born in Charleston in 1759, could in her third year "read any book."

School administration presented problems of its own. The first free school in Queen Anne's County, Maryland, procured its first teacher in 1724. Difficulty was soon experienced in securing the attendance of the "foundation" pupils. Many notices were given to the parents and guardians of these pupils requiring them to show cause why the pupils were not at school. A letter from the reverend Mr. Reed, dated at Newbern, North Carolina, in 1772, recounts trouble about an academy. "When Mr. T. opened his school, he was apprized of the excessive indulgence of American parents, and the great difficulty of keeping up a proper discipline; more especially as his school consisted of numbers of both sexes." He had to correct and turn out some for unruliness. Two trustees whose children were turned out became "his most implacable enemies. . . The correcting and turning the children of two of the trustees out of the school, was, like the sin against the Holy Ghost, never to be forgiven."

The early German settlers of North Carolina brought their religious books with them. The cabin in the clearing was followed by a schoolhouse erected in some accessible place. The youth were taught by the schoolmaster the rudiments of education. The mother tongue was used.

A writer on Highland County, Virginia, tells us that

> The Scotch-Irish set great store on schooling, but pioneer life in a thinly peopled wilderness was not favorable to effort in this direction. The more alert of those who could read and write would give their children some rudimentary training. . . A significant instance lies in the fact that an early constable of the Bullpasture, who of necessity was able to read and write, reared an illiterate family. A signature by means of a mark was very common.

Doctor Brickell of North Carolina wrote:

> The children at nine months old are able to walk and run about the house, and are very docile and apt to learn anything, as any children in Europe; and those that have the advantage to be educated, write good hands, and prove good accountants, which is very much coveted, and most necessary in these parts.

A writer on the history of Mecklenburg County and the city of Charlotte in colonial times, says that the children generally received six months of schooling for two or three years.

Observations by a traveler through the South appearing in the London *Magazine*, 1745-1746, indicate that "those that cant afford to send their children to the better schools, send them to the country school-masters who are generally servants, who after serving their terms out, set up for themselves."

A historian of Tazewell County, Virginia, wrote in 1852:

> The early settlers of this region had many difficulties to encounter in their efforts to procure homes for themselves and their children, and too frequently education appears to have been but of secondary importance in their estimation. Yet primary schools of some sort seem to have been maintained from an early date after its settlement, in those neighborhoods where children were sufficiently numerous to make up a school, and parents were able and willing to support a teacher.

Nevertheless in spite of all the desire for education and pitiful attempts to provide it the southern masses remained unenlightened. Doyle says: "In the absence of schools the small freeholder, so far as such a class existed, grew up with tastes and habits little above those of the savage whom he supplanted."[147]

Occasionally the class feeling of the aristocracy in the matter of education struck fire. Some of their ideas would bring delight to the modern advocates of caste lines in education. Thus the proceedings of the Maryland assembly for 1663 contain this item:

> Was returned the additionall act for the advancement of children's estates from the lower house wherein they desired the words [handy craft, trade] might be struck out. Ordered that answer be returned that to strike out those words . . . was to destroy the very thing intended by the act which was to breed up all the indigent youth of this province to handycraft trade and noe other.

In seventeenth century Virginia the court looked to the education of orphans. Masters were obliged to teach their bond-apprentices to read and write. For instance in 1698 "Ann Chandler, orphan of Daniel Chandler, bound apprentice to Phyllemon Miller till eighteen or day of marriage, to be taught to read a chapter in the Bible, the Lord's Prayer and Ten Commandments, and semptress work." Many negro children were taught to read and write by their parents or masters. North Carolina law required that orphans be properly educated according to rank out of the estate if it sufficed; otherwise they were to be apprenticed to handicraft or trade (not to Quakers) till of age.

The Quaker counterpart of the discrimination mentioned is seen in a query adopted by the Maryland yearly meeting in 1725 to be answered by lower meet-

[147] Doyle. *English Colonies in America*, vol. i, 394.

ings: "Whether there is any masters of trade that want apprentices[,] or children of Friends to be put forth, that they apply themselves to the monthly meetings before they take those that are not Friends, or put forth their children to such?" Another query was: "Whether have the children of the poor due education so as to fitt them for necessary employment?"

Family government in the colonies was patriarchal tho not necessarily harsh and forbidding. Pioneer exigencies magnified the family into a compendium of church, state, and school. Immigrant peoples had the same problem as modern immigrants in respect to maintaining the mother tongue and folk standards. The Mennonists in the Valley of Virginia trained their children in their peculiar religious ways. Generally they strictly forbade the dance or other juvenile amusements common to other sects of Germans. Virginia had disreputable taverns and saloons that were an offset to family interests and discipline. The Maryland Quaker queries already mentioned contain the following:

> Are all careful to keep meetings . . . bringing forth their families? . . . Do those that have children train them up in the nurture and fear of the Lord, restraining them from vice, wantonness, and keeping company with such as would teach them vain fations and corrupt ways of this world to the misspending of their precious time and substance?

An old writer remarks of the Scotch-Irish and Scotch settlers of North Carolina:

> These Presbyterian mothers gloried in the enterprise, and religion, and knowledge, and purity of their husbands and children, and would forego comforts and endure toil that their sons might be well instructed enterprising men.

Chastellux says that like the English the settlers were fond of their infants but cared little for their children. The annals and biographies do not confirm his assertion. George Wythe learned Greek at home from a Testament while his mother held an English copy and guided him. John Mason carried through life the effect of his mother's influence. She died when he was seven yet all his life "mother's room" was vivid in his memory.

Of course one can find instances to the opposite effect. Thus the reverend Mr. Urmstone writes from North Carolina that the people are unwilling to pay minister or schoolmaster, "nay they need to be hired to go to church or send their children to school." There are indications, however, that he was no model rector or pattern. Indeed he himself writes:

> I intend to send my two youngest children as a present to the society hoping they will put them into some charity school or hospitall. Whereby they may be educated and provided for, when they come to age, for I am not able to maintain them. My eldest is near twenty, capable of helping me, but is bent upon going for England. . . There is no boarding here, there is never a family that I know of that I would live in if they would hire me.

As an instance of aliens' experience with their children in the midst of the English environment we may cite the Huguenots. The children of the immigrants grew up more proficient in English than in the mother tongue. Gradually the church services became confined to the surviving refugees and such of their children as out of respect accompanied them. The second and third generations in America were ready to join the established church of the province.

With regard to the character of youth under the colonial régime the following additional citations will be suggestive. A Virginia lady of the olden time reported:

> Very little from books was thought necessary for a girl. She was trained to domestic matters, however, must learn the accom-

> plishments of the day, to play upon the harpsichord or spinet, and to work impossible dragons and roses on canvas.

Doctor Brickell wrote of early eighteenth century North Carolina:

> The young men are generally of a bashful, sober behavior, few proving prodigals, to spend what the parents with care and industry have left them but commonly improve it. . . The girls are most commonly handsome and well featur'd, but have pale or swarthy complexions, and are generally more forward than the boys, notwithstanding the women are very shy, in their discourses, till they are acquainted.

The author of *Itinerant Observations in America* which appeared in the London *Magazine* of 1745-1746, after travels in the South wrote thus:

> The girls, under such good mothers, generally have twice the sense and discretion of the boys; their dress is neat and clean, and not much bordering upon the ridiculous humour of the mother country, where the daughters seem dressed up for a market. . . Adieu Maryland.

XVIII. FAMILY PATHOLOGY AND SOCIAL CENSORSHIP IN THE COLONIAL SOUTH

The colonial South had its share of irregularities in the relations between husbands and wives, parents and children. Civic treatment of family disorders was somewhat less radical than in New England. Isolation of residence made for a low degree of civic control. Continental blood worked against tendencies to Puritan asperity in domestic life.

In 1624 in Virginia it was ordained that

> Three sufficient men of every parish shall be sworn to see that every man shall plant and tende sufficient corne for his family. Those men that have neglected so to do are to be by the said three men presented to be censured by the governor and counsell.

Sometimes Virginia church wardens relieved wives who, with children, had been ejected by husbands. Mary Laurence in 1676 complained that her husband had driven her out and refused to maintain her. The justices ordered her returned home. If the husband proved vagabond he should be put to forced labor for their support. Meanwhile the churchwarden was to see that she and the child did not lack food. In 1688 a man had deserted an old, deaf wife, who unless the rest of her estate should be sold would be thrown on the parish. The court ordered wardens to act as trustees of the property and use it for her.

In 1692 the Grand Council of South Carolina

> Upon hereing the petition of Jan La Salle ordrd that her husband Peter . . . cohibitt wth: the said Jane his wife and maintaine her in all necessaryes as his wife, or else that he allow his said wife the negro woman he had with her and pay his said wife £6 ster. p. annum.

He was charged costs.

A North Carolina law of 1755 provides that vagrants shall be whipped from constable to constable to the counties where their wives and children formerly lived and there give bond for good behavior and "for betaking him or herself to some lawful calling or honest labor." Otherwise the culprit should be hired out for one year; the money to cover expenses of arrest and any balance to go to the family.

In Georgia there was special need of social maintenance of families: it was a charity establishment in part. At a board meeting in 1735 in Palace Court was received a

> Petition of Mary Bateman, mother of Wm. Bateman now in Georgia, setting forth, that her son, William Bateman went to Georgia by the way of Charlestown at his own expense, with one servant to take possession of a grant of 75 acres of land; that his servant left him at Charles Town; that he has had great illness, and been at extraordinary expenses on other occasions; and praying credit for a years maintenance for himself and his wife in Georgia and to have the assistance of a servant. Resolved that credit be given to the said Wm. Bateman and his wife for a year's maintenance and that a servant be sent him. . .
>
> Resolvd that a town lot in Savannah be granted to Austin Weddell; And that he and his wife be sent over by the said ship and that they be maintained for a year.

In regard to Georgia the following regulation was made:

> The children of six years and upwards of [certain] servants to

be employed as the overseers shall direct; and the maintenance of them for provisions and clothing; to be paid by the week after the rate of four pence a day each . . . but those children of such servants under six years old are to be maintained by the parents out of their allowances.

At Frederica and Savannah salaries were provided for public midwives for the poor and for trust servants, besides five shillings per case, and the midwives were under obligation to attend on such as required their services.

The Savannah records for a number of years contain numerous instances of public aid to families. Many of the cases involved widowhood or bad health, and discretion was manifested in allotment of relief.

It is probable that Georgia had a greater volume of such relief cases than had the other colonies. In North Carolina in 1771 the House allowed one hundred fifty pounds to the widow of a government soldier who had fought in the battle of Alamance and one hundred pounds to each of three others, because of their distress with a number of small children; "which money shall be paid into the hands of a trustee, and by him applied to the purchase of slaves for the use of the said widows and children, and to no other purpose whatsoever."

Old records contain instances of family discord tending to separation. Some such cases have already been mentioned incidentally. In no southern colony was there a tribunal competent to grant divorce or separation. The statutes of these colonies are silent on the subject of divorce jurisdiction. Not a case has been discovered of absolute divorce by pre-revolutionary legislatures. Separations did occur and separate maintenance was sometimes granted by the court. One such case in Virginia has been cited in another connection.

Again, in 1691, the request "of Ruth Fulcher for separate maintenance against her husband, John Fulcher," was referred to county court justices, "who, after hearing the testimony, decided in favor of the plaintiff." In 1699 Mrs. Mary Taylor complained to court that her husband was "so cross and cruel" that she could not live with him. She asked for alimony in a home of her own where she would be "secure from danger." The court ordered the husband to deliver to her furniture and clothing and contribute twelve hundred pounds of tobacco or six pounds yearly to her support.

The Maryland high court of chancery took cognizance of suits for separate alimony. In 1689 the case of Galwith vs. Galwith came before the provincial court. The record of the court from which it was appealed says that at June session, 1685, "the appellee, being the wife of the appellant," presented a petition "seting forth, that within a few years certain false, evil, and scandalous reports were raised and spread abroad against her by some malicious persons," causing "great dissention and difference between her husband and herself, insomuch that he refused to entertain her in his house, or allow her a competent maintenance elsewhere, by which she was reduced to great poverty and want." In 1684 she had "applied to the county court for relief . . . at which time the court hearing and considering the premises, granted an order that her husband should allow . . . her 2000 wt. of tobacco for her maintenance the next year ensuing." But the "year was completed and ended, and her said husband not being reconciled nor willing" to take back her or the child, "which she hitherto had maintained," she would shortly "be brought to extreme poverty and necessity without further assistance from the court." She prayed the court to order her husband to "take her home to dwell with him, which she was desirous to do, or else that he might be enjoined to allow her a competent maintenance for herself and child." So he was commanded to "take home his said wife Jane Galwith, to dwell with him as man and wife ought to do; otherwise to allow . . . her 3000 wt. of tobacco a year, commencing from that day." The higher tribunal reversed the judgment. The jurisdiction in suits for alimony, assumed prior to the Revolution by the courts of equity, was confirmed by a later statute.

Troublesome cases did arise in spite of southern conservatism. The records of the Maryland provincial court show that in 1651 Robert Holt deposed that his wife had divers times threatened his life. Edward Hudson joined her in abusing him. "I goe daily in fear of my life." According to witnesses, the woman was adulteress with Hudson. A woman testified to Mrs. Holt's disposition to kill her husband. John Gent deposes "that he heard Dorothy Holt cry for many curses to God against her husband, that he might rot limb from limb, and that she would daily pray to God that such casualties might fall upon him, and likewise that her son Richard might end his days upon the gallows." On one occasion in this colony in the year 1658 a minister gave a divorce and remarried the man. Both men were indicted. In 1701 the petition of a man to the council for divorce and illegitimizing of the wife's children of the period of her elopement was sent to the house with a proposed bill. The House summoned the parties to appear at next session.

It would seem that orders of separate maintenance would be in effect decrees of separation. In seventeenth century Virginia, even orders of separation occurred only at very long intervals. They were rarely asked and more rarely granted. In 1655 Alice Clawson of Northhampton County secured some sort of "divorce" on the ground that her husband had for many years lived among the Indians and had refused to give up his Indian concubine. In the Virginia colony marriages could be annulled by the General Court if the parties were within the forbidden degrees. Before March 12, 1684 a man married his uncle's widow. How such a marriage could occur is hard to understand. After at least ten years of marriage and after the birth of children the woman seems to have been horrified at the sinfulness of her union and she secured a separation. The man agreed to pay alimony. Their daughter was to be put in school as the mother should see fit. The vestry of St. John's parish, Baltimore County, Maryland cited a man to appear and explain his marriage with his deceased wife's sister. Another was summoned for uniting himself in marriage with his late wife's niece. Both failed to justify themselves so the clerk was ordered to present them to the County Court.

An interesting personage was Mr. John Custis of Virginia. He had put on his tombstone this inscription: "Aged 71 years and yet lived but seven years which was the space of time he kept" bachelor's hall. He and his wife seem to have been very unhappy together. In 1774 they entered into the "Articles of Agreements betwixt Mr. John Custis and his wife. Whereas some differences and quarrels have arisen betwixt Mr. John Custis and Frances his wife concerning some money, plate and other things taken from him by the sd. Frances and a mor plentiful maintenance for her. Now to the end and all animostys and unkindness may cease and a perfect love and friendship may be renewed betwixt them they have mutually agreed" that she shall return things taken and not repeat the offence. She shall not run in debt without his consent. He is not to deprive her of the plate and damask during her life. She is to forbear to call him vile names or give him any ill language. He is to reciprocate. They are to live lovingly together as a good husband and wife ought. She is not to meddle with his business, nor he, in her domestic affairs. Half of the net produce of the estate shall go to her for clothing herself and children and educating them and providing things necessary for housekeeping, and physic, so long as she live quietly with him "and that he shall allow for the maintenance and family one bushel of wheat for every week and a sufficient quantity of Indian corn," also meat, "and sufficient quantity of cyder and brandy if so much be made on the plantation." If she shall exceed the allowance or run him in debt the bond shall become void and the allowance cease. She is to have the same house servants as now or others in their stead; also an errand boy. Her husband shall allow her fifteen pounds of wool and fifteen of fine dressed flax yearly to spin for any use in the family. She may give away twenty yards of Virginia cloth yearly to charity if so much remains after the servants are clothed. She may keep a white servant out of the above allowance provided he be subject to her husband. He is to give her fifty pounds now, if so much be available, in order to get things started. She is to give account under oath if he require, how said fifty pounds and yearly profits are spent.

In the latter part of the eighteenth century some Virginia husbands and wives advertised each other with abuse, in which the wife had the advantage. In one case were inserted particulars filling half a column. The indictment begins thus: "Whereas Ben Bannerman my husband has published a false and scandalous account," etc. A later writer, taking account of such instances, was impressed with the fact that all such viragoes of whom he read date from the old country. "Not one is found that does not refer to Europe; thus proving that . . . our fair countrywomen were as good-tempered as they were beautiful." It is probable that his observations refer to Richmond newspapers.[148]

In South Carolina, 1731-1732, appeared advertisements for three absconding wives. In Georgia, Whitefield's and Wesley's work, it was said, caused division among families.

While the materials at hand illustrative of marital friction and social suzerainty over the family are rather meager, it is evident that the community recognized as in New England the necessity of supplying family necessities and maintaining family integrity. The recognition of wifely claims of alimony is a tacit avowal of woman's parasitism. But some of the instances of family trouble cited suggest that some southern women were sufficiently forceful and independent. The treatment of forbidden degrees parallels that in New England. Religion as a source of family dissension recalls especially certain incidents in Rhode Island. Protestant solvent tendencies operate in both regions.

In England under Elizabeth poor children were to be trained for some trade and the idle were to be punished. In the reign of James I. the statutes of Elizabeth for binding children were utilized for sending them to America. The apprenticing of poor children to the Virginia Company began as early as 1620. In

[148] Compare Little, *Richmond*, 22.

that year Sir Edwin Sandys asked authority to send one hundred children that had been "appointed for transportation" by the city of London but were not willing to go. The apprenticeship statute of Elizabeth solved the difficulty. Children and vagrants were regularly assembled for shipment. A record of 1627 reads: "There are many ships going to Virginia, and with them 1400 or 1500 children which they have gathered up in divers places."

The jurisdiction of churchwardens in early Virginia covered indigent orphans. It seems that they were usually indentured till they were twenty-one. The parish often provided a sum for clothing. The wardens' jurisdiction extended also over parents disposed to encourage children in bad courses. In 1692 a man was reported to justices as an "idle and lazy person" whose children lived by his begging or their stealing. He refused to bind them out. The churchwardens were instructed to do so if he continued vagabond. Near the end of the seventeenth century, wardens were empowered to bind out illegitimate boys until they were thirty. Poor children whose parents could not provide for them properly were bound out for long terms. Wardens were required to supervise the treatment of those they bound out. If the master gave bad treatment the child was removed to another safe master and the offender was punished. In 1657 acts were passed forbidding any person to whom an Indian child had been entrusted from assigning or in any way transferring the child. It was ordered that such child should be free at the age of twenty-five.

Mr. H. Jones wrote of Virginia in 1724:

When there is a numerous family of poor children the vestry takes care to bind them out apprentices, till they are able to

> maintain themselves by their own labor; by which means they are never tormented with vagrant and vagabond beggars.

An act of 1748 provides that orphans whose estates will not support them shall be bound as apprentices. They shall be taught to read and write and otherwise supplied. If ill used or if training is neglected such orphans may be removed.

An instance of voluntary apprenticeship is presented in the diary of Colonel Carter:

> Billy Beale, the youngest son of the late John Beale, a lad of about eighteen, came to me Saturday on a letter I wrote to his mother. He brought with him Mr. Eustace's and Mr. Edwards' consent, his guardians, that he should be bound to me in the place of Wm. Ball, which the young gentleman very willingly agreed to. . . He is . . . to serve me three years for £10 the year in order to be instructed in the stewardship or management of a Virginia estate.

In Maryland about 1658 the assembly passed a measure to the effect that guardians should render account of minors' estates. No child was to be placed in the hands of guardians "of a contrary judgment then that of their deceased parents." In 1663 the assembly decided that no account be allowed for anything against orphans' estates unless their education is provided for out of the estate if it suffices. If the estate was too small to provide education then the orphans were to be bound apprentices to some "Handicraft, trade, or other person" till twenty-one, unless a kinsman will maintain them on the interest of the estate, the estate itself to go to the orphans at the years appointed by law. No allowance was to be made for excessive funeral expenses. The Assembly Proceedings of 1671 record the experience that former acts for the preservation of orphans' estates were inadequate. Long directions are given for safeguarding estates. It is directed explicitly that children are to be committed to persons of the same religion as the parents if the court has to make the appointment.

The early Friends in Maryland took especial care of the interests of orphans and protected their estates by extralegal guards. They had a committee to look after widows and orphans. They even had a register of wills at a time when there was no official register or at least none near at hand. Among the queries adopted by yearly meeting in 1725 to be answered by lower meetings we find this: "Whether there is any fatherless or widows that want necessarys . . . and if any want are they supplied?"

In the *Calvert Papers* occurs indication that at least one of the parochial clergy had under consideration a charitable subscription toward the support of widows and the education of children of the brethren left destitute.

In North Carolina the authorities looked after the fortunes of dependent children. Thus a Carolina court of 1694 leaves the following record:

> Upon a petition exhibited by Thomas Hassold showing that a child named Thos. Snoden was left with him by his father-in-law Edmund Perkins upon condition to pay him 600 pounds of tobacco per annum for his dyatt, ordered that the sd. Thos. Snoden serve the said Hassold until his father-in-law come for him or els till he arrive that the age of twenty one yeares.

At a later court two orphans were bound out, the boy to be taught a trade and at the end of his term to receive a heifer. The girl was to receive with her freedom a cow and calf "beside the custom of the country." Governor Johnson remarked on a North Carolina law entitled "An act concerning orphans" that this law was highly unjust and seemed designed to encourage and protect unjust guardians that robbed their wards, "a practice too common in this country." At another time attention was called to the need of further security for the estates of widows and orphans.

A statute recalling northern legislation was enacted in 1773 in a measure applying to Newbern: "Whereas sundry idle and disorderly persons as well as slaves and children under age do make a practise of firing guns and pistols within the said town," a fine of ten shillings is prescribed for the offence. If culprits are under age the parent, master, or guardian must pay.

At a meeting of the Georgia Board in Palace Court, 1735, complaint was made that William Littel, an infant in Georgia, was deprived of his patrimony by a man that had married his mother. The mother was now dead according to the complaint filed by the child's grandfather. The board ordered guardians appointed and the infant to be kept at Mrs. Parker's and proper disposal of the estate to be made for the child's benefit. The Georgia committee on accounts in 1737 recommended a budget for one year to include one hundred fifty pounds for the support of sick, widows, and orphans in the colony. A Savannah estimate in 1739 included an allowance for the care of widows of trust servants till they marry or enter service of one hundred pounds for the year. A like item of fifty pounds was made for Frederica.

Martyn's account of Ebenezer in 1738-1739 says:

> They have built a large and convenient house for the reception of orphans and other poor children, who are maintained by benefactions among the people, are well taken care of and taught to work according as their age and ability will permit.

Whitefield began an orphan asylum in Georgia in 1740. To it poor children were sent to be kept partly by charity and partly by the produce of the land cultivated by negroes. The institution did not flourish, probably on account of unhealthy location. The writer of *Itinerant Observations in America* visited the establishment soon after its foundation. He says:

> They were at dinner when we arrived, the whole family at one table, and sure never was a more orderly pretty sight: If I recollect right, besides Mr. Barber the school-master, and some women, there were near forty young persons of both sexes dressd very neatly and decently. After dinner they retired, the boys to school and the girls to their spinning and knitting: I was told, their vacant hours were employed in the garden and plantation work.

This visit to the Orphan House removed his prejudices against it. Habersham said that many of the best orphans were removed from the orphan house by justices and bound as servants.

It is evident from the foregoing pages how great a burden was imposed upon colonial enterprises (especially in Georgia) by the presence of dependent women and children. After the industrial life of a colony was under way the labor of such could be utilized; but at first they were a drag. Thus West wrote to Lord Ashley (with reference to Carolina) in 1670:

> Arrived the Carolina frigate with about 70 passengers . . . and six servants . . . viz. two men and woeman and three small children, which wilbe a great charge to the plantation, wee having nothing yet but what is brought.

A letter of Lord Ashley in 1671 warned against inviting the poorer sort, as yet, to Carolina. It is substantial men and their families that are needed. "Others relye and eate upon us."

A freeholders' petition to the Georgia trustees in 1738 says:

> None of all those who have planted their land have been able to raise sufficient produce to maintain their families in bread

> kind only, even though as much application and industry have been exerted to bring it about, as could be done by men engaged in an affair on which they believed the welfare of themselves and posterity so much depended, and which they imagined required more than ordinary pains to make succeed. . . Your honors, we imagine, are not insensible of the numbers that have left this province, not being able to support themselves and families any longer. . . [This paper is signed by one hundred seventeen freeholders.] We did not allow widows and orphans to subscribe [i.e., sign].

Habersham wrote to Oglethorpe in 1741:

> What must a poor friendless man do, with his wife and children settled upon fifty acres of land, perhaps pine barren, but suppose it the best, without either servants to help clear or steers to plow the ground?

Planters' extravagance sometimes forced a resort to the frontier. In colonial Virginia the father sometimes left his son expensive habits, a depleted plantation, and a heavy debt. Then degrading poverty, untimely death, or migration to the West were the alternatives. Many families carried to the wilderness their social refinement and dear-bought experience and commenced life afresh on a less splendid scale.

XIX. SERVITUDE AND SEXUALITY IN THE SOUTHERN COLONIES

The problem of sex morals in the colonial South was very largely an economic question and was so regarded by the authorities. Sexual morality was at a low ebb. Very early, laws had to be passed on this point.

By a Maryland act of 1650, renewed in 1654, adultery and fornication were to be censured and punished as the governor and council or authorized officials should think fit, "not extending to life or member." In 1658 an act was passed as follows:

> Whereas divers women servants within this Province not haveing husbands living with them, have bene gotten with child in the tyme of their servitude to the great dishonour of God and the apparent damage to the masters. . . For remedy whereof bee it enacted . . . that every such mother of a bastard child not able sufficiently to prove the party charged to be the begetter of such child, in every such case the mother of such child shall only be lyable to satisfy the damages soe sustained by servitude, or other wayes . . . provided that when the mother of any such child as aforesaid shalbe able to prove her charge either by sufficient testimony of wittnesses or confession, then the party charged, if a servant to satisfie half the said damages, if a freeman then the whole damages by servitude or otherwise as aforesaid. And if any such mother . . . be able to prove . . . that the said party charged (being a single person and a freeman) did before the begitting of such child promise her marriage, that then hee shall performe his promise to her, or recompense her abuse, as the court before whom such matter is brought shall see convenient, the quallity and condition of the persons considered.

This act was to continue for three years or to the end

of the next General Assembly. According to Maryland law, polygamy, sodomy, and rape were capital offences.

The author of *Leah and Rachel* notes regarding Virginia that "if any be known . . . to . . . commit whoredome . . . there are . . . severe and wholesome laws." An act of 1657-1658 deprived males guilty of bastardy of the right to testify in court or hold office – a severe penalty when everyone wanted some office. But the colony could not afford to support illegitimates! An act was passed giving the master an additional time of service if a bastard was born to his servant. This law put a premium on immorality and there seem to have been masters base enough to profit by it. The evil was restrained by an act of 1662 which provided that the maid servant should be sold away from her master in such cases without compensation to him for the loss of her time. By a law of 1705 "every person not a servant or slave, convicted of adultery or fornication by the oaths of two or more credible witnesses, or confession, shall, for every offense of adultery, pay 1000 lbs. of tobacco and cost; and of fornication, 500 . . . to be recovered by . . . churchwardens of parish where offense was committed." In default of payment he should receive twenty-five lashes By an act of 1727 the mother of a bastard was subject to fine or flogging. The person in whose house the birth occurred was responsible for giving notice. A servant woman had to serve an extra year or pay her owner one thousand pounds of tobacco. The reputed father, if free, had to give security to maintain the child. If he was a servant he had to render satisfaction to the parish, after expiration of his term, for keeping the child. If the master was the father he could claim no extra service but the parish could sell the mother for one extra year.

North Carolina bastardy laws were similar to Virginia's. A law of 1715 provided that a woman servant bearing a bastard was liable to two years extra servitude besides punishment for fornication. If she came into the province with child she was not liable. If with child by the master she was to be sold for two years after expiration of her time; the money to go to the parish. The act left the master unpunished except as he lost her service or was liable for fornication or adultery. The act of 1741 was milder. "Whereas many women are begotten with child by free men or servants, to the great prejudice of their master or mistress" such must serve one year extra. If the master is the father the woman should be sold by the church wardens for one year. There was no punishment for the seducing master. Instructions to Governor Dobbs in 1754 directed that laws against adultery, fornication, polygamy, and incest were to be enforced and extended.

A recent writer says that the sanctity of the marriage vow was inviolable in early Maryland. Citations that might be given for the period between 1650 and 1657 convey a quite different impression; the extant record of fornication and adultery is appalling.

Alsop in his *Character of Maryland* suggests that while male immigrants had less luck than female in getting mates unless they were good talkers and persuaders, this fluent sort stood a chance of injecting "themselves in the time of their servitude into the private and reserved favor of their mistress, if age speak their master deficient." An Episcopal rector in 1676 wrote of Maryland: "All notorious vices are committed; so that it is become a Sodom of uncleanness, and a pest house of iniquity."

In 1685 Anne Thompson, convicted of bigamy, was pardoned on agreement to abandon the second husband. In 1696,

> Vpon representacōn . . . that Thomas Hedge Clerk . . . had lately been marryed to another woman notwithstanding his having a wife now living in England and that one Lieut. Coll. Richardson tho conscious thereof did presume to perform tht office; ordered thereupon that Mr Attorney and Sollictor Genll. make due proceedings agt them.

About 1697 Governor Nicholson reported to the Board of Trade that "some of the men having two wives, and some of the women, two husbands, whoring . . . were too much practised in the countrey, and seldom any were punished for these sins."

A letter of the reverend Thomas Bray in 1702 says:

> How else could it be that such an infamous vile man as Holt who is expelled out of Virginia for adultery should be received in Maryland and presented to one of the best livings in the province. And were any one amongst you to govern the clergy such a miscreant who I hear has attempted to poison his own wife and has lately had a bastard by the woman he kept would have been so far from being permitted to enjoy his place and to exercise the ministry of his holy calling that he would not only long ere this have been deprived of his living but degraded from his function. I hear there is another scandalous vagrant come into the province, one Butt as wicked as the other and yet put into a place.

In All Saints Parish in 1736,

> Mr. Richard Blake, vestryman, reported to this vestry that himself and Mr. Jas. Hughes church warden forewarned George —— and Mary —— not to cohabit tegether for the future upon their penalty as the law in that case provides.

In the province at a later date a case of bastardy and forced marriage was burlesqued by vulgar officials.

In Virginia persons were presented for adultery and fornication by the church-wardens at the annual visitations; and the culprits had to submit to fines or whipping. The following judgment was given by the governor and council in 1627:

> Upon the presentment of the church-wardens of Stanley Hundred for suspicion of incontinency betweene Henry Kinge and the wife of John Jackson, they lyinge together in her husband's absence; it is thought fitt that the sayd Kinge shall remove his habitation from her, and not to use or frequent her company until her husband's return.

In 1631, "Because Edw. Grymes lay with Alice West he gives security not to marry any woman till further order from the governor and council."

Bruce in his *Institutional History of Virginia in the Seventeenth Century* treats at length of sex sin. He asserts that one of the commonest sins committed in the lower levels of society was bastardy. Numbers of women servants came over either free or bound by indenture. These generally belonged to the lowest class in the home country and not all were trained in virtue. In Virginia as contract servants it was not easy for them to marry. Masters did not want this species of cattle laid by for pregnancy and childbirth with the risk of death. Licentious masters were in a position also to utilize the sex services of such as they chose. Moreover the unfortunate women were thrown in contact with the lowest class of men and immorality was practically inevitable especially as kinship ties and responsibility had been broken by the migration.

At a very early period punishment was inflicted for incontinence even tho the guilty persons had married and their children had been born in wedlock. In 1642 a couple were arrested for living unlawfully together.

They were sentenced to thirty lashes each and thereafter were kept apart till legally united. Another man for like offense was compelled to give one hundred fifty pounds of tobacco towards the erection of stocks. The same year a woman was convicted of bearing two bastards. J. Pope, summoned for improper intimacy with a woman, was tried and sentenced to build a ferry boat or receive forty lashes and acknowledge his fault in the parish church. In another case the father of a bastard was sentenced to go before the congregation and confess. The mother was to receive thirty lashes on her bare back. One woman led into church was impenitent. She was lashed and required to appear again. It was generally the man that escaped whipping.

After the middle of the century bastardy became more frequent than ever, owing to the increase in number of female domestic and agricultural servants. The burden of maintaining illegitimates weighed heavily on the colony. In the House of Burgesses Colonel Lawrence Smith offered a petition in which after stressing "the excessive charge" that rested on the parishes "by means of bastards born of servant women" he asked for more stringent measures. The House, however, deemed the existing laws sufficient.

One of the church wardens' most important duties was to protect the parish from the expense of bastards. Sometimes the father of a bastard was required to give bond to protect the parish from expense while the mother was in his service. Always the master, if not guilty of the bastardy, could pay such sum as would safeguard the parish. Servants would have to serve extra time.

In 1663 fourteen cases of bastardy were tried at one county court session. In 1688, at least three servant women of one master gave birth to illegitimate children. If wardens neglected to bind till the age of thirty unprovided-for bastards they might be prosecuted in county court.

County courts protected women of loose reputation from undue severity. In 1693 Elizabeth Paine was ordered by the wardens of York to leave the plantation where she was living. She appealed as the ground was ready for a crop and she did not want to lose it from herself and her "poor children." The court granted leave to stay until the crop was secured.

The court of Norfolk County, 1695, took the following action:

> Whereas Captain J—— H—— hath been prsented to this court by the grand jury for entertaining another man's wife, contrary to lawe, the woman being the wife of B—— S—— blacksmith late of this county, who hath been sometimes absent out of this county and the said Capt. J—— H—— apearing upon sumons from this court, pleading in his vindication, this court hath thought fit and doe order that the church wardens of Eliza R. parrish doe repair forthwith to the said Capt H—— house and admonish him and the said woman not to frequent or be seene in each other's company for the future and that the said Capt H—— put her away from his house imeadiately after such admonicon and make report of theire soe doing at the next court and that the said H—— doe accordingly put the sayd woman away from his house and that they doe not frequent each other's company hereafter upon payne of the penalty of the lawes in such cases provided and Sd. H—— pay cost.

Stories of scandal in high society can be found in the histories of all old Virginia and Carolina towns.[149]

The contemporary authorities usually speak in unfavorable terms of the morals of the first settlers in North Carolina. Graffenried speaks of lewd fellows

---

[149] Giddings. *Natural History of American Morals*, 34.

among the Palatines. The reverend Mr. Urmstone in a letter from the colony dated 1711 says:

> This is a nest of the most notorious profligates on earth. Women forsake their husbands come in here and live with other men they are sometimes followed then a pull is given to the husband and madam stays with her gallant a report is spread abroad that the husband is dead then they become man and wife make a figure and pass for people of worth and dignity. What to do with such I know not . . . for I have not been wanting in my endeavors.

Brickell says of the North Carolinians in 1737: "The generality of them live after a loose and lascivious manner." In 1760 Woodmason said:

> The manners of the North Carolinians in general are vile and corrupt and the whole country is a stage of debauchery dissoluteness and corruption, and how can it be otherwise? The people are composed of the outcasts of all the other colonies. . . Marriages (through want of Clergy) are performed by every ordinary magistrate – poligamy is very common – celibacy much more – bastardy no disrepute, concubinage general.

The reverend gentleman quoted above was later forced to turn his son adrift. "He got a servant wench with child who had two years to serve rendered her not only useless but even a burden to me yet am forced to keep her not knowing where to get a better." But a letter to the secretary accuses this clerical gentleman of drunkenness, profanity, and lewdness.

A Carolina general court in 1727 entertained

> A presentment against Solomon Hews for leaving his lawful wife and cohabiting with another woman in which time the woman have had two children. . . A presentment against John Brown for having left his wife . . . and cohabits with another which he acknowledges to be his lawful wife both of said women within this Government.

On another occasion a grand jury presented James Boulton for cohabiting with and seducing Mary Jennings from her husband. Brickell notes an Indian's attempt to seduce a planter's maid. Locke's Carolina Memoirs refer to one "O'Syllivan . . . illnatured buggerer of children." At one time, probably about 1760, a minister complained against his vestry:

> One of them declared that the money he is obliged to give to the maintaining a minister he would rather give to a kind girl. Another is a person who committed incest with his own uncle's widow and has a child by her which he owns publicly.

The House in 1766 appointed a committee to investigate a complaint of Solomon Ewell of the elopement of his wife and her living in adultery. Solomon asked divorce.

Charges of loose living in early North Carolina may have been exaggerated. But probably the inaccessibility of the settlements and the lack of religion and education favored the coming of undesirables.

Georgia was not free from sex sin. For Savannah, 1735, we find the following record:

> Att our last Court Wm. Watkins . . . was prosecuted for misdemeanor and the late wife of James Willoughby for Bigamy. . . Watkins in April had procured a person unknown . . . to marry him to the widow . . . in consequence of which she proved with child; soon after this, he received advice by letter and message that his wife was alive and well in England; and he had not made his marriage publick, he proposed to her, that as he had a wife in England, he should be liable to be troubled, and therefore dared not own it; and as she was with child the world would soon discover it, and believe she had played the whore, therefore persuaded her to marry R. Mellichamp. They were married by Mr. Irving Watkins being present; Mellichamp soon discovered her being with child, and his own misfortunes in marrying her; Watkins and the woman were at Richard Turner's one night, when Mellichamp came in and desired her to go home, but as she was not willing, he said, that he would sell such a wife for a

groat at any time, declaring he believed she loved Watkins better than he; one in the company jocularly said he would give a shilling for her, severall others bidding by way of auction she was declared to be sold for £5 sterling; Mellichamp seemed satisfyed, and the woman declared she would go with the buyer and behaved immodestly. One Langford then in company at their desire conveyed them to his lodging, where they were bedded in publick, and the £5 paid and accepted of. . . Watkins was whipt (unpittyed) on a muster day at the carts tail round the town and remains in gaol for want of surety. The woman is held in gaol as being with child; but as we think her crime is within the benefit of the clergy her confinement is enlarged; Langford was very instrumental in the discovery of the whole matter and gave a clear evidence therefore was only bound over for his future good behavior, and Mellichamp, being a sufferer was acquitted.

One of the Wesleys' first experiences was with two coarse women with tainted virtue who they supposed had repented. The brothers persuaded Oglethorpe to accept the women as respectable and then attempted to reform the other female colonists.

Illegitimacy sometimes led to infanticide. In Maryland, 1656, a woman was accused (probably on suspicion of bastardy) of murdering her child. A jury of women was appointed to examine her. They testified that she had not had a child within the time in question. In other case a wretched girl bore an illegitimate child in secret. It died soon and was privately buried by the mother. According to English law this furtiveness was proof presumptive of infanticide and the girl was condemned to death. But the council, considering that the body showed no marks of violence and that its being wrapped in clean linen showed "a tender care and affection on the part of the mother," commuted the sentence to a fine of six thousand pounds of tobacco. Thereupon her old father sent a pathetic petition to the council representing that he was miserably poor and crushed with grief and shame. The fine was then reduced to five hundred pounds, or between four and five pounds sterling. In 1711 in Virginia there was an act to prevent murder of bastard children. In North Carolina at an early date occurred the case of a woman accused of killing her bastard child. She was found not guilty.

The Revolution doubtless brought a degree of the sex vice that is inseparable from warfare. In seaboard Georgia, women and children were driven from their homes. "The obscene language which was used and personal insults . . . offered to the tender sex soon rendered a residence in the country insupportable." They were obliged to abandon the country in great distress.

The presence of African slaves and Indians early gave rise to the problem of miscegenation. It took some time for standards of race integrity to become thoroly set and indeed while they did take shape in sanctimonious professional abhorrence they never eliminated intercourse between the male white and women of the inferior race. It was otherwise with the females of the white race. They belonged to their males.

In 1609 a sermon was preached at Whitechapel in presence of many adventurers and planters for Virginia from *Genesis*, xii, 1-3. The sermon taught that

> Abrams posteritie [must] keepe to themselves. They may not marry nor give in marriage to the heathen, that are uncircumcised. . . The breaking of this rule, may breake the necke of all good successe of this voyage, whereas by keeping the feare of God, the planters in shorte time, by the blessing of God, may grow into a nation formidable to all the enemies of Christ.

The only marriage with an Indian during the company's rule was in the case of Pocahontas. But in the early days no great antipathy to amalgamation with the Indians was shown. Through most of the seventeenth century there was no prohibition of marriage with Indians. Numerous instances of marriage with Indians are on record. There are instances in which the county courts granted express permission to a white man to espouse an Indian servant.

Pocahontas's marriage was thought to be a surety of peace and so it turned out to be. Sir Thomas Dale (with a wife in England) asked Powhatan for the hand of a favorite daughter. He meant to live for the remainder of his days in Virginia, he said, and he wanted to conclude with Powhatan a "perpetual friendship." Powhatan was not beguiled; he replied that his daughter was already disposed of. But the incident is an incisive commentary on the standards of the day. Rolfe, even, failed to provide in his will for his child by Pocahontas.

Governor Charles Calvert wrote to Lord Baltimore in 1672:

> Major Fitzherberts' brother who maryed the Indian Brent, has ciuilly parted with her and (as I suppose) will neuer care to bed with her more, soe that your Lopp need not to fear any ill consequence from that match butt what has already happened to the poore man who vnaduisedly threw himself away vpon her in hopes of a great portion, which now is come to little.

Doctor Brickell wrote of North Carolina:

> I knew an European man that lived many years amongst the Indians and had a child by one of their women, having bought her as they do their wives, and afterwards married a Christian. Sometimes after, he came to the Indian town [and wanted] to pass away a night with his former mistress as usual, but she made answer, that she then had forgot that she ever knew him, and that she never lay with another woman's husband; so fell a crying, took up the child she had by him, and went out of the

cabin in great disorder, altho he used all possible means to pacify her. . . She would never see him afterwards, or be reconciled. . . There are several Europeans and other traders which travel and abide amongst them for a long space of time, sometimes a year, two or three, and those men commonly have their Indian wives or mistresses, whereby they soon learn the Indian tongue and keep in good friendship with them, besides having the satisfaction they have of a bed-fellow, they find these girls very serviceable to them upon several occasions; especially in dressing their victuals, and instructing them in the affairs and customs of the country. . . One great misfortune that generally attend the Christians that converse with these women as husbands, is that they get children by them, which are seldom otherwise brought up or educated than in the wretched state of infidelity [for according to Indian custom, the children go to the mother, and it is hard for the white men to get them away. Some white men stay thus permanently among the Indians]. These Indian girls that have frequently conversed with the Europeans, never much care for the conversation of their own countrymen afterwards.

One trader from the Carolinas is said to have boasted that he had upwards of seventy children and grandchildren among the Indians.

Bosomworth, chaplain in Oglethorpe's regiment, married a half-breed much respected by the Indians. He hoped thus to get a great fortune.

Mixture with negroes was a more serious southern problem and called forth severe penalization. White servitude, assimilating European men and women to the servile status, was a potent factor in the demoralization. Planters sometimes married women servants to negroes in order to transform the women and their offspring into slaves.[150]

Something of the colonial attitude in the South on the question of miscegenation may be gathered from such terminology as "unnatural," "inordinate" unions. The

150 Compare McCormac. *White Servitude in Maryland*, 67-70.

offending white "defiled his body" and "abused himself to the dishonor of God and shame of Christianity."

Slavery of course had small regard for sex morality on the part of the chattels. Something of the economic spirit at work may be seen even in the legal protection given to the slaves. In Virginia even before 1705 the courts attempted to check the growth of the right to separate husband and wife and larger children. Devises of children, particularly of children not born before the testator's death (which devises were adjudged void), were declared by the general court in 1695 to be neither "convenient nor humanitarian" as the mother's owner would not be careful of her in pregnancy nor of the child "and many children might hence die; and besides it was an unreasonable charge" without benefit to the owner of the mother.

In North Carolina in the first half of the eighteenth century in disposing of slaves some care was used not to part the men and their wives and children. Such an instance is shown in the will of Cullen Pollock in 1749. Doctor Brickell wrote that negro marriages had little ceremony. If the woman returned the pledge the union was ruptured. If a woman proved unfruitful by her first husband the planter required her to take a series if necessary for the sake of procuring offspring. Rivals fought desperately. Slave children, he said, were carefully brought up and provided for by planters. Negro children wore little or no clothing save in winter. Many young men and women worked in hot weather nude save for a piece of cloth to "cover their nakedness."

The author of *Itinerant Observations in America* who visited Maryland, Virginia, and Carolina, wrote that with slavery

> Several brutal and scandalous customs . . . are too much

practised: such as giving them a number of wives, or in short, setting them up for stallions to a whole neighborhood; when it has been prov'd, I think, unexceptionably that polygamy rather destroys than multiplies the species . . . and were these masters to calculate, they'd find a regular procreation would make them greater gainers.

John Woolman in 1757 wrote after a trip through Maryland to Virginia:

Many of the white people in these provinces take little or no care of negro marriages; and when negros marry after their own way, some make so little account of these marriages that with views of outward interest they often part men from their wives by selling them far asunder, which is common when estates are sold by executors at vendue. . . Men and women have many times scarcely clothes sufficient to hide their nakedness, and boys and girls ten and twelve years old are often quite naked amongst their master's children. Some of our society, and some of the society called Newlights, use some endeavors to instruct those they have in reading; but in common this is not only neglected, but disapproved.

Instructions by Richard Corbin to an agent for the management of a plantation in Virginia in 1759 direct as follows:

The breeding wenches more particularly you must instruct the overseers to be kind and indulgent to, and not force them when with child upon any service or hardship that will be injurious to them and that they have every necessary when in that condition that is needful for them, and the children to be well looked after and to give them every spring and fall the jerusalem oak seed for a week together and that none of them suffer in time of sickness for want of proper care.

In North Carolina the reverend Mr. Reed wrote in 1760:

I baptise all those blacks whose masters become sureties for them, but never baptize any negro infants or children upon any other terms.

An advertisement of a runaway in the Virginia *Ga-*

zette, 1767, illustrates the scattering of slave families: "Has a wife at Little Town, and a father at Mr. Philip Burt's quarter." A slave-owner in North Carolina in 1774 wrote: "I have a Congoer who wants to be sold along with his wife and two children. I do not wish to sell him, tho I would not refuse to do so, if I find he will not stay here." A letter of John Peck (presumably in Virginia) in 1788 says: "My man George Jones has a wife at Colespoint."

The conditions of slavery and servitude were conducive to rape by negroes and whites. In Virginia in the seventeenth century we find reference to strong measures to be taken for apprehending Robin, a negro that had ravished a white woman. In the latter half of the eighteenth century the rigor of the criminal code was lessened. Slaves attempting rape, etc., had been castrated. But later the ability of county court to order castration was limited to cases of blacks convicted of attempt to ravish white women.

The effect of slavery on the morals of white children was beginning to be evident. The author of the *Itinerant Observations* previously cited says with reference to the using of negro males as "stallions:"

> A sad consequence of this practice is, that their childrens morals are debauched by the frequency of such sights, as only fit them to become the masters of slaves.

They suffer the children when young "too much to prowl amongst the young negros, which insensibly causes them to imbibe their manners and broken speech."

Chastellux, a French traveler, frequently remarks on the masses of the poverty-stricken people he saw in Virginia, some dressed in rags and living in miserable huts. They were indolent and hopeless, a product of the slave system, which degraded useful effort. From them sprang many of the "poor whites" of later days.

The record of southern servile institutions even in colonial days shows with sufficient plainness that fundamental morality is a very scarce commodity among people of the ruling class. At best they are willing to skim the surface of moral issues provided this can be done with advantage to their pocketbooks or their public treasury. It becomes evident from the study of servitude and slavery if not before that the family is the creature of economic conditions and that sentimental morality is an aftergrowth of economic improvement. The large reason why the ethics of the aristocratic family differed from that of the slave union was that the members of the former were a product of economic prowess while the latter were the victims of economic exploitation. The indictment that enlightened judgment brings against the industrial system in the colonial South is precisely that which to-day is due against the capitalist system as the subverter of family morality and the enemy of the home.

XX. FRENCH COLONIES IN THE WEST

The French settlements in the Gulf region, unlike those in the northern part of the Mississippi Valley, left an impress sufficiently permanent and important to make them worthy of special attention.

A colony was established at Mobile in 1701 and New Orleans was founded in 1718. From the outset there was a constant appeal to the mother country for wives. The Canadians of standing that were married brought their families to Louisiana. Many had grown daughters and these married young Canadians of good position. The French officers, younger sons of the nobility, could not condescend to lower grade so they lived in gay and careless bachelorhood. Some of them perhaps were relieved rather than distressed by the lack of wives. But the crude pioneers of the wilderness needed wives. "With wives," wrote Iberville, "I will anchor the sorry coureurs de bois into sturdy colonists." "Send me wives for my Canadians," write Bienville; "they are running in the woods after Indian girls."

In the summer of 1703 twenty-three young women of good character and appearance arrived. In 1706 Louis XIV. sent a number of girls to Louisiana. They were to have good homes and to be well married. It was thought that they would soon teach the squaws many useful domestic employments. But the girls rebelled against Indian corn, threatened to run away, and stirred up an imbroglio known as the Petticoat Rebellion, bringing much ridicule on the governor.

In 1713 the commissary-general wrote to the minister that twelve girls had lately arrived from France who were too ugly and badly formed to win the affections of the men and that only two of them had found husbands. He feared that the other ten would remain in stock for a long time. He thought fit to suggest that in future those that sent girls should attach more importance to beauty than to virtue as the Canadians were not particular about what sort of lives their spouses had formerly led whereas if they were supplied only with such ugly girls they would prefer to take up with Indian women, especially in the Illinois country where the Jesuits sanctioned such alliances by the marriage ceremony.

The same year Governor Cadillac wrote that the inhabitants were "a mass of rapscallions from Canada, a cut-throat set, without subordination, with no respect for religion and abandoned in vice with Indian women whom they prefer to French girls" and that the soldiers all had Indian wives who cooked for them and waited on them. With regard to a consignment of girls from Europe the sea-captain had seduced more than half the girls on the passage and this was why they had not found respectable husbands. It seemed to him best under the circumstances that the soldiers should be allowed to marry them lest their poverty should drive them to prostitution.

In 1714 the Curate La Vente suggested to the minister that Louisiana be colonized with Christian families or else that the French be allowed to marry the Indian women with religious rites; or if these ideas were not feasible that a large number of girls "better chosen than the last, and especially some who will be sufficiently pleasing and well-formed to suit the officers of the garrisons and the principal inhabitants" should be sent over from France as a partial remedy.

From time to time the paternal government responded to such requests with cargoes of women. In 1721 twenty-five prostitutes came from Salpetriere, a house of correction at Paris, sent as wives for the colonists. In 1726 the Company of the Indies contracted with the Ursuline sisters to teach girls and to serve as the means of transporting girls of good character and training to supply the need of suitable wives for the officers and for the farmers and artisans of "the better sort." The degraded women first sent over had often been not only unfit but unwilling for marriage and domesticity. Even the policy of granting discharges to the soldiers and offering them land and exemption from taxation as an inducement to marry these women had failed to solve the problem. The colony needed mothers.

The strength of the demand is illustrated in a passage by Dumont in reference to one cargo of women:

> When landed all were lodged in the same house, with a sentinel at the door. They were permitted to be seen during the day in order that a choice might be made, but as soon as night fell, all access to them was guarded. . . It was not long before they were married and provided for.

Indeed the supply never went round. The last one left on one occasion became the object of dispute between two bachelors that wanted to fight for her tho she was somewhat of an Amazon. The commandant required them to draw lots for the prize. Once a girl refused to marry tho "many good partis had been offered her."

The year after the Ursulines a cargo of girls came who had been chosen for character and skill in housewifery. They came of their own accord. Each was dowered with a chest of clothing. They came with the understanding that their vocation was to be wifehood and motherhood but the choice of husbands was to be voluntary from among such suitors as the sisters, under whose care the girls were, should approve.

Louisiana must have been indeed a region of loose morals. Sieur Charle, merchant, admitted that he had a child in 1709 by an Indian slave. Hervé mentions one, Jean Baptiste, child of an Indian woman of Sieur d'Arbanne, "whose son it is held to be, not only by public rumor, but by the voluntary account of the mother." The church did not sanction marriages with Indians but such unions occurred and were classed in the church records as *mariages naturels.* We find record also in Hervé's writings of one Capinan's forsaking a slave woman with whom he had lived in a marriage of this irregular species. The man had found a more desirable partner.

Cadillac refers to women of irregular life. Mere transplanting of the refuse of hospital and prison to the New World could not metamorphose them into good wives and mothers. In spite of great influx of people to Louisiana in the boom days, population does not seem to have grown fast. Gradually, however, there grew up an American generation of women ready for matrimony. Girls were often married at twelve or fourteen, some of them "not even knowing how many gods there are and you can imagine the rest."[151] Girls of bad conduct were "severely punished by putting them upon wooden horses and having them whipped by the regiment of soldiers that guard the town."[152] A house for the detention and reform of immoral women was built and intrusted to the sisters. Gradually the imported dregs of vice were submerged by the natural conse-

[151] Phelps. *Louisiana,* 83.

[152] — *Idem.*

quences of degeneracy. Many officials had their wives and families with them and kept clear of inferior mixture. On the Mississippi the Germans had German homes. Only a few Louisiana settlers had been persons of rank. Many of the population descended from the "casket girls" and from stock that society considers no account.

Family life was subject to pioneer exigencies. In the first half of the eighteenth century two hundred fifty women and children taken by the Natchez, and retaken, were brought to New Orleans. The orphan girls were adopted by the Ursulines. The boys found homes in well-to-do families. All the refugees were absorbed, many of the widows finding new husbands. In 1734 occurred the marriage of one Baudran with the publication of only one ban. The reason for this abridgment of the preliminaries was doubtless that the priest came so seldom. In 1720 provision was made (Mobile) for registration of baptisms, marriages, and deaths.

A side-light on the desire for growth in numbers in the colony is seen in the fact that during the Spanish régime the governor arrested the grand inquisitor and packed him off to Spain in order not to scare off population.

A Spanish precontract of marriage in 1786 is interesting for comparison with English usage. The instrument provides for a Catholic marriage, to take place as soon as either person requests it. Neither is to be liable for the ante-nuptial debts of the other; but they shall hold in common all property, movable and immovable, according to the custom of Spain, all other customs being renounced. In case of death of either without issue the survivor is to receive the whole property.

Children brought up on the coarse rough frontier were also spoiled by slavery. The girls caught less coarseness from slavery and less roughness from the wilderness. They were thus, in a way, superior to the men. In old Louisiana before annexation to the United States the lives of the women of the well-to-do were taken up mainly with the supervision of their servants and in exaggerated devotion to their children. Tho they were personally attractive and of natural intelligence they appeared but little interesting to the French traveller, or indeed to their husbands. Quadroons attracted the men.

This brief view of the southern French colony is useful in two ways: it shows the origin of the unique social institutions of New Orleans and it illuminates by way of contrast the English development on the Atlantic coast and helps us to appreciate the distinctive quality of the English institutions from which the American family derives its main features. There was apparently less solidity and seriousness in the French territory. The Puritan blood of France, or, if that be too strong a term, the bourgeois fibre of the nation, was by short-sighted intolerance excluded from French America, and English America profited by the Huguenot strains. Thus the foundations for the modern, as contrasted with the medieval family, were laid on the Atlantic coast rather than in the valley of the Mississippi. By the same token England was destined to possess the continent.

BIBLIOGRAPHY[153]

ABBOTT, EDITH. Study of the early history of child labor in America.

In the *American Journal of Sociology* (Chicago, 1908-1909), vol. xiv, 15-37.

ABRAM, A. English life and manners in the later middle ages (London, 1913).

ADAMS, BROOKS. Law of civilization and decay (New York, 1896).

ADAMS, C. F. Familiar letters of John Adams and his wife Abigail during the Revolution (New York, 1876).

—— Letters of Mrs. Adams, wife of John Adams, fourth edition (Boston, 1848).

—— Sexual morality and church discipline in colonial New England.

In *Massachusetts Historical Society Proceedings*, second ser. (Boston, 1873), vol. vi, 477-516.

ADAMS, H. B. Tithingmen (Baltimore, 1883).

Reprinted from the American Antiquarian Society, *Publications*, new ser., vol. i, part 3.

ARTHUR, T. S. and W. H. Carpenter. History of Georgia (Philadelphia, 1861).

BALLAGH, J. C. History of slavery in Virginia (Baltimore, 1902).

—— White servitude in the colony of Virginia (Baltimore, 1895).

In Johns Hopkins University *Studies in Historical and Political Science*, thirteenth ser., nos. vi-vii, 261-357.

BARBER, J. W. History and antiquities of the Northern States, third edition (Hartford, 1846).

BARING-GOULD, S. Germany present and past (London, 1879), 2 vols.

BARTON, R. T., editor. Virginia colonial decisions (Boston, 1909), vol. i.

---

153 This is complete as to source materials, but contains only the more important of secondary authorities.

BASSETT, J. S. Slavery and servitude in the colony of North Carolina (Baltimore, 1896).

In Johns Hopkins University *Studies in Historical and Political Science*, fourteenth ser., nos. iv-v, 169-254.

BEBEL, A. Woman and socialism, fiftieth edition, translated by Meta L. Stern (New York, 1910).

BICKLEY, G. W. L. History of the settlement and Indian Wars of Tazewell County, Virginia (Cincinnati, 1852).

BJÖRKMAN, F. M. and Porritt. Woman suffrage – history, arguments, results (New York, 1915).

BLISS, W. R. Side glimpses from the colonial meetinghouse (Boston, 1894).

BRACE, C. L. Gesta Christi (New York, 1883).

BRACKETT, J. R. The Negro in Maryland (Baltimore, 1889).

BRADFORD, WILLIAM. Plymouth Plantation, from the original manuscript (Boston, 1898).

BRADLEY, R. M. The English housewife in the seventeenth and eighteenth centuries (London, 1912).

BRAY, REVEREND THOMAS, by B. C. Steiner (Baltimore, 1901).

In Maryland Historical Society *Fund Publications*, no. 37.

BRENTANO, L. History and development of gilds.

Preliminary essay to T. Smith, *English gilds* (London, 1870; reprinted in 1892).

BRICKELL, J. Natural history of North Carolina (Dublin, 1737; reprinted [Raleigh, 1910?]).

BROWN, ALEXANDER. Genesis of the United States (Boston, 1890).

BROWN, E. H., JR. First free school in Queen Anne's County (Baltimore, 1911).

In Maryland *Historical Magazine* (Baltimore, 1911), vol. vi, 1-15.

BROWNE, W. H. Maryland (Boston, 1884).

BRUCE, P. A. Institutional history of Virginia in the seventeenth century (New York, 1910).

—— Social life of Virginia in the seventeenth century (Richmond, 1907).

BUCKINGHAM, J. S. Slave states of America (London, 1842).

BURK, J. [D.]. History of Virginia (Petersburg, 1822), vol. ii, Appendix xviii.

BYINGTON, E. H. Puritan in England and New England (Boston, 1897).

CABLE, G. W. Creoles of Louisiana (New York, 1884).

CAIRNS, W. B. Selections from early American writers (New York, 1909).

CALVIN, JOHN. Institutes of the Christian religion (Philadelphia, 1844).

CAMPBELL, D. The Puritan in Holland, England, and America, third edition, revised and corrected (New York, 1893), 2 vols.

CAMPBELL, H. Women wage-earners (Boston, 1893).

CARROLL, B. R., editor. Historical collections of South Carolina (New York, 1836), vol. ii.

CLAPP, T. Memoirs of a college president – Womanhood in early America (Transcript by E. S. Welles), (Hartford, 1908).

In Connecticut *Magazine*, vol. xii, 233-239.

COCKSHOTT, W. Pilgrim fathers (New York, 1909).

COLEMAN, W. M. History of the primitive Yankees, or the Pilgrim fathers (Washington, 1881).

CONNECTICUT Colonial Records (Hartford, 1850-1890).

CONRAD, H. C. History of the state of Delaware (Wilmington, 1908), vol. i.

COOKE, G. W. Woman in the progress of civilization.

In the *Chautauquan* (Chautauqua, N. Y.), September, 1909-May, 1910.

COOKE, J. E. Virginia (Boston, 1884).

CORNISH, F. W. Chivalry (London, 1908).

COWLEY, C. Our divorce courts, their origin and history. . . (Lowell, Mass., 1879).

COXE, MISS —. Claims of the country on American females (Columbus, 1842).

DAVENPORT, C. B. Heredity in relation to eugenics (New York, 1911).

DEALEY, J. Q. The family in its sociological aspects (Boston [1912]).

DELAWARE historical and biographical papers (Wilmington, 1879-1914).

DELAWARE HISTORICAL SOCIETY. Papers (Wilmington), vol. ix (1890), vol. liv (1909).

DINSMORE, J. W. Scotch-Irish in America (Chicago [1906]).

Documentary History of American Industrial Society (Cleveland, 1910-1911), 11 vols.

DOYLE, J. A. English colonies in America: Virginia, Maryland, and the Carolinas (New York, 1889), vol. i.

EARLE, A. M. Child-life in colonial days (New York, 1909).

—— Colonial dames and goodwives (Boston, 1895).

—— Colonial days in old New York (New York, 1896).

—— Customs and Fashions in Old New England (New York, 1893).

EARLY, R. H. By-ways of Virginia history (Richmond, 1907).

EARLY RECORDS of the town of Providence (Providence, 1892-1906).

EDWARDS, J. Works (Worcester, 1808; reprinted, New York, 1844).

ELLIOTT, C. W. New England History (New York, 1857), 2 vols.

FAUST, A. B. German elements in the United States (Boston, 1909), vol. ii.

FERNOW, B., editor. Records of New Amsterdam (New York, 1897).

FERRIS, B. History of the original settlements on the Delaware (Wilmington, 1846).

FIELD, E., editor. State of Rhode Island and Providence Plantations at the end of the century (Boston, 1902), vol. iii.

FISHER, S. G. Men, women, and manners in colonial times (Philadelphia, 1898), 2 vols.

—— The making of Pennsylvania (Philadelphia, 1896).

FOOTE, W. H. Sketches of North Carolina (New York, 1846).

—— Sketches of Virginia (Philadelphia, 1850).

FORCE, P. Tracts and other papers (Washington, 1836-1846).

FORD, W. C., editor. Writings of George Washington (New York, 1889-1893).

FORREST, J. D. Development of Western civilization (Chicago, 1907).

FORREST, W. S. Historical and descriptive sketches of Norfolk and vicinity . . . (Philadelphia, 1853).

FRANKLIN, JAMES. Philosophical and political history of the thirteen United States of America (London, 1784).

GAGE, M. J. Woman, church, and state (Chicago, 1893).

GEORGIA Colonial Records (Atlanta), vol. ii (1904), vol. iv (1906), vol. vi (1906), vols. xviii and xxi (1910), vol. xxii, part 1 (1913).

GEORGIA HISTORICAL SOCIETY. Collections (Savannah), vol. i (1840), vol. ii (1842), vol. iii (1873), vol. iv (1878).

GIDDINGS, F. H. Natural history of American morals.

In *Times Magazine*, December, 1906, p. 34.

GODFREY, E. Home life under the Stuarts, 1603-1649 (New York, 1903).

GOODSELL, W. History of the family as a social and educational institution (New York, 1915).

GOODWIN, J. A. The Pilgrim Republic (Boston, 1888).

GOODWIN, M. W. The colonial cavalier, or southern life before the Revolution (New York, 1894).

GRAHAM, A. A. Vincennes, Indiana, a century ago (Philadelphia, 1879).

In Potter's *American Monthly*, vol. xii, 161-171; 289-298.

GRANT, A. M. Memoirs of an American lady (London, 1808).

GRIFFIS, W. E. Story of New Netherlands (Boston, 1909).

GUIZOT, F. P. History of civilization in Europe.

HALL, C. C. Narratives of early Maryland (New York, 1910).

—— The Lords Baltimore and the Maryland Palatinate (Baltimore, 1904).

HALL, G. S. and T. Smith. Marriage and fecundity of colonial men and women (Worcester, 1903).

In *Pedagogical Seminary*, vol. x, 275-314.

HALSEY, F. W., editor. Great epochs in American history (New York [1912]), vol. ii.

HAMILTON, P. J. Colonial Mobile, revised and enlarged edition (Boston, 1910).

HART, A. B. American history told by contemporaries (New York, 1897), vol. i.

—— Source book of American history (New York, 1903).

HECKER, E. A. Short history of woman's rights (New York, 1911).

HENNIGHAUSEN, L. P. History of the German Society of Maryland (Baltimore, 1909).

—— Redemptioners and the German Society of Maryland (Baltimore, 1888).

In Society for History of the Germans, *Second Annual Report.*

HILL, G. Women in English life (London, 1896), 2 vols.

HOLCOMB, T. Sketch of early ecclesiastical affairs in New Castle, Delaware, and history of Immanuel Church (Wilmington, 1890).

HOLDER, C. F. Quakers in Great Britain and America (New York, 1913).

HOLY TRINITY – Old Swede – Church. Records, 1697-1773 (Wilmington, 1890).

In Delaware Historical Society *Papers*, vol. ix.

HOWARD, G. E. History of matrimonial institutions (Chicago, [1904]), 3 vols.

HOWE, D. W. Puritan republic of Massachusetts Bay (Indianapolis [1899]).

HOWE, H. Historical collections of Virginia (Charleston, 1852).

INGLE, E. Parish institutions of Maryland (Baltimore, 1883).

In Johns Hopkins University *Studies in Historical and Political Science*, first ser., Local Institutions, no. vi.

IRVING, W. Knickerbocker history of New York (Philadelphia, 1836).

ITINERANT Observations in America (Savannah, 1878).

Reprinted from the London *Magazine*, 1745.

JAMES, E. W., editor. Lower Norfolk County, Virginia Antiquary, vol. i (Richmond, 1897).

KERCHEVAL, S. History of the Valley of Virginia (Winchester, Va., 1833).

KEYSER, N. H. et al. History of old Germantown (Philadelphia, 1907).

KING, G. New Orleans, the place and the people (New York, 1896).

KINGSBURY, S. M., editor. Records of the Virginia Company (Washington, 1906).

KUHNS, O. German and Swiss settlements of colonial Pennsylvania: a study of the so-called Pennsylvania Dutch (New York, 1901).

KULTURGESCHICHTE des Mittelalters mit Einschluss der Renaissance und Reformation (Leipzig, 1897).

LEE, F. B. New Jersey as a colony and as a state (New York, 1902).

LETTERS from Virginia; translated from the French (Baltimore, 1816).

LIPSON, E. Introduction to the economic history of England (London, 1915), vol. i.

LITTLE, J. P. Richmond (Richmond, 1851).

LOGAN, Mrs. J. A. The part taken by women in American history (Wilmington, Del., 1912).

LOW, A. M. The American people: I. The planting of a nation (Boston, 1909).

MCCORMAC, E. I. White servitude in Maryland, 1634-1820 (Baltimore, 1904).

In Johns Hopkins University *Studies in Historical and Political Science*, twenty-second ser., nos. 3-4, pp. 113-224.

MACGILL, C. E. Myth of the colonial housewife (New York, 1910).

In *Independent*, vol. lxix, 1318-1322.

MACKENZIE, E. Historical, topographical, and descriptive view of the United States of America and of Upper and Lower Canada (Newcastle upon Tyne [1819]).

MARYLAND. Archives (Baltimore, 1883-1914).

MARYLAND HISTORICAL SOCIETY. Fund Publications (Baltimore, 1867-1900).

MARYLAND, Society for History of Germans in Sixth Annual Report, 1891-1892 (Baltimore).

MASSACHUSETTS. Colonial Laws (Boston, 1889).

MASSACHUSETTS BAY. Acts and Resolves of the Province of (Boston, 1869), vol. i.

MASSACHUSETTS COLONIAL SOCIETY. Publications (Boston), vol. vii (1905), vol. xii (1911).

MASSACHUSETTS HISTORICAL SOCIETY. Collections (Boston, 1792-1915).

—— Proceedings, second ser. (Boston, 1906), vol. xix.

MATHER, C. Magnalia (Hartford, 1855), vol. i.

—— Diary.

In Massachusetts Historical Society *Collections*, seventh ser., vols. vii and viii.

MEILY, C. Puritanism (Chicago [1911]).

MILLIGAN, DOCTOR —. Short description of the province of South Carolina, 1763 (Charleston, 1858).

In Carroll, *Historical Collections of South Carolina*, vol. ii.

MOORE, G. H. Notes on the history of slavery in Massachusetts (New York, 1866).

MORONG, T. Puritan life and manners (Boston, 1871).

MORTON, O. F. History of Highland County, Virginia (Monterey, Va. [1911]).

MOTLEY, J. L. Rise of the Dutch Republic (Philadelphia, n. d.), 3 vols.

MYERS, A. C. Immigration of the Irish Quakers into Pennsylvania, 1682-1750 (Swarthmore, 1902).

MYERS, G. History of the Supreme Court of the United States (Chicago, 1912).

NEAL, D. History of New England (London, 1747), 2 vols.

NEILL, E. D. Virginia Carolorum (Albany, 1886).

—— Virginia Vetusta (Albany, 1885).

NEW HAVEN Colony and Plantation, Records (Hartford, 1857-1858).

NEW PLYMOUTH COLONY. Laws (Boston, 1836).

NEW YORK. Documents relating to the colonial history of the state (Albany, 1853-1887).

NIESEN, —. Abridgment of public acts of Assembly of Virginia in force Jan. 1, 1758 (Glasgow, 1759).

NOBLE, F. A. The Pilgrims (Boston, 1907).

NORRIS, J. S. The early Friends in Maryland (Baltimore, 1862).

In Maryland Historical Society *Publications*.

NORTH CAROLINA Baptist Historical Papers, April, 1898 (Henderson, N. C.).

—— Booklet (Raleigh, 1903-1908), vols. iii-v, vii, viii.

—— Colonial record (Raleigh, 1886-1890).

OGLETHORPE, J. E. New and accurate account of the Provinces of South Carolina and Georgia (London, 1732).

[OLDMIXON, J.]. The British Empire in America (London, 1741).

ONEAL, J. Workers in American History, third edition, revised and enlarged (St. Louis, 1912).

OTTO, E. Deutsches Frauenleben im Wandel der Jahrhunderte (Leipzig, 1903).

PAINTER, F. V. N. Luther on education (Philadelphia [1889]).

PALFREY, J. G. Compendious history of New England (Boston, 1884).

PARCE, L. Economic determinism (Chicago, 1913).

PASTON Letters (London, 1872-1875).

PATTEN, S. N. Development of English thought (New York, 1899).

PENNSYLVANIA GERMAN SOCIETY. Publications (Lancaster, Pa.), vol. x (1900), vol. xiii (1902).

PENNYPACKER, S. W. Settlement of Germantown (Lancaster, Pa., 1899).

In Pennsylvania German Society, *Publications*, vol. ix, 53-345.

PETRIE, G. Church and state in early Maryland (Baltimore, 1892).

PHELPS, A. Louisiana, a record of expansion (Boston, 1905).

PHILLIPS, L. A. Home life and training of New England children in the seventeenth century (Boston, 1896).

In the *Bostonian*, vol. iii, 329-334.

PICKETT, A. J. History of Alabama, new edition (Charleston, 1896).

PIERCE, C. H. New Harlem past and present (New York, 1903).
PIERCE, M. B. Shreds and patches of Virginia history (East Aurora, N. Y. [1906]).
PLYMOUTH COLONY Laws (Boston, 1836).
—— Records, vol. iii (Boston, 1855).
POLLARD, A. F. Factors in modern history (London, 1907).
POSITION of women: actual and ideal, with preface by Sir Oliver Lodge (London, 1911).
POWELL, L. P. History of education in Delaware (Washington, 1893).
RAPER, C. L. Social life in colonial North Carolina (Raleigh, 1903).

In North Carolina *Booklet*, vol. iii, no. 5.

RAVENEL, MRS. ST. J. Charleston, the place and the people (New York, 1906).
RHODE ISLAND Colonial Records (Providence, 1856-1865).
RICHARD, E. History of German Civilization (New York, 1911).
RICHARDSON, H. D. Sidelights on Maryland History (Baltimore, 1913), vol i.
RIDGELY, H. W. The old brick churches of Maryland (New York, 1894).
ROSS, E. A. Origins of the American people.

In the *Century* (New York, 1913-1914), new ser., vol. lxv, 712-718.

RUSH, B. Account of the manners of the German inhabitants of Pennsylvania (1789), edited by Rupp (Philadelphia, 1875).
SALLEY, A. S., editor. Narratives of Early Carolina (New York, 1911).
SALLEY, A. S., editor. Marriage notices in the South Carolina *Gazette* and its successors, 1732-1801 (Albany, 1902).
SCHANTZ, F. J. T. Domestic life and characteristics of the Pennsylvania German Pioneer (Lancaster, Pa., 1900).

In Pennsylvania German Society, *Publications*, vol. x.

SCHERR, J. Geschichte der deutschen Frauenwelt (Leipzig, 1873), 2 vols.
SCHOULER, J. Americans of 1776 (New York, 1900).
SCRIBNER'S Magazine (New York, 1911), vol. l, 761-764.
SEIGNOBOS, C. History of Medieval and Modern Civilization (New York, 1909).
SEWALL, S. Diary (Boston, 1882).

In Massachusetts Historical Society, *Collections*, fifth ser., vol. vii.

SINGLETON, E. Dutch New York (New York, 1909).

SIOUSSAT, A. Colonial women of Maryland (Baltimore, 1907).

In Maryland *Historical Magazine*, vol. ii, 214-226.

SMITH, WILLIAM. History of New York (1756).

SMYTHE, W. E. Conquest of arid America (New York, 1900).

SOLLERS, B. Transported convict laborers in Maryland during the colonial period (Baltimore, 1907).

In Maryland *Historical Magazine*, vol. ii, 17-47.

SOUTH CAROLINA historical and genealogical magazine (Charleston, 1900-1911), *passim*.

SOUTH CAROLINA HISTORICAL SOCIETY. Collections (Charleston, 1897), vol. v.

SOUTH CAROLINA HUGUENOT SOCIETY. Transactions (Charleston, 1889-1897), nos. 2-5.

SOUTHERN HISTORICAL ASSOCIATION. Publications (Washington), vol. i (1897), vol. vi (1902), vol. vii (1903).

STANTON, MRS. E. C., et al., editors. History of woman suffrage (Rochester, 1889-1902), 4 vols.

STEINER, B. C. Beginnings of Maryland, 1631-1639 (Baltimore, 1903).

In Johns Hopkins University *Studies in Historical and Political Science*, twenty-first ser., nos. 8-10, pp. 353-464.

STILES, H. R. Bundling (Albany, 1869).

STILLÉ, C. J. Studies in Medieval History, second edition (Philadelphia, 1883).

SUMNER, W. G. Folkways (Boston, 1911).

TAILFER, P. True and historical narrative of the colony of Georgia (Charleston, 1741).

THOM, W. T. The struggle for religious freedom in Virginia: the Baptists (Baltimore, 1900).

In Johns Hopkins University *Studies in Historical and Political Science*, eighteenth ser., nos. 10-12, pp. 477-581.

THWAITES, R. G. Colonies, 1492-1750, second edition (New York, 1891).

TOMPKINS, D. A. History of Mecklenburg County and the city of Charlotte (Charlotte, N. C., 1903).

TRAILL, H. D. and J. S. Mann, editors. Social England (New York [1902-1903]), vols. iii, iv.

TURNER, E. R. History of slavery in Pennsylvania (Baltimore, 1911).

TURNER, C. H. B. Some records of Sussex County, Delaware (Philadelphia, 1909).

NORTH CAROLINA University. James Sprunt Historical Publications (Chapel Hill, N. C., 1912), vol. ii.

VAN RENSSELAER, MRS. J. K. The goede Vrouw of Mana-ha-ta at home and in society, 1609-1760 (New York, 1898).

VAN RENSSELAER, MRS. S. History of the city of New York in the seventeenth century (New York, 1909).

VEDDER, H. C. The Reformation in Germany (New York, 1914).

VINCENT, F. History of the state of Delaware (Philadelphia, 1870), vol. i.

VIRGINIA HISTORICAL SOCIETY. Collections (Richmond), new ser., vol. i (1882), vol. x (1891).

VIRGINIA Magazine of History and Biography (Richmond).

WARD, L. F. Pure sociology (New York, 1911).

WEEDEN, W. B. Early Rhode Island (New York [1910]).

—— Economic and social history of New England (Boston, 1890), 2 vols.

WEEKS, S. B. Church and state in North Carolina (Baltimore, 1893).

WERTENBAKER, T. J. Patrician and plebeian in Virginia (Charlottesville, 1910).

WHARTON, A. H. Colonial days and dames (Philadelphia, 1895).

WHITE, HENRY. Early history of New England (Boston, 1841).

WHITTEMORE, W. H. Colonial laws of Massachusetts, 1660-1672 (Boston, 1889).

WINTHROP, J. Journals, edited by J. K. Hosmer (New York, 1908).

WISE, J. C. Ye Kingdom of Accawmacke or the eastern shore of Virginia in the seventeenth century (Richmond, 1911).

WOOLSEY, T. D. Divorce and divorce laws in the United States (New Haven, 1868).

In the *New Englander*, vol. xxvii, 517-550.

YONGE, S. H. The site of old "James Towne" (Richmond, 1907).

YOUNG, A. Chronicles of the first planters of the colony of Massachusetts Bay, from 1623 to 1636 (Boston, 1846).

ZWIERLEIN, F. J. Religion in New Netherland (Rochester, 1910).

A CATALOG OF SELECTED
DOVER BOOKS
IN ALL FIELDS OF INTEREST

A CATALOG OF SELECTED DOVER BOOKS IN ALL FIELDS OF INTEREST

CATALOG OF DOVER BOOKS

FRANK LLOYD WRIGHT'S DANA HOUSE, Donald Hoffmann. Pictorial essay of residential masterpiece with over 160 interior and exterior photos, plans, elevations, sketches and studies. 128pp. $9\frac{1}{4}$ x $10\frac{3}{4}$. 29120-0

THE MALE AND FEMALE FIGURE IN MOTION: 60 Classic Photographic Sequences, Eadweard Muybridge. 60 true-action photographs of men and women walking, running, climbing, bending, turning, etc., reproduced from rare 19th-century masterpiece. vi + 121pp. 9 x 12. 24745-7

1001 QUESTIONS ANSWERED ABOUT THE SEASHORE, N. J. Berrill and Jacquelyn Berrill. Queries answered about dolphins, sea snails, sponges, starfish, fishes, shore birds, many others. Covers appearance, breeding, growth, feeding, much more. 305pp. $5\frac{1}{4}$ x $8\frac{1}{4}$. 23366-9

ATTRACTING BIRDS TO YOUR YARD, William J. Weber. Easy-to-follow guide offers advice on how to attract the greatest diversity of birds: birdhouses, feeders, water and waterers, much more. 96pp. $5\frac{3}{16}$ x $8\frac{1}{4}$. 28927-3

MEDICINAL AND OTHER USES OF NORTH AMERICAN PLANTS: A Historical Survey with Special Reference to the Eastern Indian Tribes, Charlotte Erichsen-Brown. Chronological historical citations document 500 years of usage of plants, trees, shrubs native to eastern Canada, northeastern U.S. Also complete identifying information. 343 illustrations. 544pp. $6\frac{1}{2}$ x $9\frac{1}{4}$. 25951-X

STORYBOOK MAZES, Dave Phillips. 23 stories and mazes on two-page spreads: Wizard of Oz, Treasure Island, Robin Hood, etc. Solutions. 64pp. $8\frac{1}{4}$ x 11. 23628-5

AMERICAN NEGRO SONGS: 230 Folk Songs and Spirituals, Religious and Secular, John W. Work. This authoritative study traces the African influences of songs sung and played by black Americans at work, in church, and as entertainment. The author discusses the lyric significance of such songs as "Swing Low, Sweet Chariot," "John Henry," and others and offers the words and music for 230 songs. Bibliography. Index of Song Titles. 272pp. $6\frac{1}{2}$ x $9\frac{1}{4}$. 40271-1

MOVIE-STAR PORTRAITS OF THE FORTIES, John Kobal (ed.). 163 glamor, studio photos of 106 stars of the 1940s: Rita Hayworth, Ava Gardner, Marlon Brando, Clark Gable, many more. 176pp. $8\frac{3}{8}$ x $11\frac{1}{4}$. 23546-7

BENCHLEY LOST AND FOUND, Robert Benchley. Finest humor from early 30s, about pet peeves, child psychologists, post office and others. Mostly unavailable elsewhere. 73 illustrations by Peter Arno and others. 183pp. $5\frac{3}{8}$ x $8\frac{1}{2}$. 22410-4

YEKL and THE IMPORTED BRIDEGROOM AND OTHER STORIES OF YIDDISH NEW YORK, Abraham Cahan. Film Hester Street based on *Yekl* (1896). Novel, other stories among first about Jewish immigrants on N.Y.'s East Side. 240pp. $5\frac{3}{8}$ x $8\frac{1}{2}$. 22427-9

SELECTED POEMS, Walt Whitman. Generous sampling from *Leaves of Grass*. Twenty-four poems include "I Hear America Singing," "Song of the Open Road," "I Sing the Body Electric," "When Lilacs Last in the Dooryard Bloom'd," "O Captain! My Captain!"–all reprinted from an authoritative edition. Lists of titles and first lines. 128pp. $5\frac{3}{16}$ x $8\frac{1}{4}$. 26878-0

MY BONDAGE AND MY FREEDOM, Frederick Douglass. Born a slave, Douglass became outspoken force in antislavery movement. The best of Douglass' autobiographies. Graphic description of slave life. 464pp. 5⅜ x 8½. 22457-0

FOLLOWING THE EQUATOR: A Journey Around the World, Mark Twain. Fascinating humorous account of 1897 voyage to Hawaii, Australia, India, New Zealand, etc. Ironic, bemused reports on peoples, customs, climate, flora and fauna, politics, much more. 197 illustrations. 720pp. 5⅜ x 8½. 26113-1

THE PEOPLE CALLED SHAKERS, Edward D. Andrews. Definitive study of Shakers: origins, beliefs, practices, dances, social organization, furniture and crafts, etc. 33 illustrations. 351pp. 5⅜ x 8½. 21081-2

THE MYTHS OF GREECE AND ROME, H. A. Guerber. A classic of mythology, generously illustrated, long prized for its simple, graphic, accurate retelling of the principal myths of Greece and Rome, and for its commentary on their origins and significance. With 64 illustrations by Michelangelo, Raphael, Titian, Rubens, Canova, Bernini and others. 480pp. 5⅜ x 8½. 27584-1

PSYCHOLOGY OF MUSIC, Carl E. Seashore. Classic work discusses music as a medium from psychological viewpoint. Clear treatment of physical acoustics, auditory apparatus, sound perception, development of musical skills, nature of musical feeling, host of other topics. 88 figures. 408pp. 5⅜ x 8½. 21851-1

THE PHILOSOPHY OF HISTORY, Georg W. Hegel. Great classic of Western thought develops concept that history is not chance but rational process, the evolution of freedom. 457pp. 5⅜ x 8½. 20112-0

THE BOOK OF TEA, Kakuzo Okakura. Minor classic of the Orient: entertaining, charming explanation, interpretation of traditional Japanese culture in terms of tea ceremony. 94pp. 5⅜ x 8½. 20070-1

LIFE IN ANCIENT EGYPT, Adolf Erman. Fullest, most thorough, detailed older account with much not in more recent books, domestic life, religion, magic, medicine, commerce, much more. Many illustrations reproduce tomb paintings, carvings, hieroglyphs, etc. 597pp. 5⅜ x 8½. 22632-8

SUNDIALS, Their Theory and Construction, Albert Waugh. Far and away the best, most thorough coverage of ideas, mathematics concerned, types, construction, adjusting anywhere. Simple, nontechnical treatment allows even children to build several of these dials. Over 100 illustrations. 230pp. 5⅜ x 8½. 22947-5

THEORETICAL HYDRODYNAMICS, L. M. Milne-Thomson. Classic exposition of the mathematical theory of fluid motion, applicable to both hydrodynamics and aerodynamics. Over 600 exercises. 768pp. 6⅛ x 9¼. 68970-0

SONGS OF EXPERIENCE: Facsimile Reproduction with 26 Plates in Full Color, William Blake. 26 full-color plates from a rare 1826 edition. Includes "The Tyger," "London," "Holy Thursday," and other poems. Printed text of poems. 48pp. 5¼ x 7. 24636-1

OLD-TIME VIGNETTES IN FULL COLOR, Carol Belanger Grafton (ed.). Over 390 charming, often sentimental illustrations, selected from archives of Victorian graphics–pretty women posing, children playing, food, flowers, kittens and puppies, smiling cherubs, birds and butterflies, much more. All copyright-free. 48pp. 9¼ x 12¼. 27269-9

PERSPECTIVE FOR ARTISTS, Rex Vicat Cole. Depth, perspective of sky and sea, shadows, much more, not usually covered. 391 diagrams, 81 reproductions of drawings and paintings. 279pp. 5⅜ x 8½. 22487-2

DRAWING THE LIVING FIGURE, Joseph Sheppard. Innovative approach to artistic anatomy focuses on specifics of surface anatomy, rather than muscles and bones. Over 170 drawings of live models in front, back and side views, and in widely varying poses. Accompanying diagrams. 177 illustrations. Introduction. Index. 144pp. 8⅜ x11¼. 26723-7

GOTHIC AND OLD ENGLISH ALPHABETS: 100 Complete Fonts, Dan X. Solo. Add power, elegance to posters, signs, other graphics with 100 stunning copyright-free alphabets: Blackstone, Dolbey, Germania, 97 more–including many lower-case, numerals, punctuation marks. 104pp. 8⅛ x 11. 24695-7

HOW TO DO BEADWORK, Mary White. Fundamental book on craft from simple projects to five-bead chains and woven works. 106 illustrations. 142pp. 5⅜ x 8. 20697-1

THE BOOK OF WOOD CARVING, Charles Marshall Sayers. Finest book for beginners discusses fundamentals and offers 34 designs. "Absolutely first rate . . . well thought out and well executed."–E. J. Tangerman. 118pp. 7¾ x 10⅝. 23654-4

ILLUSTRATED CATALOG OF CIVIL WAR MILITARY GOODS: Union Army Weapons, Insignia, Uniform Accessories, and Other Equipment, Schuyler, Hartley, and Graham. Rare, profusely illustrated 1846 catalog includes Union Army uniform and dress regulations, arms and ammunition, coats, insignia, flags, swords, rifles, etc. 226 illustrations. 160pp. 9 x 12. 24939-5

WOMEN'S FASHIONS OF THE EARLY 1900s: An Unabridged Republication of "New York Fashions, 1909," National Cloak & Suit Co. Rare catalog of mail-order fashions documents women's and children's clothing styles shortly after the turn of the century. Captions offer full descriptions, prices. Invaluable resource for fashion, costume historians. Approximately 725 illustrations. 128pp. 8⅜ x 11¼. 27276-1

THE 1912 AND 1915 GUSTAV STICKLEY FURNITURE CATALOGS, Gustav Stickley. With over 200 detailed illustrations and descriptions, these two catalogs are essential reading and reference materials and identification guides for Stickley furniture. Captions cite materials, dimensions and prices. 112pp. 6½ x 9¼. 26676-1

EARLY AMERICAN LOCOMOTIVES, John H. White, Jr. Finest locomotive engravings from early 19th century: historical (1804–74), main-line (after 1870), special, foreign, etc. 147 plates. 142pp. 11⅜ x 8¼. 22772-3

THE TALL SHIPS OF TODAY IN PHOTOGRAPHS, Frank O. Braynard. Lavishly illustrated tribute to nearly 100 majestic contemporary sailing vessels: Amerigo Vespucci, Clearwater, Constitution, Eagle, Mayflower, Sea Cloud, Victory, many more. Authoritative captions provide statistics, background on each ship. 190 black-and-white photographs and illustrations. Introduction. 128pp. 8⅞ x 11¾. 27163-3

LITTLE BOOK OF EARLY AMERICAN CRAFTS AND TRADES, Peter Stockham (ed.). 1807 children's book explains crafts and trades: baker, hatter, cooper, potter, and many others. 23 copperplate illustrations. 140pp. 4⅝ x 6. 23336-7

VICTORIAN FASHIONS AND COSTUMES FROM HARPER'S BAZAR, 1867–1898, Stella Blum (ed.). Day costumes, evening wear, sports clothes, shoes, hats, other accessories in over 1,000 detailed engravings. 320pp. 9⅜ x 12¼. 22990-4

GUSTAV STICKLEY, THE CRAFTSMAN, Mary Ann Smith. Superb study surveys broad scope of Stickley's achievement, especially in architecture. Design philosophy, rise and fall of the Craftsman empire, descriptions and floor plans for many Craftsman houses, more. 86 black-and-white halftones. 31 line illustrations. Introduction 208pp. 6½ x 9¼. 27210-9

THE LONG ISLAND RAIL ROAD IN EARLY PHOTOGRAPHS, Ron Ziel. Over 220 rare photos, informative text document origin (1844) and development of rail service on Long Island. Vintage views of early trains, locomotives, stations, passengers, crews, much more. Captions. 8⅞ x 11¾. 26301-0

VOYAGE OF THE LIBERDADE, Joshua Slocum. Great 19th-century mariner's thrilling, first-hand account of the wreck of his ship off South America, the 35-foot boat he built from the wreckage, and its remarkable voyage home. 128pp. 5⅜ x 8½. 40022-0

TEN BOOKS ON ARCHITECTURE, Vitruvius. The most important book ever written on architecture. Early Roman aesthetics, technology, classical orders, site selection, all other aspects. Morgan translation. 331pp. 5⅜ x 8½. 20645-9

THE HUMAN FIGURE IN MOTION, Eadweard Muybridge. More than 4,500 stopped-action photos, in action series, showing undraped men, women, children jumping, lying down, throwing, sitting, wrestling, carrying, etc. 390pp. 7⅞ x 10⅝. 20204-6 Clothbd.

TREES OF THE EASTERN AND CENTRAL UNITED STATES AND CANADA, William M. Harlow. Best one-volume guide to 140 trees. Full descriptions, woodlore, range, etc. Over 600 illustrations. Handy size. 288pp. 4½ x 6⅜. 20395-6

SONGS OF WESTERN BIRDS, Dr. Donald J. Borror. Complete song and call repertoire of 60 western species, including flycatchers, juncoes, cactus wrens, many more–includes fully illustrated booklet. Cassette and manual 99913-0

GROWING AND USING HERBS AND SPICES, Milo Miloradovich. Versatile handbook provides all the information needed for cultivation and use of all the herbs and spices available in North America. 4 illustrations. Index. Glossary. 236pp. 5⅜ x 8½. 25058-X

BIG BOOK OF MAZES AND LABYRINTHS, Walter Shepherd. 50 mazes and labyrinths in all–classical, solid, ripple, and more–in one great volume. Perfect inexpensive puzzler for clever youngsters. Full solutions. 112pp. 8⅛ x 11. 22951-3

PIANO TUNING, J. Cree Fischer. Clearest, best book for beginner, amateur. Simple repairs, raising dropped notes, tuning by easy method of flattened fifths. No previous skills needed. 4 illustrations. 201pp. 5⅜ x 8½. 23267-0

HINTS TO SINGERS, Lillian Nordica. Selecting the right teacher, developing confidence, overcoming stage fright, and many other important skills receive thoughtful discussion in this indispensible guide, written by a world-famous diva of four decades' experience. 96pp. 5⅜ x 8½. 40094-8

THE COMPLETE NONSENSE OF EDWARD LEAR, Edward Lear. All nonsense limericks, zany alphabets, Owl and Pussycat, songs, nonsense botany, etc., illustrated by Lear. Total of 320pp. 5⅜ x 8½. (Available in U.S. only.) 20167-8

VICTORIAN PARLOUR POETRY: An Annotated Anthology, Michael R. Turner. 117 gems by Longfellow, Tennyson, Browning, many lesser-known poets. "The Village Blacksmith," "Curfew Must Not Ring Tonight," "Only a Baby Small," dozens more, often difficult to find elsewhere. Index of poets, titles, first lines. xxiii + 325pp. 5⅜ x 8¼. 27044-0

DUBLINERS, James Joyce. Fifteen stories offer vivid, tightly focused observations of the lives of Dublin's poorer classes. At least one, "The Dead," is considered a masterpiece. Reprinted complete and unabridged from standard edition. 160pp. 5$\frac{3}{16}$ x 8¼. 26870-5

GREAT WEIRD TALES: 14 Stories by Lovecraft, Blackwood, Machen and Others, S. T. Joshi (ed.). 14 spellbinding tales, including "The Sin Eater," by Fiona McLeod, "The Eye Above the Mantel," by Frank Belknap Long, as well as renowned works by R. H. Barlow, Lord Dunsany, Arthur Machen, W. C. Morrow and eight other masters of the genre. 256pp. 5⅜ x 8½. (Available in U.S. only.) 40436-6

THE BOOK OF THE SACRED MAGIC OF ABRAMELIN THE MAGE, translated by S. MacGregor Mathers. Medieval manuscript of ceremonial magic. Basic document in Aleister Crowley, Golden Dawn groups. 268pp. 5⅜ x 8½. 23211-5

NEW RUSSIAN-ENGLISH AND ENGLISH-RUSSIAN DICTIONARY, M. A. O'Brien. This is a remarkably handy Russian dictionary, containing a surprising amount of information, including over 70,000 entries. 366pp. 4½ x 6⅛. 20208-9

HISTORIC HOMES OF THE AMERICAN PRESIDENTS, Second, Revised Edition, Irvin Haas. A traveler's guide to American Presidential homes, most open to the public, depicting and describing homes occupied by every American President from George Washington to George Bush. With visiting hours, admission charges, travel routes. 175 photographs. Index. 160pp. 8¼ x 11. 26751-2

NEW YORK IN THE FORTIES, Andreas Feininger. 162 brilliant photographs by the well-known photographer, formerly with *Life* magazine. Commuters, shoppers, Times Square at night, much else from city at its peak. Captions by John von Hartz. 181pp. 9¼ x 10¾. 23585-8

INDIAN SIGN LANGUAGE, William Tomkins. Over 525 signs developed by Sioux and other tribes. Written instructions and diagrams. Also 290 pictographs. 111pp. 6⅛ x 9¼. 22029-X

PHOTOGRAPHIC SKETCHBOOK OF THE CIVIL WAR, Alexander Gardner. 100 photos taken on field during the Civil War. Famous shots of Manassas Harper's Ferry, Lincoln, Richmond, slave pens, etc. 244pp. 10⅝ x 8¼. 22731-6

FIVE ACRES AND INDEPENDENCE, Maurice G. Kains. Great back-to-the-land classic explains basics of self-sufficient farming. The one book to get. 95 illustrations. 397pp. 5⅜ x 8½. 20974-1

SONGS OF EASTERN BIRDS, Dr. Donald J. Borror. Songs and calls of 60 species most common to eastern U.S.: warblers, woodpeckers, flycatchers, thrushes, larks, many more in high-quality recording. Cassette and manual 99912-2

A MODERN HERBAL, Margaret Grieve. Much the fullest, most exact, most useful compilation of herbal material. Gigantic alphabetical encyclopedia, from aconite to zedoary, gives botanical information, medical properties, folklore, economic uses, much else. Indispensable to serious reader. 161 illustrations. 888pp. 6½ x 9¼. 2-vol. set. (Available in U.S. only.) Vol. I: 22798-7
Vol. II: 22799-5

HIDDEN TREASURE MAZE BOOK, Dave Phillips. Solve 34 challenging mazes accompanied by heroic tales of adventure. Evil dragons, people-eating plants, blood-thirsty giants, many more dangerous adversaries lurk at every twist and turn. 34 mazes, stories, solutions. 48pp. 8¼ x 11. 24566-7

LETTERS OF W. A. MOZART, Wolfgang A. Mozart. Remarkable letters show bawdy wit, humor, imagination, musical insights, contemporary musical world; includes some letters from Leopold Mozart. 276pp. 5⅜ x 8½. 22859-2

BASIC PRINCIPLES OF CLASSICAL BALLET, Agrippina Vaganova. Great Russian theoretician, teacher explains methods for teaching classical ballet. 118 illustrations. 175pp. 5⅜ x 8½. 22036-2

THE JUMPING FROG, Mark Twain. Revenge edition. The original story of The Celebrated Jumping Frog of Calaveras County, a hapless French translation, and Twain's hilarious "retranslation" from the French. 12 illustrations. 66pp. 5⅜ x 8½. 22686-7

BEST REMEMBERED POEMS, Martin Gardner (ed.). The 126 poems in this superb collection of 19th- and 20th-century British and American verse range from Shelley's "To a Skylark" to the impassioned "Renascence" of Edna St. Vincent Millay and to Edward Lear's whimsical "The Owl and the Pussycat." 224pp. 5⅜ x 8½. 27165-X

COMPLETE SONNETS, William Shakespeare. Over 150 exquisite poems deal with love, friendship, the tyranny of time, beauty's evanescence, death and other themes in language of remarkable power, precision and beauty. Glossary of archaic terms. 80pp. 5 3/16 x 8¼. 26686-9

THE BATTLES THAT CHANGED HISTORY, Fletcher Pratt. Eminent historian profiles 16 crucial conflicts, ancient to modern, that changed the course of civilization. 352pp. 5⅜ x 8½. 41129-X